MULTIETHNIC
MOMENTS

2.00

Multiethnic Moments

The Politics of Urban Education Reform

Foreword by

CLARENCE N. STONE

Susan E. Clarke,
Rodney E. Hero, Mara S. Sidney, Luis R. Fraga,
Bari A. Erlichson

TEMPLE UNIVERSITY PRESS
Philadelphia

*To current and future generations of public school children, in
hopes for a world with greater social and educational equality*

TEMPLE UNIVERSITY PRESS
1601 North Broad Street
Philadelphia PA 19122
www.temple.edu/tempress

∞

The paper used in this publication meets the requirements
of the American National Standard for Information Sciences—
Permanence of Paper for Printed Library
Materials, ANSI Z39.48-1992

Library of Congress Cataloging-in-Publication Data
Multiethnic moments : the politics of urban education reform /
by Susan E. Clarke ... [et al.] ; foreword by Clarence N. Stone.
p. cm.
Includes bibliographical references and index.
ISBN 1-59213-536-6 (hardcover : alk. paper) — ISBN 1-59213-537-4
(pbk.: alk. paper)
1. Education, Urban—United States—Case studies. 2. United
States—Ethnic relations—Case studies. 3. Educational change—United
States—Case studies. I. Clarke, Susan E., 1945-
LC5131.M85 2006
370.117—dc22
2006011162

2 4 6 8 9 7 5 3 1

CONTENTS

FOREWORD

Clarence N. Stone

Consider a thought experiment. Suppose in the 1950s that employment, rather than education, had been the opening wedge for bringing an end to racial discrimination and promoting equal rights. Suppose also that the primary responsibility for this push had lain with Congress and the White House, not the Supreme Court. Coalition building across racial lines would have had a much different springboard. The nation's politics might have evolved in a much different way. Perhaps white flight and the construction of residential boundaries of race and class privilege would have been more tempered, and attachment to place might have proven more durable. Above all, school reform might have taken a different form.

The spotlight on academic performance might even have come earlier if there had been an initial concentration on employment. As it was, the judicial approach to racial change focused on school-enrollment practices as the means to bring about equal rights. And, in this book, Susan E. Clarke, Rodney E. Hero, Mara S. Sidney, Luis R. Fraga, and Bari A. Erlichson show that a body of policy principles and institutional embodiments of those policies were built on the legal foundation of *Brown v. Board of Education*. By putting separate-but-equal to rest as a constitutional doctrine, the Court made an essential step toward ending second-class citizenship for African Americans and other minorities. Yet the stubborn reality is that the *Brown* case could declare racial separation to be inherently unequal, but the Supreme Court did not determine how race and education would play out. De jure segregation is gone, but de facto segregation of schools is, nevertheless, a widespread fact.

Education is a distinct policy arena on several grounds. One is that school districts are local, often with their own elections for school board and sometimes even with their own power of taxation. Despite the fact that we are now in a new information age that has given education a heightened level of social and economic significance, the nation continues in many ways to treat education as a local matter. To be sure, there are national goals, national commissions, and national legislation. All are important, as is the fact that education is a major state function. State-delineated school districts, state regulations, and state funding are fundamental features of how education is structured in the United States. Yet the local school district is the testing ground for determining which policies and practices will take hold.

While ideas set the stage, the pull of particulars is nevertheless strong in education. Much is at stake both materially and symbolically. School districts have often been among the largest employers in the local community—sometimes they are indeed the biggest single employer. School facilities involve large expenditures, and they are a large factor in education politics at both state and local levels. Collective bargaining contracts cover an enormous variety of topics. And nothing packs more emotional punch than pupil assignments. Residential property values are tied closely to perceived quality of schools in the attendance area. Many particulars have a potential to generate a level of intensity that totally eclipses large issues of educational policy. On occasion, a reverse pattern takes shape. Big issues of educational policy become the vehicles by which local and particular frustrations are voiced.

On many counts, then, education is a high reverberation policy arena. Value conflicts are often intense and material stakes are high, but at the same time the pattern of group engagement fluctuates because the scope of the policy arena shifts as issues rise and fade. Such issues included in this volatile mix include pedagogy, schools as a source of peer influence, the cost of housing, neighborhood stability, level of taxation, expressions of cultural identity, philosophies of youth development, jobs and contracts for adults, and the scope of opportunities available to the rising generation—all this and more are part of a volatile mix. Educators and parents are constant players, but many others come and go as the kaleidoscope of issues changes.

Yet education has had periods of stability. The first part of the twentieth century was a time when education expertise was on the rise, and a reservoir of deference to this expertise insulated schools from some of the crosscurrents of social conflict. That time has now passed. Desegregation battles contributed to the destabilization of those arrangements, but a general decline in deference to expertise was also a factor. One might be tempted to see a pattern of stability followed by ferment and then reform. However, such a crude characterization of the process of change misses much that is of great importance.

Through the experiences of Boston, Denver, Los Angeles, and San Francisco, *Multiethnic Moments* enables us to see that ferment does not lead automatically to reform, and that the scope and direction of reform can be very much in question. The authors bring a highly fragmented policy landscape under close examination at just such a transitional moment. They show us that even when change is needed, far-reaching reform can be difficult. Fragmentation is only one hurdle. Their analysis reminds us that two-tiered pluralism continues to be a factor, affirming equality as a formal legal principle, but leaving forces of race, class, and ethnicity as barriers to equal educational opportunity. Surface ferment and reform activity have not yet penetrated the deepest structural barriers. Yet with phrases like "no child left behind," we continue to treat school reform as the *only* means by which a grand dream can be realized.

Ideas, interests, and institutions combine to provide a complex tapestry for understanding reform. Sometimes reform makes them congruent in ways that a new and stabilized policy order can take shape, but Clarke, Hero, Sidney, Fraga, and Erlichson show that instability can have a long life when congruence is low. They give us an illuminating close-up of the growth and perpetuation of fragmentation. The decline of professional expertise as the accepted guardian of public-service performance is a major factor in today's world. It has proven to be a Humpty Dumpty scenario. No one knows how to put it back together.

This book is part of a larger project, Civic Capacity and Urban Education, officially launched in the spring of 1993. This was ten years after the release of *A Nation at Risk*, the report of the National Commission on Excellence in Education and nine years before the enactment of No Child Left Behind. The period proved to be an especially turbulent time in education reform. Very fundamental changes were proposed at the national level. The states became increasingly active in fostering change, and much local experimentation occurred. Yet a broadly supported program of coherent reform has yet to take hold. Urban school districts have been the special target of reform talk, but urban constituencies and reform programs remain weakly aligned.

In this four-city study of urban education, we see that the effort to bring about school desegregation, important as it was in the struggle for civil rights, is now caught in limbo. It framed a defining approach to school reform, but could not contend with population movement and demographic change. The civil rights movement altered local political life, but for a changing and diversifying urban population, its legacy has failed to unify those most in need of a "new deal" in education.

The overall project launched in 1993 covered eleven cities across all regions of the country. Well populated by people of color and those from lower-income households, the student bodies in these schools stood in sharp contrast with stereotypical suburban student bodies. These cities were and remain the places of greatest education challenge—the places where reform was most needed. The Civic Capacity and Urban Education project had as a central aim the examination of school reform coalitions, their nature, and their impact. Few of us at that launching had a full appreciation of how strong the forces of fragmentation in education are. We expected resistance to reform, but underestimated the many crosscutting forces that would make mounting a sustained reform effort so difficult. By concentrating on four highly multiracial/multiethnic cities, *Multiethnic Moments* offers a close look at the special challenge of putting together "rainbow" coalitions behind a sustained reform effort. It shows us the importance of paying attention to the specifics of history while following the interplay of ideas, interests, and institutions.

Readers will find that *Multiethnic Moments* brings a complex reality into view. Aspirations and dreams are important, but their realization in education requires that reforms be wide in scope and broad in constituency support, while at the same time solidly grounded in a world of interests, institutions, and implementable practices. Vague talk about rainbow coalitions does not carry reform very far. The rainbow metaphor has great appeal in the abstract, but as a guide to coalition building it leaves much to be desired. Perhaps symbolic stances have a place in the politics of reform—certainly ideas are important, but readers will learn from the authors that sustained and concrete engagement cannot be finessed. Reform cries for policy solutions that are politically sustainable at both a macro and a micro level. Both the specifics of context and those of reform are matters to be attended to with great care. Let us hope that reformers of the future will read this book and learn its lessons well.

PREFACE

ARK TWAIN, eminent writer and observer of American race relations, once said, "Everyone talks about the weather, but nobody
does anything about it." Until recently, the same could be said
about theorizing race and ethnicity in the study of American politics. As 2000
Census data were released and analyzed, we saw a spate of stories in major
newspapers detailing the growth and urban concentration of Latinos and the
increasing political participation of Asian Americans. But for all the talk, there
has been less progress in developing theoretical and analytical frameworks that
can help us understand these important political and social developments.

While mindful of the many complex factors hampering theory development, our goal here is to provide theoretically grounded, empirical scholarship
about the politics of race/ethnicity in multiethnic settings. This book is structured around and emphasizes the development of an analytic framework to
analyze the politics of race and education in four multiethnic cities (Denver,
San Francisco, Los Angeles, and Boston). But the book is not intended as a
comparative case study per se, with the attendant detailed evidence harnessed
to explain similarities and differences across cases. Instead, this book represents an initial, though extended, effort to come to grips with the multiethnic
city as a distinctive setting and, within that setting, the politics of education
reform—a policy arena commonly perceived as most critical to equality of
opportunity in America.

Our analytical efforts face daunting obstacles in several ways, distinct from
those facing scholarship that seeks to explain black politics and education
reform issues (see Henig et al. 1999; Portz et al. 1999; Henig and Rich 2003;

Chambers 2002). While certainly not simple, the centrality of the black/African American situation in American politics is well recognized. Black political incorporation into formal governing institutions (at least at local levels) is well established, a sense of group awareness and shared identity among black people is relatively clear, and education policy (and other policy) issues facing blacks are less likely to encompass the language and related cultural issues that appear where Latinos and Asians make up significant portions of school populations.

Analyzing multiethnic local politics requires a different approach. In studying multiethnic cities, we seek to understand groups whose place in the U.S. political system is ambiguous or "in between" (Hero 1992; Jones-Correa 1998), whose sense of "groupness" may be "ambivalent" and complicated by intra- and intergroup factors, and to analyze aspects of education policy that are more elusive. In short, to a considerable degree we are treading uncharted substantive as well as theoretical terrain as we move beyond the black/white paradigm to search for ways to understand racial and multiethnic conflicts that are taking urban politics in new directions.[1]

As the American "dilemma" of race/ethnicity evolves and as "newer" groups become more salient, it is important to take stock of the changing situation within a general analytical framework. Our study focuses on a particularly important historical moment—when multiethnic politics began to displace biracial politics in many American cities. To capture the unfolding of this moment in the 1980s and 1990s, we take a developmental perspective that portrays the particular political experiences in our four cities while also anticipating future patterns.

The research and interviews that provide the evidentiary basis for our analysis took place in the mid-1990s (primarily 1993 and 1994) when a particular set of choice-oriented reform ideas were prominent, such as school vouchers and charter schools, as court-ordered desegregation orders were being lifted in many cities. This convergence of events created a window of opportunity for less visible groups to more strongly and clearly articulate their voices. We place this critical moment and those occurring in earlier eras in a broader historical perspective, emphasizing the many outcomes possible in cities experiencing similar "moments."

In retrospect, our study's time frame proved especially apt. The 2000 Census revealed what we heard on the ground—that officials in many American cities, especially school officials, were experiencing a uniquely complex surge of ethnic and demographic change during the 1990s. Our research led us to talk and listen to a broad range of local officials and citizens coping with complex changes on an everyday basis. Indeed, significant developments were unfolding in the midst of our research (see especially Chapters 3 and 6) and have continued to unfold since our data collection ended. Like other scholars of education politics, we recognize the "churning," "faddism," "spinning

wheels" (Hess 1998), and "reforms that go nowhere" (Henig et al. 1999) that
seem common to this policy arena. This fluidity means that we cannot provide
an up-to-the minute play-by-play account of educational politics in each city—
nor is this our aim.

Indeed, it is precisely because there are so many rapid developments in
local education politics and policy that it is imperative to develop broad frameworks for understanding them. As we see it, particular configurations of interests, ideas, and institutions shape and limit the churning and faddism of
education programs; these configurations are at the heart of our analytical
framework (see Heclo 1994; Hall 1997). By emphasizing the intersection of
interests, ideas, and institutions in each city, we are able to move beyond an
emphasis on structural features such as district autonomy or school budgets to
take into account the contingent nature of school politics in each city. This sen-
sitivity to context and history seems critical to making sense of the complex
politics in the multiethnic settings we study. It is especially important to understand how our current education problems and reforms are shaped by the
political legacy and policy context of the past in each of our cities. Our intention, therefore, is to map the lay of the land in each city; to identify, describe,
and explain the general factors or forces that created this terrain and whose
relevance is likely to endure; and to discuss specific manifestations of these
larger factors.

This book grew out of a larger study of "civic capacity" and education in
urban politics (see Stone et al. 2001).[2] Civic capacity refers to the extent to which
various sectors of a community develop formal and informal means to identify
common objectives and pursue common goals. The argument of the larger
project, and of two books based on it (Henig et al. 1999; Portz et al. 1999), was
that greater civic capacity might lead to better educational policy outcomes.
But those studies, in cities characterized primarily by black and white school
populations, concluded that although blacks gained substantial representation
in governing bodies and ostensible institutionalization of their policy views,
they did not achieve substantive educational change. In each of these cities,
context, history, and contingency proved more powerful than general structural
features in shaping outcomes. The findings for these "black and white" cities
are instructive and suggestive, but only partly relevant to our study. Latinos and
Asians in multiethnic cities, despite their numbers, have little representation,
and on the whole have had little ability to significantly shape policies, much
less to institutionalize them. Indeed, this "nonrepresentation" or lack of influence is a major puzzle we seek to explain.

Therefore, this book is a first step toward creating a distinct analytical
approach to an emerging, significant set of phenomena. We need to begin to
understand multiethnic school districts and their historical backgrounds, contexts, dynamics, and so on, *before* we can appropriately compare them to

districts in black/white cities, lest we "compare apples and oranges." That is, we cannot simply take what we know about black/white cities, and apply it to the study of multiethnic cities. In places where, for example, Latinos are the largest group—a group that is understudied in political science—the issues and issue frames pertinent and significant in black/white cities are less salient. The history of race relations in black/white cities is different and sometimes longer than in cities where Latinos and Asians are concentrated.

At the same time, the black/white paradigm importantly affects the empirical reality and the scholarly and popular understanding of minority group politics, a point we stress in this book. And in some respects, the analytical approach adopted here draws from and builds on previous studies of biracial cities. For example, a study by Henig and others (1999)—which focuses on Washington DC, Detroit, Baltimore, and Atlanta—emphasizes "stakeholders" and their competition and interactions, including the racial dimensions thereof. Our study also examines stakeholders in our discussion of interests as a dimension of analysis. However, a major point we make is that stakeholders' interests are more ambiguous and complex in multiethnic settings where, for a variety of reasons, the newer groups are less cohesive, have less clearly formed views, and have views shaped by the context of an earlier paradigm of black/white school desegregation that complicates, rather than clarifies, the current situation of new "minority" groups. Similarly, a study by Portz and others (1999) that focuses on Pittsburgh, St. Louis, and Boston emphasizes "institutions and leadership," as does our analytical framework. But aside from Boston, "leadership" is less prominent in the multiethnic cities we study, in part because of the patterns of multiethnicity, ideational ambiguity, institutional fragmentation, and other variables we describe. Delineating and beginning to explain these distinctive circumstances using our "interests, ideas, and institutions" framework thus represents a significant step.

To summarize, multiethnic cities where Latinos and Asians figure prominently—often located in the West and shaped by Western political traditions, but now emerging across the United States—present unique social and political settings and unique education issues. Along with other researchers (e.g., Lien 2001; Lien et al. 2004; Kim 1999; Schmidt 2000), we find that the repertoire of ideas and theories about race politics, understandably framed by a biracial black/white paradigm, has only a limited ability to illuminate these distinct circumstances and issues. And Latinos and Asians, at least to this point, have been hampered in formulating and articulating distinctive and coherent political and educational policy visions. Given the inherently complex nature of these issues, these first steps towards rethinking our analytical and theoretical approaches to the study of race and ethnicity are important but difficult efforts. We hope our work will be read in this spirit and we appreciate and respect the growing community of scholars sharing these concerns.[3]

ACKNOWLEDGMENTS

THIS BOOK REFLECTS a particularly long period of development, so we think back on this process with an especially heartfelt appreciation for those who helped us reach this stage. Clarence Stone, Jeff Henig, and Bryan Jones developed the larger civic capacity and education project that supported our efforts. As Principal Investigators and fellow researchers, each championed our work and helped us clarify the unique cases we were dealing with. Clarence especially proved a stalwart, optimistic, patient, and supportive advocate for our extended research efforts; we suspect we finally wrapped this up because he expected us to, but we know we never could have done so without his support. While the NSF funding (Education and Human Services Directorate, National Science Foundation RED9350139) for this multicity project was critical, the collaborative nature and congenial exchange characteristic of the larger project proved invaluable. We continue to enjoy the friendship and intellectual community of our Civic Capacity project colleagues: Marion Orr, John Portz, Fernando Guerra, Mara Cohen Marks, Lana Stein, Robin Jones, Ric Hula, John D. Hutcheson, Desiree Pedescleaux, Carol Pierannunzi, Richard Jelier, Mark Schauer, and Thomas Longoria, as well as the colleagues and students who worked with them on their city teams. We feel privileged to have been part of this remarkably successful, complex, decentralized, collaborative research project.

By design, each city "team" enjoyed considerable autonomy in carrying out a common research design and data collection strategy. Thus we each incurred our own set of debts to be acknowledged. Susan E. Clarke, Rodney E. Hero, and Mara S. Sidney began work on the Denver case while at the University of Colorado at Boulder. In addition to the intangible ways in which universities contribute to faculty research, their work enjoyed support from the Center for Policy Research in the Department of Political Science, the Center to Advance Research and Teaching in the Social Sciences (CARTSS), as well as grants from the University's Council for Research and Creative Work and the Provost's Office. Jose Marichal, Matt Greene, Eric Hirsch, Meg McCroskey Blum, Roger Pielke, Jr., and Brad Baca worked on the data collection while graduate students. McNair Scholar Saundra Locke helped design and carry out a supplemental study of Latino and African American perspectives on school reform in Denver. Coming full circle, Rob Preuhs, Director of the Social Science Data Lab at Boulder, helped us untangle last minute data problems. Alex Medler offered cogent and incisive comments on the entire manuscript while completing his doctoral research on state level education reforms.

Rodney E. Hero, now at the University of Notre Dame, thanks his collaborators on this project and gratefully acknowledges the support of the University of Colorado at Boulder and from the Packey J. Dee professorship in American Democracy at Notre Dame.

Mara S. Sidney, now at Rutgers University-Newark, thanks Katalin Dancsi, Koushiki Mukherjee, Linda Weinstein, and Vivian Pacheco for research assistance.

It is much more difficult to convey our appreciation to the many Denver parents, teachers, activists, and policymakers who generously shared their time and experiences with us, but we would like to acknowledge their importance here.

The San Francisco team of Luis R. Fraga and Bari A. Erlichson gratefully acknowledge the contributions of Gloria M. Rodriguez, Jorge Ruiz-de-Velasco, Sandy Lee, and Racy Ming. Understanding the inner workings of school politics in this city was enhanced beyond measure by the insight and guidance of Robert Harrington, John Flores, Bonnie Bergum, Dee Dee Desmond, Ritu Khanna, Henry Der, and many principals, teachers, and community leaders with whom we spoke.

Our analysis of Los Angeles draws on the project work of Fernando Guerra and Mara Cohen Marks, both at Loyola Marymount University. Their continued interest and guidance has been invaluable. Our inclusion of the Boston case is only possible because of the generous assistance from John Portz, who headed up the Boston study. His work, incorporated in Portz, Stein, and Jones (1999) and Portz (1996) remains the authoritative Boston case. Our decision to include Boston reflected our conviction, prior to the 2000 census, that many cities are becoming multiethnic and facing the types of dilemmas we present here. Boston allows us to make this larger point and enriches the comparisons across cities and over time. It also indicates the value of framing research on race and ethnicity in cities historically characterized by black/white tensions in terms of multiethnic dynamics. We hope to see more such work in the future.

Peter Wissoker first brought our book to Temple University Press and continued as our advocate even after moving on to Cornell University Press. Alex

Holzman made things work at Temple University Press, with good humor, dispatch, and insight; we are fortunate indeed to have had the benefits of their professional acumen and editorial expertise. The final version of our book is much improved, thanks to the copyediting of Stephanie Roulias and the help from David M. Wilson at Temple University Press.

Finally, life happens while books are being written. Our Sunbelt cities "team" was one of the largest involved in the NSF project, including scholars at every career stage and experiencing numerous challenges: Weddings were celebrated, babies were born, dissertations were finished, other books and articles were written, jobs were changed, parents died, tenure was granted, and children grew up and went off to college. We especially appreciate the good-natured support and patience generously expressed by our partners and families throughout what seemed, especially to them, a very protracted research process. Anyone involved in collaborative work understands the pleasures and penalties of such intense and interdependent work: It was not always an easy path but we all take great pride and satisfaction in arriving at this final stage with our friendships and scholarly ties intact and strong.

Interests, Ideas, and Institutions: The Politics of School Reform in Multiethnic Cities

I N DENVER, two African American families mulled over the options for their children.[1] Ronnie and Judy Young started their sons in Denver Public Schools (DPS) and then moved them to private schools due to overcrowding. But their sons were not doing as well as they had hoped despite the comfortable surroundings. Citing teachers' inflexibility about teaching methods, they moved their boys back into DPS. "They are in the mix of things at school just as they will be in society," they wrote.

Sherrie and Kermit Queenan's children also tried public and private schools, but they took the opposite stand. Starting in an African American private school—Union Baptist Excel Institute—the kids did well, but the Queenans sent them to public school when they had difficulty paying tuition. There, the kids lost ground. Thus the Queenans "scraped and scrimped," and reenrolled Thanes, Kelsianna, and Kershena in Excel. To these parents, the difference between the schools was that Excel teachers valued all children. They asked, "How can a system as large and well-funded as DPS be failing our children?" Their answer is the lack of competition: "As the only game in town, DPS has little incentive to improve."[2] The Queenans wanted to know "How can many private schools educate a child better than DPS for far less money [per student]?"

These questions trouble many parents, but they especially affect parents of color. To them, public schools continue to be the last, best hope for their children's future. Yet, like the Queenans, many wonder why these schools fail to meet their expectations and to address their concerns. As one headline in the *Denver Post* put it, "DPS gets passing grade in teaching white children."

(Illescas 1998); the implication being that, unlike white students, Latino, African American, and Asian children remain poorly served by the public school systems in many American cities.[3] To many Latino and Asian parents, especially in multiethnic cities like Denver, the apparent success of African Americans in shaping school reform may now seem to be part of the problem. The mobilization and collective action of the civil rights campaigns in the 1950s, 1960s, and 1970s remain inspirational models for other minority groups in the United States. Ironically, however, these historic political successes can appear as political barriers to other groups seeking access and influence in local education politics. These barriers are not intentional, nor are they permanent. Thus, to begin to understand the politics of school reform in multiethnic cities, we must consider instances in which past reforms privileged certain definitions of school problems and created educational institutions in which school officials initially had few incentives to respond to newly emerging school constituencies.

As court-ordered desegregation plans were challenged, relaxed, and eventually lifted in many cities in the 1980s and 1990s, a window of opportunity seemed to open for new, more diverse voices, and for the expression of new ideas about school reform. This "multiethnic moment," which occurred at different points in each of the cities studied—San Francisco, Boston, Denver, and Los Angeles (see Figure 1.1)—did not lead to greater responsiveness to new multiethnic school constituencies. Indeed, all students of color appear to be doing little better this decade than in the 1990s. This book addresses this puzzle—the difficulties in taking advantage of this historical multiethnic moment to pursue more responsive school reforms—by analyzing the interests, ideas, and institutions in play during this period in the cities studied. Our story about the multiethnic moment emphasizes how these configurations contributed to each city's lagged responses to new multiethnic school constituencies in the 1990s. We see these dynamics taking place in a larger context of "two-tiered pluralism," in which historical, socioeconomic, and cultural forces blunt the prospects for responding to racial and ethnic claims. The emergence during this period of national school-reform movements that centered on market mechanisms and emphasized "choice" rather than equity—characterized here as the "new educational populism"—also limited the ability of new multiethnic interests to take advantage of this window of opportunity.

The Puzzle of School Reform
in Multiethnic Cities

All parents share a common interest in the quality of their children's education. In a survey of eight hundred African American and eight hundred white parents, majorities of both groups agreed on the primacy of basic education needs;

eight in ten black parents said the goals of integration and diversity should be secondary to raising academic standards and achievement (Morin 1998). But how best to meet these basic needs remains a contentious question.

The question of school reform is an increasingly salient one for American cities. While many cities can boast of a string of redevelopment projects through the 1990s and into the current decade, they appear stalemated in responding to the educational needs that leaders and the public see as central to future development. It is not that leaders resist demands to do something about education. Rather, city officials and citizens cannot agree on appropriate strategies and have trouble linking education with other city priorities.

Multiethnic school constituencies further complicate this problem. While multiethnic local politics are the distinctive stuff of U.S. political and social history, their resurgence and distinct form in recent years merits greater attention. This is particularly so where cities are now dealing with levels of ethnic and racial diversity comparable to those at the turn of the nineteenth century in older industrial cities. History is only a partial guide, however, to understanding current realities. Structural reforms of local governments in the intervening years, national and state intervention in local education policies, and the arrival and growth of different racial and ethnic groups with distinctive histories ensure that local responses will depart significantly from those of the last century. And most importantly, new school constituencies are emerging in nearly every American city; the majority of children in many public school districts now are from "minority group" backgrounds—Latino and Asian as well as African American.[4]

Our story about school reform in multiethnic cities is complex and, we think, compelling. We argue that the current mismatch of school reform agendas with the concerns of new school constituencies is partially rooted in the bittersweet legacy of African Americans' experience in gaining control of local schools from white professionals and experts. While these victories rarely led to the improvement of educational achievement sought by black parents, the programs and personnel associated with desegregation initiatives became institutionalized. As Latinos and Asians become the new school majorities, these institutional legacies inevitably shape—and often seem to frustrate—their interests and rebuff their ideas.

This is not new. Over time, many conflicts over educational priorities stem from institutional lags and competing problem definitions (see Peterson 1985). But the contemporary education debate is notable for decoupling equity concerns from school reform proposals. In the postdesegregation era, without strong public institutions promoting educational equity for racial and ethnic minority groups, we witness the emergence of a new policy paradigm—one we call "the new educational populism"—that features market efficiency and privatization for the provision of public education. We hear a shift from equity to commodity in the dominant talk about school reform, and see the impacts

FIGURE 1.1 TIMELINE: SAN FRANCISCO

1960	1965	1970	1975	1980	1985	1990	1995	2000	2005
1962 *Brock v. Boardman*: CORE sues SFUSD on segregation, wants race-based school assignments	1969 District seeks targeted desegregation, Mayor opposes any busing and puts referendum on ballot: voters reject busing	1970 *Johnson v. SFUSD*: NAACP sues to prevent efforts to halt desegregation	1978 Superintendent replaces plan with percent-based formula.	1981 Court appoints Settlement Team.	Four phases of CD then implemented with uneven effects.	1992 Committee of Experts evaluates CD: finds more integration but not much academic excellence	1997 Judge rejects Ho plaintiffs	2000 SFUSD develops index of 6 socioeconomic indicators to assign students to over-subscribed schools.	2005 Judge denies request to extend CD
1963 District concedes, NAACP drops suit	District continues work on desegregation plans	1971 Court orders SFUSD to desegregate all elementary schools in 4 months	NAACP tries to reopen Johnson case, but is dismissed	1982 Agree to Consent Decree (CD)	1986 Ramon Cortines is new Superintendent: openly hostile to CD	1993 SFUSD: Comprehensive School Improvement Plan to identify low-performing schools who will face reconstitution.	1999 Judge and SFUSD agree to end use of racial and ethnic criteria in school assignment; decision to end court-ordered desegregation efforts by 2002.	New Supt. promises to expand reconstitution in Dream Schools Initiative.	Arlene Ackerman resigns as 1st African American SFUSD Superintendent. Later succeeded by Gwen Chan, 1st Chinese American in post
		SFUSD adopts Horseshoe Plan: desegregation zones. White flight and Chinese withdrawal to Freedom Schools.	*NAACP v. SFUSD*: alleges Bayview-Hunters Point area shows deliberate racial concentration, underrepresentation of African Americans on teaching and administration, unequal access to school and after-school programs.	1983 CD approved to end NAACP desegregation suit. Sets guidelines on student assignment and academic excellence goals. Approves reconstitution strategy.		1994 Latino and Chinese attempt to become parties to Overseeing Committee of CD: denied by judge but given amicus status.		2004 Monitoring Committee requests extension of CD beyond 2005 to meet achievement goals.	2005 CD set to formally terminate in 2005.

FIGURE 1.1 TIMELINE: SAN FRANCISCO (*continued*)

1960	1965	1970	1975	1980	1985	1990	1995	2000	2005
						1994 *Ho v SFUSD*: Chinese American parents claim CD is uncon- stitutional system of racial classifi- cation, denies them access to preferred schools.			

FIGURE 1.1 TIMELINE: BOSTON

1960	1965	1970	1975	1980	1985	1990	1995	2000	2005
		1972 *Morgan v. Harrigan*: Black parents sue, claim BPS schools are intentionally segregated. 1973 MA Board of Education mandates a racial balance plan for Boston. 1974 State passes "Racial Imbalance Law" prohibiting imbalance and discourging schools from student enrollments that are more than 50% minority.	1975 SC fails to submit plan. Judge appoints 4-member committee to create a Master Plan for BPS integration. Master Plan divides city into community districts for paired school assignments. Sets up 32 citywide magnet schools; judge sets aside 35% of seats at top 3 exam schools for black and other minority students.	1982 Court cites BPS "good faith effort," begins "transitional disengagement," and assigns monitoring task to State Dept. of Education.	1985 Judge enters final orders: sets affirmative action goals for student assignment, teachers, and administrators. BPS and BTU appeal orders. 1986 Supt. and Task Force suggest changes to Plan: the implementation of district-wide school choice, the opening of parent information centers, the end of magnet schools, the decentralization of assignment process.	1990 Judge issues final judgment, approves Controlled Choice to replace busing; SC responsible for student assignments. Controlled Choice set for K-12. 1991 Latino parents' El Comite joins black plaintiffs. 1992 Mayor gains power to appoint 7-member School Committee.	1996 Successful challenge to set-asides in exam school admissions; SC relaxes racial guidelines. 1997 BPS Desegregation case officially closed. 1999 Boston's Children First sues, seeking race-neutral school-admissions policy and mandatory neighborhood school assignments.	2003 U.S. District Court rejects BCF, upholds BPS walk-zone policy, says 3 master zones no longer being used for racial balancing. SC and Supt. begin public forums to devise new assignment plans.	2005 SC decides to retain existing plan and develop indicators of school quality to inform parents' choice. BPS simplifies choice process to allow students to attend nearby schools BPS builds 19 pilot schools over last 10 years BPS converts four high schools to 13 smaller specialty schools

FIGURE 1.1 TIMELINE: BOSTON *(continued)*

1960	1965	1970	1975	1980	1985	1990	1995	2000	2005
		BPS ordered to change assignment procedures Judge finds BPS is racially segregated, orders implementation of state racial balance plan, orders School Committee (SC) to create plan. Orders state racial balance plan as temporary remedy: Phase I includes busing. Busing between Roxbury and South Boston begins with many disturbances.			1987 Experimental Community District 8 set up to increase school choice in 4 areas heavily impacted by busing. U.S. Court of Appeals finds BPS attained "unitary status." Can design own assignment plan. 1989 SC adopts Controlled Choice for K–6 50.8% Boston voters approve referendum giving Mayor direct control of schools	1993 State passes legislation authorizing charter schools, district-wide choice, fiscal equalization across the district, core learning, and statewide testing.	SC votes to end use of race in school assignments, end Controlled Choice, and move to neighborhood schools. SC adopts New Choice Plan with assignments based on walking zones to nearby schools.		

FIGURE 1.1 TIMELINE: DENVER

1960	1965	1970	1975	1980	1985	1990	1995	2000	2005
	1969 Keyes v. DPS: claims segregated schools in Northeast Denver. Judge rules intentional segregation, orders desegregation of Northeast schools.	**1973** Judge orders complete desegregation of Northeast Denver schools. **1974** Busing begins: about 1/3 in district bused. State voters approve Constitutional amendment prohibiting busing for racial purposes. State voters approve constitutional amendment prohibiting annexations by Denver without voter approval.	**1975** DPS makes numerous appeals in late 1970s to be released from desegregation order; refused by judge.	**1984** DPS asks to be released from court order. Judge upholds court order, says DPS not meeting needs of bilingual students. Court accepts DPS and Congress of Hispanic Educators' new bilingual program.	**1986** Judge orders DPS to improve integration at 3 elementary schools: DPS proposes magnet schools. **1987** Judge relaxes oversight.	**1991** State sets up Collaborative Decision Making units at all schools. **1992** DPS again asks for release. DPS switches from at-large to district election for school board. **1993** State adopts statewide standards-based education. State Charter Schools Act signed. DPS again asks for release.	**1995** Judge releases DPS from court orders. DPS approves plan for 9 neighborhood walk-in schools to attract whites back to district. **1997** Busing ends. Board allows Supt. to identify failing schools for possible reconstitution.	**2000** State passes statewide standards program with penalties for failing schools. **2003** Mayor Hickenlooper supports, voters approve $312M DPS bond	**2005** Padres Unidos issues report critical of Latino outcomes measures in DPS. Mayor's Chief of Staff named DPS Superintendent. DPS faces budget shortfall blamed on loss of students to charter schools. Denver voters approve $25M teacher-pay-for-performance plan. Superintendent Bennett announces "Denver Plan," overhauling DPS.

FIGURE 1.1 TIMELINE: LOS ANGELES

1960	1965	1970	1975	1980	1985	1990	1995	2000	2005
	1968 *Serrano v. Priest*: to end pupil funding inequalities based on property tax. 1970 Court-ordered desegregation.	1972 LASB appeals desegregation. 1974 NAACP sues LASB.	1976 *Crawford v LA School Board*: CA Supreme Court upholds desegregation order but relaxes enrollment criteria; gives LA Superior Court authority to approve plan. 1977 LASB proposes voluntary plan. U.S. Supreme Court rules against LASB: busing begins. Superior Court rules against LASB plan. 1979 Board changes to district-based elections.	1980 State voters approve Prop.1 stopping mandatory integration. Court jurisdiction ends. LAUSD adopts voluntary desegregation plan focused on blacks, Latinos, Asians. Magnet schools used for desegregation. 1981 Busing ends.	1986 LASB approves bilingual program.	1991 LEARN forms 1992 *Rodriguez v LAUSD*: consent decree for uniform per-pupil funding in district. 1993 Board adopts LEARN reforms. 1994 State voters pass Proposition 187: teachers must notify if undocumented immigrant students in classroom; no access to public education for undocumented immigrants. Not implemented.	1995 LAAMP forms: *Metro v. LAUSD* reform focus, excludes education system members 1998 State voters pass Proposition 227 eliminating/revamping bilingual education.	2000 Roy Romer becomes LAUSD Superintendent. LEARN and LAAMP merge. 2001 Initiative to break up LAUSD fails to make ballot. Supporters include whites and Asians in Valley; opposed by Latinos and African Americans. 2002–2004 Four bond measures pass to support new school construction. 2004 Board agrees to small schools initiative.	2005 Mayor Villaraigosa seeks greater control over city schools; School Board and unions oppose. Conflict over LAUSD breakup views ongoing.

inherent in many of the reform ideas enacted and proposed across our cities. The specific reforms couched in these terms have serious distributional consequences for parents and students of color—some benefits, perhaps, but also significant risks.

Throughout this book, we emphasize the ways in which current educational problems and reforms are shaped by the political and policy legacies of the past. In particular, the multiethnic "moment" emerging in the 1980s and 1990s as court-ordered desegregation plans were lifted in many American cities presented an opportunity for schools to adjust to increasingly diverse multiethnic student populations and new educational reform strategies. Their difficulties in doing so exemplify the puzzle of school reform in multiethnic cities. From the critical juncture created by challenges to and eventually the lifting of court sanctions, cities took different paths as they dealt with new interests and new ideas about schools. New school constituencies of Latino and Asian parents often defined "the problem with schools" differently than many African American and Anglo parents. Our research indicates these are competing definitions of problems rather than ideological differences per se: Parents of color brought different preferences for policy solutions to the table. And, critically, these groups were often unable to articulate preferences with a coherent and consistent voice. This underscores our argument that demographic change and new interests alone are insufficient to change local education policies, and highlights the ways in which institutions shape preferences and filter reform ideas. We organize our findings with an analytical framework that directs attention to the ways in which the intersection of interests, ideas, and institutions drives policy change. Based on fieldwork in four cities, our work differs from a conventional case study approach as well as an exclusive focus on structural or behavioral features in that ours takes into account the importance of history and contingency to school reform in each of the cities studied. This necessarily leads us to acknowledge the persistence of two-tiered pluralism as the context for school reform politics.

The Mismatch of School Reform Agendas and Multiethnic Constituencies

To many Latino and Asian parents, there is a mismatch between what they believe their children need and what school reforms define as the problem. Local education policy often appears to lag behind the new realities of increasing social diversity and new school constituencies, resulting in a striking dissonance between the problems and solutions that new school constituencies articulate and the dominant reform ideas school district leaders and other policy actors promote for restructuring public schools. Latinos and Asians are caught in a bind: In the school districts we studied, they found remnants of desegregation initiatives that they either thought irrelevant or objectionable, but the reforms that school officials promoted in place of or in addition to desegregation did not necessarily address their concerns. The ironic conflict between programs developed to accommodate past demands for desegregation and the dramatic shift in the students served by public schools often put parents of color at odds and at a loss for influencing school policies.[5]

In substantial part, this mismatch stemmed from the persistence of a historical policy paradigm centered on school integration. School policymaking, personnel, and programs in multiethnic cities often continued to reflect the interests and ideas packaged together by African Americans decades ago when *they* challenged the professional elites controlling educational policy. By adopting policies and programs responding to blacks' interests and values, school districts regained the stability and equilibrium threatened by the tumult of the integration struggles. But from the viewpoint of new school constituencies, blacks' hard-won gains in the desegregation struggles of the 1960s and 1970s became the institutions, programs, and privileges of the 1980s and 1990s. In multiethnic settings then, group relations are often substantially more complicated than the biracial or black/white model recognizes. Many assumptions or recommendations about "cooperation" between minority groups overlook real divisions.

As new school constituencies bring different interests and values into the educational arena, they confront the institutionalization of past demands and the structures—both formal and informal—set up by other groups. Their stories about "the problem with schools" threaten to disrupt the policy stability gained by the institutionalization of an educational agenda grounded in the black/white paradigm (Baumgartner and Jones 1993). Certainly these constituencies differ among themselves in how they see "the problem with schools" and what they want to do in response. But they increasingly challenged both the extant definition of school problems as rooted in racial segregation, and also the institutional solutions established to address the segregation.

Instead, new school constituencies in our study tended to emphasize educational achievement goals for their children, but also sought greater cultural tolerance through bilingual education arrangements and better teacher awareness of cultural pluralism. Our research indicates that many of their concerns focused on the uncertain classroom consequences of institutional redesign schemes like vouchers and charter schools. They also reported more basic concerns about class size and teaching methods, and they supported efforts to link other social agencies with schools. While these ideas appear innocuous, they are only pieces of a larger potential reform package in the process of construction. What is apparent is that that they were not part of the wave of school reforms that aimed to restructure public schools and to introduce more choices for parents and students. Not that parents of color necessarily opposed such "big" reforms; rather, they remained unconvinced that institutional redesigns served their interests or broader political principles—to the extent these newer groups were even part of the debate and able to tentatively understand the consequences of the proposed reforms.

Locking in Agendas

The puzzle at the heart of this analysis of multiethnic cities is this mismatch of current reforms emphasizing school restructuring and "choice" with the more pragmatic preferences of new school constituencies and their desires for equity. Although Latinos or Asians constituted the majority of the school-age populations in three of our cities in the 1990s and a growing share of the school-age population in the fourth city, their interests and ideas remained marginal in educational institutions and in school administration and policy-making networks. Despite the desires and efforts of multiethnic school constituencies with different ideas about the causes of education problems and appropriate solutions, this mismatch between the needs articulated and the solutions adopted continued to be a feature of the local education policy agendas. The composition and relative needs of school constituencies changed, but education policies seem locked into paths advocated from outside the growing Latino and Asian communities in the case cities.

Notwithstanding some representation on school boards, the relative absence of both Latinos and Asians from the education policy arena in these multiethnic cities and also their lack of policy influence were striking. When Asian and Latino voices were present, they were rarely engaged in basic framing and formulation of reforms. As we characterize it in Chapter 2, they were relegated to a second tier of influence; at best, they experienced policies designed *for* their communities rather than having the opportunity to design policies themselves.

Our purpose in examining this school reform puzzle is not to argue that one set of interests and stories should replace—or displace—another. Nor is it to assess and evaluate specific reforms or to grade cities on their reform efforts. Instead, we want to understand how and why certain groups are not fully incorporated in education reform debates in the first place; and also to explore how the limited inclusion of such groups and their ideas affects how a community deals with educational problems.

Why the Resurgence of Education Politics?

The continuing sense of crisis, particularly for urban school districts, is clear. There is no denying that many—maybe even the majority—of the 11 million children in urban public schools do not have the same educational resources and experiences as students in other settings. The facts are striking: Compared to students in nonurban districts, children in urban schools are less likely to graduate on time, less likely to meet minimum standards on national tests, less likely to have parental involvement in their schools, more likely to face violence in their schools, more likely to have teachers with only temporary licenses, more likely to go to school in deteriorating buildings, and more likely to be in schools where a majority of the students are poor and where most are ethnic and racial minorities (*Education Week* 1998).

These conditions are not new. From a historical perspective, educational policy reform activities appear to be cyclical (Tyack and Cuban 1995). Yet the attention to education is rarely related simply to changing conditions in the schools: Policy attention is often independent of significant problems or dramatic changes in indicators of educational achievement. Indeed, despite the escalating critique of public education, there is also consistent evidence of relatively effective public school performance overall. To begin to make sense of this paradoxical situation, we put the recent attention to public education in the broader context of localized tensions and anxieties associated with major economic and social changes.

Major social and economic transformations reconfigure interests and introduce competing ideas about city fortunes and children's futures. The growth of multiethnic school constituencies is a significant local impact of these larger changes. We highlight three ways that larger social and economic trends matter for local education politics: They bring new interests with new values into the political process (Inglehart 1990), they introduce new ideas linking economic development with human capital development, and they underscore the degree to which local political institutions lag in responding to new realities. Social and economic forces also exacerbate the poverty, crime, racism, and economic displacement long viewed as contributing to the problems in urban schools. As we see it, the distinctive local context emerging in response to these changing conditions in the last two decades sets boundaries for what is possible, but does not determine what will happen in local educational reform politics.

New Interests: Economic Trends and Immigration Flows

What appeared initially to be a process of deindustrialization in the 1970s and 1980s—an absolute decline in the number of industrial jobs—is now recognized as a shift from manufacturing employment to service industries and a shift in the location of jobs in these new sectors. The U.S. employment structure is changing from the production and shift work associated with industrial production to the knowledge-based jobs of design, marketing, finance and other specialized services; there is also a shift from full-time to part-time jobs. The number of production workers in the U. S. has been declining since 1973; along with increased substitution of capital for labor, there is a shift from labor-intensive to capital-intensive production modes. A two-tiered wage structure is emerging at every scale to reflect these differential skill needs; increasingly educational attainment drives earnings. Over the years, this has become increasingly true independent of race: Christopher Jencks and Meredith Phillips (1998) report that earnings of black and white men scoring above the 50th percentile on national tests are nearly equal.

Globalization and economic restructuring are open to conflicting interpretations. But nearly every version paints a gloomy picture for American workers who lack the skills and education needed in a knowledge-based economy. These work and wage pressures create new educational agendas in cities. Business interests clearly desire an educational system that will supply them with the symbolic analysts and the specialized expertise necessary to remain competitive. Parents want an educational system that will prepare their children for an uncertain and volatile future—one increasingly less receptive to undereducated, hard-working employees. To parents of color, the experience of African Americans proves that better education holds the key to better earnings. Local government officials want a public educational system that responds to their electorates' needs and, increasingly, is capable of attracting, retaining, and graduating well-prepared students. Even though state and national officials increasingly speak out on educational matters, and despite the mandates of the national 2002 *No Child Left Behind* legislation (NCLB), core education decisions remain in the hands of local officials. In making these decisions, they face an array of new interests and values in a context of growing diversity.

Social Diversity

Because of jurisdictional fragmentation and class- and race-based suburbanization patterns, many metropolitan areas resemble mosaics of racial and ethnic groupings (Table 1.1). Blacks and Latinos now make up almost half the population in many large U.S. cities; most American cities are now multiethnic. Denver, Los Angeles, San Francisco, and Boston—the cities studied in this book—represent this shift toward multiethnic populations, both in the city generally, and, even more so, in the public schools.

Despite some upward mobility associated with education, blacks, Latinos, and Asians have made only modest economic gains relative to whites overall; this persistent gap exacerbates tensions among groups (Table 1.2). Where these groups are segregated and isolated, they are often poor and jobless or, at best, working poor. The concentrated poverty resulting from unemployment undermines social organization in urban neighborhoods and further distances these groups from gaining access to high-quality jobs and schools (Wilson 1996). As a result, many observers view the metropolitan multiethnic mosaic as the facade of a dual city characterized by economic and social polarization between affluent groups with valued skills and lesser-skilled, marginalized groups.

Increased immigration is part and parcel of globalization and economic restructuring, and is felt keenly at the local level (Ramakrishnan 2005). The 1980s and 1990s had the second largest wave of legal immigration in U.S.

TABLE 1.1 CITIES AND SCHOOLS: MULTIETHNIC CONSTITUENCIES

	Denver	Los Angeles	San Francisco	Boston
2000 Population	554,636	3,694,820	776,733	589,141
% Non-Hispanic White	51.9	29.7	43.6	49.5
% Non-Hispanic Black	11.6	11.4	8.2	25.7
% Hispanic	31.7	46.5	14.1	14.4
% Asian	3.3	10.8	32.6	8.0
1990 Population	467,610	3,485,398	723,959	574,283
% Non-Hispanic White	61.4	37.3	46.6	59.0
% Non-Hispanic Black	12.4	13.0	10.5	23.8
% Hispanic	23.0	39.9	13.9	10.8
% Asian	2.4	9.8	29.1	5.3
Public School Enrollment 2003/04	72,489	746,610	58,750	58,600
% Non-Hispanic White	19.7	9.4	9.6	14
% Non-Hispanic Black	18.9	12.1	14.4	46
% Hispanic	57.0	71.9	21.8	31
% Asian	3.1	3.9	38.8	9
1994/95	62,771	700,000	64,422	60,172*
% Non-Hispanic White	29	11	14	19
% Non-Hispanic Black	21	14	19	48
% Hispanic	45	68	20	23
% Asian	4	7	25	9

* 1992/93 data

TABLE 1.2 ECONOMIC STATUS BY RACE/ETHNICITY IN MULTIETHNIC CITIES

	Denver	Los Angeles	San Francisco	Boston
Household Median Income	$39,500	$36,687	$55,221	$39,629
Non-Hispanic White	44,022	51,516	65,431	47,668
Non-Hispanic Black	30,895	27,236	29,561	31,061
Hispanic	32,636	28,759	46,553	27,141
Asian	36,194	37,195	49,607	27,732
Poverty Rate	14.3	22.1	11.3	19.5
Non-Hispanic White	7.8	10.0	7.7	13.1
Non-Hispanic Black	19.2	28.0	25.0	21.9
Hispanic	22.4	29.6	15.6	30.5
Asian	17.0	16.9	10.7	30.0

Source: U.S. Census, 2000.

history; by 2000, more immigrants lived in the United States than at any other historical period (28.4 million), making up about 10 percent of the population. The origins of immigrants in the 1970s and 1980s primarily included countries in the Caribbean, Central and South America, and Asia. These newcomers are concentrated in ten metropolitan areas (including Boston, Los Angeles, and San Francisco).[6] While the percentage of immigrants with professional and technical skills is higher than the U.S. average, this varies by group. It is also clear that immigrants often bring entrepreneurial initiatives to communities, creating jobs and providing for unmet market needs in many areas. Thus the local impacts of immigration include labor market effects and public costs—especially for education and social services—which will vary according to the particular characteristics of the local immigrant communities.

Greater social diversity introduces new school constituencies into most American cities. With higher birth rates among Latinos and Asians relative to blacks and Anglos, these will be growing school constituencies for years to come. Currently, 43 percent of racial/ethnic minority children go to urban public schools, as do 35 percent of poor children (*Education Week* 1998). The contrast between the public school constituency and the city population is especially stark in multiethnic cities, where white people often are the majority or the plurality in the city but children of color are the majority in the school population.[7] For example, during our study period, about 50 percent of Boston's residents were white, but only 14 percent of the public school population was white. As one commentator put it, two Bostons exist—one white, with "high numbers of childless households, and one nonwhite and Hispanic, dominated by families with children" (Sege 1991). Such developments diminish a sense of common ownership of a city's public school system. Given that these demographic changes intertwine with economic shifts that create a dual economy in cities, social diversity may occur alongside greater fiscal uncertainty and distress. For many cities, these tensions appear to be manageable only by seeking greater support for schools from the private sector. But the business sector is undergoing significant transformations as well.

The Business Sector

Large-scale transformations do not challenge the privileged role of business in local politics; indeed, many would argue that globalization of the economy and the emergence of multinational corporations means that business interests will increasingly prevail in competition with any other local interests. Businesses that depend on strong human capital, as well as those with geographically specific assets (Berk and Swanstrom 1995), may see local education policies as influencing their competitive position within a global economy. This segment of the business sector may now be more attentive and responsive to education issues, more willing to negotiate with school officials, and more committed to establishing the alliances that would support their human capital concerns. But dialogue will not occur simply because the composition of the business community has changed, or because of the presence of visionary business leaders; it also depends on whether local institutional arrangements allow diverse voices and new agendas to be heard and whether they enable the development of shared understandings.

Boston provides a telling example. For over 35 years, the Coordinating Committee in Boston—known locally as "the Vault"—brought together the CEOs of about 30 major businesses to address policy issues. In 1982, members of the Vault joined leaders of higher education, labor, city government, and public schools to sign the Boston Compact to support improved school performance and to link schools with employers. Yet there was little meaningful African American, Latino, or Asian representation in Boston's longstanding business-dominated education coalitions (Nelson 1999). Now the Vault no longer functions, while the Compact continues to play a lead role in school reform initiatives.

New Ideas: Linking Human Capital and Economic Growth

In addition to new sets of interests, the transformations of globalization and economic restructuring bring new ideas about the significance of education. Much of the energy and attention now directed toward education reform stems from the conviction that human capital is critical to future economic growth (Reich 1991). Today, innovation rather than factor costs determines productivity and profit in dynamic new sectors. Changes in the nature of competition, growth processes, and production systems require rethinking accepted economic assumptions. There is growing consensus that a base of knowledge and skills is essential both to individual success and to community well-being (Clarke and Gaile 1998).

But neoclassical economic models analyzing the role of physical capital in economic growth are less useful when considering how human capital fosters economic growth. As Figure 1.2 indicates, the attributes of physical capital differ dramatically from those of human capital. These differences pose challenges to community leaders in government and business when they attempt to rethink education policy in their cities. Indeed, uncertainty about how to link human capital development to economic development marked education politics in the studied cities. Local business leaders in these cities were forthright in contrasting their greater success in economic development projects with their difficulties investing in human capital through education reform. They pointed out that human capital projects lack a profit incentive to stimulate participation and action, lack an obvious set of operating procedures, require interaction with educational bureaucracies (about whom they are wary), involve long-term time horizons, and risk "leakage" of local investment due to labor mobility. The knowledge base for human capital strategies is neither

FIGURE 1.2 A COMPARISON OF HUMAN AND PHYSICAL CAPITAL

ATTRIBUTE	HUMAN CAPITAL	PHYSICAL CAPITAL
Global Economic Importance	Increasing	Decreasing
Policy Goals	Often Diffuse	More Focused
Mobility	Relatively high	Relatively low
Returns over time	Increase	Diminish
Assets	Non-ownable	Ownable
Flexibility	High	Low
Measurability of Success Complex Measures	Ambiguous, Multiple, and Concrete Measures	More Tangible and
Federal Policy Tools	Modest grants	Capital Gains Exemptions, Investment Tax Credits
Political Dynamics	Competitive and Client Politics	Entrepreneurial and Short Majoritarian Politics

Source: Original figure in Clarke and Gaile (1998). Revised by Rodney Hero.

coherent nor consensual; the policy community is fragmented by specialization as well as ideological differences. Disagreements arise about the very nature of human capital problems, the appropriate policy goals and strategies, and the appropriate methods of evaluating success.

Yet the American context of federalism, and a political climate emphasizing devolution, means that local actors must struggle with such issues if they are to address the locally felt deficits in human capital. Only 7 percent of the nation's education spending derived from the national government during our study period, making the American education system one of the most highly decentralized in the world (Applebome 1997). National education initiatives, such as the Clinton Administration's proposals to improve state teaching standards or encourage development of a national curriculum and voluntary national tests, were labeled as creeping "federalization" of American education (Applebome 1997). An exception is the bipartisan congressional support for the federal Charter School Grant Program, launched in 1995 with a modest appropriation of six million dollars and the goal of creating three thousand charter schools by the turn of the century.

Now, the ambitious agenda embedded in the 2002 reauthorization of the Elementary and Secondary Education Act alters the education landscape. The NCLB legislation means that states now must test all students annually from third to eighth grades and there is a federal drive for universal literacy among school children. Far from abolishing the Department of Education, as advocated by Republican Party leaders, President George W. Bush embarked on a significant redefinition of the federal role in education and provided for substantial increases in federal school funding. This funding increase, however, was dedicated to standardized testing—not to educational equity directly. At best, the implication was that more testing and accountability would lead to greater equity. Beyond charting differential test scores by race and ethnicity, however, there is little federal attention to the distinctive and dramatic concerns of ethnic and racial minority populations with low education outcomes. Indeed, the emphasis on standardized testing is perceived as diverting resources from substantive educational programs needed by disadvantaged students.[8] To many education experts, as test-based accountability came to dominate the public education agenda, achievement gaps of racial and ethnic minority students increasingly challenged existing approaches (Hendrie 2004). As one analyst put it, "there was a tremendous amount of gap-narrowing in the 1970s and 1980s, and somewhere around 1990, that gap-narrowing stopped" (Hendrie 2004).

In our cities, many Latino, Asian, and African American respondents believed that local schools were "falling short" of what they could and should do (see Chapter 5). What this means, however, is a matter for debate. Although most Americans say minorities receive an equal education in local schools, for example, more than half of black parents call underachievement among black students a "crisis." Two-thirds of Americans say children of recent immigrants should take all their classes in English while Latinos are more likely to say that children of immigrants should be able to take some courses in their native language. In 1999, African Americans (50 percent) and Latinos (40 percent) were more likely than whites (27 percent) to perceive racism in education. But only 54 percent of whites, compared to 90 percent of blacks, think more should be done to integrate schools (Publicagenda.org 2000). Different racial and ethnic groups see schools in markedly different ways.

Changing Institutions

Globalization and economic restructuring bring more—and more diverse—actors into the local political arena, along with the greater complexity of human capital investment needs. The emergence of a third sector of nonprofit organizations challenges the local institutional infrastructure to accommodate different bargaining and negotiating processes. These broad changes add to the already fragmented education policy environment. In many cities, school districts are independent political entities; much of the difficulty in reforming education stems from the problems of overcoming this fragmentation between city and school governments. With the rise of the charter school movement, nonprofit organizations now also supply public education. Local officials must play a more activist role in interactions with nonstate sectors by moderating and managing interests and providing resources on a conditional basis. As new actors and organizations crowd into the educational arena, the fragmentation and complexity increases.

The expansion of the local sphere and the increase in different types of actors exacerbates the dilemma of generating "enough cooperation" to get things done (Stone 1989). Bringing the necessary actors to the table and then negotiating cooperation are new local government responsibilities. The need is to find new institutional and organizational arrangements with sufficient scope, responsiveness, and flexibility to accommodate this complexity and interdependence of government and nongovernment actors. Often, however, these models will operate outside formal government structures; the public sector may no longer be the center of negotiations and decision making about public resources.

Interest, Ideas, and Institutions in Multiethnic Cities

Our study analyzes how the reciprocal influence of interests, ideas, and institutions shapes educational reform politics in multiethnic cities. This analytic framework draws on work by Hugh Heclo (1994) and others (Hall 1997; Blyth 1997); it also resonates with David Tyack and Larry Cuban's depiction of public school reform as "an interaction of long-term institutional trends, transitions in society, and policy talk" (1995, 58). These scholars recognize the significance of new interests that emerge from societal transitions, but they also emphasize the importance of the rhetoric used to diagnose problems and advocate solutions, and of the institutions established to implement reforms. As Heclo puts it (1994), these three elements are the building blocks for political analysis. Whereas other theoretical perspectives focus on interests and coalitions (as in urban regime theory, see Henig et al. 1999; Stone et al. 2001), interests and ideas (as in agenda-setting models, see Kingdon 1995), or institutions and ideas (as in historical institutionalism, see Steinmo et al. 1992), this framework brings all three dimensions together.

Our starting point is Heclo's contention that "ideas tell interests what to mean," that "interests tell institutions what to do, and that "institutions tell ideas how to survive" (1994, 383). To understand school politics in multiethnic cities, we must take account of the interactions of ideas, institutions, and interests in the broader context of two-tiered pluralism. These two perspectives— both the configurations of interests, ideas, and institutions, and also two-tiered pluralism—provide the framework for our analysis. As we detail in subsequent chapters, configurations of interests, ideas, and institutions drive policy change by differentially enabling and constraining mobilization around education reform and by blunting the impacts of this mobilization through institutional barriers to nonincremental change.

Mobilizing for School Reform

One way to examine this mobilization is to think about a community's civic capacity—its ability to generate and sustain cooperative efforts across sectors, groups, and institutions (Henig and Stone 1994; Jones et al. 1997; Stone 1998;

Stone et al. 2001). Given the political fragmentation of American local governments, the prospects for generating civic capacity will matter for any local policy initiative, but especially so for education issues in racially and ethnically diverse communities. Civic capacity is problematic in these communities not only because of the variable resources available to different groups, but because the "rhetoric[s] of reform" (Tyack and Cuban 1995, 42) are often dissonant and the institutions available for policymaking and implementation are often perceived as unresponsive to new voices.

We find it impossible to talk about civic capacity and educational reform without directly considering how race and ethnicity both structure and are structured by local politics. It is equally unproductive to think about race independent of the interests, ideas, and institutions that give multiple meanings to race and ethnicity as identities and structures. The very notions of race and ethnicity and their salience are amenable to reformulation, redefinition, and reinvention over time. Because these reinvention processes emerge from power relations, there is no universal pattern; rather they vary by community and context. Thus, in our analysis of four cities with multiethnic populations (Denver, Los Angeles, San Francisco, and Boston), we anticipate variation in the processes by which race and ethnicity are constructed as significant identities and interests, in the rhetoric of reform adopted by different groups, and in their mobilization around distinctive reform initiatives. We expect these processes to mark educational reform politics.

Race, Ethnicity, and Common Grounds for School Reform

The time frame of our analysis begins with each city's court-ordered desegregation ruling that validated African Americans' charges of racial discrimination in education. San Francisco's ruling came in 1971, Denver's in 1973, Boston's in 1974, and Los Angeles's in 1976. These judicial decisions epitomize "punctuated equilibriums" (Baumgartner and Jones 1993): They disrupted a stable policy regime in which professional administrators and teachers controlled education decisions. The rulings set timetables for increasing African American representation in education decisions, and they established state and federal judges as monitors of desegregation's implementation. It is hard to imagine a better example of such abrupt policy change.

We recognize that desegregation "victories" were bittersweet and fleeting: Integration did not bring the degree of improvement in black children's educational achievement that civil rights activists sought, and resegregation occurred rapidly when courts stepped out of the picture. With white flight in response to busing in many communities, a continued reluctance to equalize financing across and within school districts, and the devastating impacts of drugs and gangs in a deindustrializing economy, racially integrated public schools often seemed hollow prizes. African American children remain ill served by public education in the United States, particularly those children in impoverished neighborhoods. To that extent, African Americans, Latinos, and Asians share a common interest in improving public education, but there are few occasions where this common interest prompts multiracial coalitions and mobilization around shared educational reform agendas.

As these court orders were challenged and lifted in the 1980s and 1990s—creating the multiethnic moment of interest here—we found a stalled transition from the desegregation policy paradigm to a new paradigm reflecting the claims of today's new school constituencies. Instead, coexisting with the remnants of the desegregation paradigm, we found the emerging new educational populism paradigm. These initiatives to restructure public schools—often introduced by national policy entrepreneurs lobbying state legislatures—were the most prominent local education policy agenda in the cities at the time of our study. Even now, few policy initiatives are aimed directly at the distinctive needs of new school constituencies or at guaranteeing their attainment of educational equity.

Prospects for Multiethnic Reform Coalitions

To understand the marginalization of Latinos and Asians in urban education, it is important to understand how the desegregation movement privileged definitions of school problems centered on racial equity and created institutions—including rules and laws enforced by court orders—that offered school officials few incentives to respond later to emerging school constituencies.

The irony is that these privileged definitions and institutions persisted, even as consent decrees were lifted in many cities and black children became smaller proportions of school populations in multiethnic cities. They were challenged by advocates of choice and race-neutral policies, but no alternative vocabulary for addressing equity concerns emerged. Some of this persistence and stalemate might be attributed to political coalitions capable of resisting change, which some have even characterized as "cartels" (Rich 1996), but we instead direct attention to the volatile and complex contexts in which educational issues are debated. This context includes the ambiguous ethnic identities and political resources of Latinos and Asians, the difficulties of reaching shared understandings of school problems that would lead to consensus on a new policy paradigm, and the institutional incentives that encourage the churning of educational reforms (Hess 1998). The importance of the institutional contexts in each city—those sites where issues are raised and sometimes resolved—cannot be underestimated. And it is unclear whether the institutional restructuring at the heart of school reforms incorporating consumer choice will be enough to enable parents and students of color to overcome the larger social and economic constraints they face in exercising their choices.

INTERESTS, IDEAS, AND INSTITUTIONS

Analyzing the Local Politics of School Reform

In part, the historical legal separation and institutional autonomy of most big-city school districts and local governments encourages analyses of school politics as isolated from the politics of the city. Furthermore, urban political-economy perspectives slight education issues in their focus on the tensions between market and government actors over local land development. To undertake this study, we realized we needed to move beyond these unnecessary divisions to a more integrative approach.

Bringing Together Interests, Ideas, and Institutions in School Reform

By bringing interests, ideas, and institutions into the analysis, we are not asking which is a superior explanation, but rather, how they go together (Heclo 1994). In local politics, their interplay is immediately and directly complicated by race and ethnicity: These factors shape the ability to mobilize "civic capacity" to address educational reform issues and bring about policy change (see also Wells and Scott 1999). We looked at the educational agendas adopted in each city and asked whether there was a gap or mismatch between items on the agenda and the preferences and needs of new constituencies articulated during our fieldwork in each city. Where these gaps existed—and we found them to varying degrees in each of our cities—we asked how the configuration of interests, ideas, and institutions explained them, and shed light on the difficulties of overcoming them. The analysis highlights the coalitions controlling educational reform choices, but also underscores the importance of policy ideas and institutions that can lock these regimes into certain ways of seeing the world and solving problems.

Interests

We ground our analysis in the material conditions and everyday realities of the citizens of Denver, Los Angeles, San Francisco, and Boston. Their concerns about their children's education are strong and valid. These concerns were intense enough in some instances that groups mobilized and formed organizations articulating their needs and advocating particular solutions. Organization was contingent on group resources, including not only material resources— time, money, and organizational skills—but also social capital on which the group could draw to articulate and act upon their problems. The stock of social capital varied by community; it stemmed from the trust and mutuality built by citizens sharing a place, common activities, and often, common cultural features such as language and religion.

Taking a simple interest-group model, the new school constituencies' internal resources and dynamics initially appeared to explain the marginalization

puzzle for our cities. Their lack of spatial concentration, insufficient social capital, multiple cultural identities, low socioeconomic status, mix of citizenship
statuses, among other features, all seemed plausible explanations for Latinos'
and Asians' lack of political access and influence. But as we argue in Chapter
4, it is essential to probe further the mobilization and representation of racial
and ethnic minorities. Attributing lack of access and representation to weak
organization and incoherent voices within these multiethnic communities is
only a starting point, not the conclusion.

Any explanation of educational reform is inadequate if based solely on
the differential efforts and resources—common measures of self-interest—
of the groups involved, and thus their coalitional prospects. Both the climate of
ideas and the institutional opportunity structures in a particular city will shape
group resources and motivations in important ways. Notably, interest-group
analyses tend to slight governance issues, particularly the difficulties of organ-
izing coordination to promote agendas in a complex decision setting.

But if not the groups themselves, perhaps it is a matter of linkages between
groups. Some analysts of school politics draw on regime theory to bring issues
of cooperation and agendas to the forefront (Henig et al. 1999; Portz et al.
1999; Stone et al. 2001). In regime theory, the ability to get things done is an
important aspect of power. The formation of governing regimes—here, education policy regimes—that bring together groups with access to critical
resources is essential to school reform. Regime models emphasize that
"resource-rich" sectors, such as business, are attractive coalition prospects
while, implicitly, resource-poor groups such as racial and ethnic minorities may
be more problematic partners. New school constituencies control few material
resources; furthermore, cleavages of ethnicity, race, and class may make these
school constituencies less attractive coalition members because of a lack of
internal coherence. In contrast to the iterative exchanges that produce some
trust, reciprocity, and internal cohesion within the business community, the
multiethnic composition of school constituencies often stymies such efforts.
Indeed, the typical use of selective incentives or small opportunities (Stone
1989) to maintain coalitions may exacerbate competition in multiethnic constituencies and destabilize coalitional arrangements.

On the other hand, strategic knowledge is also a resource that gives some
groups privileged access to governing coalitions (Stoker 1995). And community
and civic groups have noncredentialed knowledge of their communities and
constituencies essential for implementing reforms; this makes them potentially
more attractive as coalition members. From a regime perspective, the influence
wielded by racial and ethnic groups in education politics may be less a function
of their internal resources than their control over external resources and strategic knowledge essential for "getting things done" in the education arena.

This coalitional perspective moves attention away from the assets of particular groups and draws attention to the conditions under which reform interests

mobilize. Clearly, educational reform is no longer only, or largely, a matter of working through the district hierarchy to carry out district-devised initiatives. The increasing role that state officials and nonprofit organizations play in education politics means that reform now entails creating coalitions that reach across sectors and government levels. Often, the ideas driving local mobilization are promoted by foundations and policy entrepreneurs operating in national arenas. These external actors can intervene in local decisions, advocating policy solutions for motives that may have little to do with the local situation. Policy regime members are less likely to be coherent or even in frequent contact. Policy windows open and policy entrepreneurs emerge from outside the local system, with the critical agenda-setting processes often occurring independently of local dynamics. In addition, state and federal governments can both create and contribute to local problems as well as constrain the solutions possible at the local level. Reaching consensus on appropriate policy solutions becomes that much more difficult with multiple actors involved at different scales. Once consensus is reached or reforms are imposed on local school systems, the complexity of actors and scales exacerbates path dependency and makes policy change more difficult.

Coalitional strategies are key to contemporary school reform struggles. Nevertheless, coalitional perspectives alone cannot account for the ideas about school reform that gain ground in cities and shape school reform struggles before they ever reach the decision stage.

Ideas
Coalitional approaches to political analysis may acknowledge the importance of cognitive and symbolic elements but they focus on decisions. In contrast, ideational approaches shift the focus to *pre*decision processes that set the agenda of possible choices and the range of feasible solutions. Competing definitions of problems and preferred solutions were integral parts of the predecision and agenda-setting processes in our four cities, as set out in Chapter 5. According to Frank R. Baumgartner and Bryan D. Jones (1993), once agendas are set, policy monopolies emerge with distinctive institutional infrastructures that limit further access to the policy process and highlight certain images and symbols. To bring about change, policy entrepreneurs must advocate new images and symbols and seek different policy venues where decisions favoring their views might be made (Mintrom 2000). This element of path dependency underscores the difficulty of policy change and the importance of understanding the contextual conditions under which new directions are possible.

In the multiethnic cities we studied, competing problem definitions, path dependency, and the search for new symbols were at the heart of school reform politics. It is not that ideas independently affected outcomes, but they set boundaries for action when elites used them to frame their preferred solutions. As Hall puts it, "While material conditions may delimit what is possible, policy paradigms delimit what is practical in a given political struggle" (Blyth 1997, 237).

An ideational perspective is especially important in the education arena. Education differs from distributive policies because it incorporates values, status, history, tradition, and other normative expectations. Dominant policy ideas can preclude the ability of some groups to access power and influence. As Gerry Stoker (1995) notes, we can characterize regimes by the reform agendas they promote as much as by the sectors or groups their participants represent; agendas shape access to coalition membership as much as group resources do. Policy ideas thus can explain regime continuity and change; turning to ideas can be a fruitful means of bringing racial and ethnic differences into the analysis without presuming that these differences tell the story on their own.

We don't assume that race and ethnicity are the central explanatory factors in our analysis of education politics, but neither do we anticipate that a common understanding of how to pursue, much less ensure, quality education will emerge when the social, historical, and cultural experiences of African Americans, Latinos, Asians, and whites differ so markedly (Hero 1992, 1998; Meier and Stewart 1991). By focusing on competing reform agendas, we gain a better understanding of what different school constituencies want, what they actually get, and what factors shape their access and influence.

Stalemates in education reform may exist because of *segmented agendas* as much as from entrenched interests resisting new demands. Differences in how groups see "the problem with schools" set the stage long before outright conflicts occur. Our interviews with Latino, African American, Asian, and Anglo community leaders delineated important differences in problem definition that shaped the capacity for collective action. Although there was a multitude of problems with schools, groups in each city varied in the extent to which they attributed these to the school district itself, to school-community relations, or to larger social problems. Furthermore, racial and ethnic groups within these cities varied in their agreement on these problem definitions. Indeed, the four cities varied in terms of whether there was a consensus among groups as to what, precisely, the concerns were, their relative priority, how they should be addressed, and even a broad sense of "where we go from here."

The politics of ideas are therefore critical to our analysis: We ask whether court-ordered desegregation in the 1960s and 1970s locked in a particular definition of education problems and prescribed particular solutions and institutional arrangements that contributed to policy monopolies and path dependency in urban education. The notion of a multiethnic moment directs our attention to both the different paths on which cities embarked when these conditions changed with the lifting of court orders, and the interests, ideas, and institutions that shaped these paths.

Although ideas play a significant role in the puzzle of school reform, we find that coalitional and ideational perspectives can understate the ways in

which institutions construct racial and ethnic identities and educational interests. A stronger institutional perspective provides the strategic context necessary for explaining how policy conflicts and multiethnic politics play out
across cities.

Institutions

We draw on new institutionalism to characterize institutions as settings with
features that help or hinder reaching agreements, coordinating preferences,
and providing options (Heclo 1994; Steinmo et al. 1992). Institutions can
change how groups understand their own interests and affect the types of coalitions that form (Heclo 1994; Croucher 1997). In many ways, this "new institutionalism" resonates with E. E. Schattschneider's (1960) classic argument that
"the nature of political organization depends on the conflicts exploited in the
political system" and the ability of some particular cleavages to gain a dominant
position. As he puts it, "every shift in the line of cleavage affects the nature of
the conflict, produces a new set of winners and losers and a new kind of result."
This provides an incentive to seek institutional change since "organization is
the mobilization of bias," the ability to define alternatives and to organize some
conflicts into politics and some out.

More explicit emphasis on how institutions form and channel goals and
preferences distinguishes historical institutionalism from rational choice versions (Thelen and Steinmo 1992). By seeing institutions in relational terms, we
examine how they structure distributions of power among contending groups
and shape both the strategies and the goals of political actors. Yet this is not a
determinate argument for institutions. As Thelen and Steinmo put it, "institutions constrain and refract politics but they are never the sole 'cause' of outcomes" (1992, 3).

Overall, we view institutions as the legacy of past conjunctures of interests
and ideas, and as the framework for current politics: They articulate working agreements on what can and can't be done, how reforms will be implemented,
and how costs and benefits are to be distributed (Hudson 1995). Legislatures and
courts shape local school politics by presenting distinctive incentives to actors.
By focusing on institutional changes, salient ideas, and levels of interest group
influence is understood in the context of local decision-making processes
rather than seen as a matter of symbolic politics, group resources, or other factors external to the groups (Immergut 1992, 66).

Two-tiered Pluralism

The interests, ideas, and institutions shaping school politics in U.S. cities play
out in a multiethnic and multiracial setting. The two-tiered pluralism model we
employ develops a more structural or institutional and historical outlook on
minority politics than do other analytic models (Hero 1992). It also acknowledges

that conditions may be modified by specific circumstances, including patterns of racial and ethnic diversity (Hero 1998; cf. Lieberman 1993, 1995).

The notion of two-tiered pluralism suggests that pluralism functions to some degree in U.S. politics, but that there are two tiers or levels in play. Two-tiered pluralism describes a situation of formal and legal equality (as suggested by standard pluralism) across groups coexisting with actual practices in which tacit handicaps undercut equality for most members of minority groups, although individuals may register significant achievements and occasional policy successes may occur (cf. Hochschild 1984, 169; Smith and Feagin 1995, 5–9). At the same time, the different histories and circumstances of minority groups lead to somewhat different patterns across and within groups of interest and interest competition, problem definitions, and stances toward institutions.

Two-tiered pluralism implies that pluralism exists in form but not fully in fact for groups whose "formative" or initial relationship with the United States was not entirely voluntary or consensual. Groups predominantly located within this second level—Latinos, African Americans, Native Americans, and Asians—have the formal rights of citizens. Indeed, they may be given special protection, being among the "protected classes" in a legal sense. But two-tiered pluralism implies a marginal inclusion of minorities in most or all facets of the political process that coexists with stigmatization. This marginalization affects minority groups differently, shaping their interactions with the dominant group, and with each other. "Conventional" pluralist analysis focuses on explaining politics and policy within the first tier and is reasonably successful. But this is not an adequate or appropriate explanation when trying to explain politics of the second tier, particularly in multiethnic contexts. The second tier, where minority groups are concentrated, has fewer economic resources and less political and social influence.

The concept also implies differences in the kind of situations faced by some groups; there are not only differences in degree, as is the case within the "mainstream," or first tier, of pluralism (cf. Stone 1986, 1980). For example, Latinos' political and social status has been formally shaped through laws and political processes, although less starkly and visibly than for blacks and Native Americans. In important respects, the Latino situation has been seen as different and less directly a normative or moral "dilemma" in U.S. political history. On the whole, the position of Latinos in the U.S. political structure has been less explicitly articulated than the position of blacks. The Latino experience has in many respects revolved around and been shaped by cultural and linguistic factors. Latinos' inferior status also often has been attributed to or explained and "legitimated" by these same factors. These points seem central to understanding the Latino lag in political influence and in educational achievement, and also help explain relations with other groups. The Asian American situation is different yet. It is less well articulated and data on Asians in cities are still underdeveloped relative to other groups (see Lien 2001; UCLA 2005;

Kim and Lee 2001). This relative silence of Asian voices is part of the story we tell here.

Two-tiered pluralism structured the politics of school reform in Boston, Denver, Los Angeles, and San Francisco. In Boston, racial and ethnic minorities had only modest success in gaining political incorporation; they remained distinctly in the second tier, with Latinos and Asians worse off than blacks (Nelson 1999; Nelson 2005; Portz et al. 1998). In Denver, Los Angeles, and San Francisco, it is fair to say racial and ethnic minorities were relatively incorporated into electoral politics but their incorporation into education policy decision structures was much weaker. In part, this reflects difficulties of collective action within the Latino community. In San Francisco, Los Angeles, and Boston, political mobilization and policy incorporation for Latinos was and continues to be complicated by the presence of significant immigrant communities; but in Denver, with a historic, primarily Mexican American community, the Latino voice was also weak. In contrast to African Americans, Latino political mobilization in these cities was relatively recent, and less clearly articulated.

Plan of the Book

Education in general and school reform in particular are problematic in multiethnic settings not only because of the variable resources available to different groups but also because the "rhetoric of reform" (Tyack and Cuban 1995, 42) is often discordant and the institutions available for policymaking and implementation are often perceived as biased and unresponsive. In each instance, the dynamics of race and ethnicity contribute to skewed resources, dissonance, and wariness. Interest-based perspectives are important but insufficient without attention to the competing values and problem definitions, argumentation, and terms of discourse in a policy arena. Institutions, of course, shape argumentation and discourse, as well as the emergence of shared interests. The institutional context provides a mix of incentives and disincentives for overcoming the stalemate created by contested problem definitions and segmented agendas in a multiethnic context.

This chapter set out the framework—centering on ideas, interests, and institutions and two-tiered pluralism in multiethnic cities—we used to compare local responses to educational issues in multiethnic cities when court orders for desegregation were challenged and lifted.[9] It highlighted the difficulties of school reform in multiethnic cities and the context for the resurgence of educational reform initiatives. We also assessed the strengths and limitations of existing approaches to analyzing the problems we are interested in—multiethnic constituencies, competing ideas about educational reform, and lagging local institutions. Chapter 2 goes on to argue that race and ethnicity have long been viewed as critical to understanding urban politics but that relatively few

analyses systematically assess the politics in contemporary cities with multiethnic and multiracial minority populations. Thus we incorporate arguments that
explicitly focus on explaining power relationships where race and ethnicity
issues are central and complex, relying on the two-tiered pluralism (Hero
1992) model to frame our analysis of these dynamics. Our intent is not to grant
primacy or priority to racial and ethnic interests in explaining educational
reform politics but to consider the many ways in which race and ethnicity, particularly multiethnicity, complicate the ability to mobilize civic capacity.
Chapter 3 considers whether reforms in our cities—which aimed to restructure public schools in market-like terms—effectively addressed the needs of
emerging constituencies.

The hazards of educational reform in multiethnic cities stem from the ways
that configurations of interests, ideas, and institutions hamper further policy
changes by "locking in" particular solutions. In Chapters 4, 5, and 6, we present comparative empirical analyses of the competing interests, ideas, and institutional factors shaping school reform politics in the four cities. Essentially,
each chapter attempts to explain the marginalization of Latinos and Asians in
school politics through interest-based, ideational, and institutionalist perspectives, respectively. To inform this analysis, we draw on nearly 200 interviews
with community, professional, and political leaders in these four cities, as well
as aggregate data on the cities and their school systems. Our multimethod
approach includes drawing together archival and descriptive data, text analysis
techniques, and case study materials to make comparisons across the cities.

Looking ahead, our empirical analyses lead us to recognize both the utility
and limits of interest-based arguments stressing group factors and coalitional
strategies in explaining mismatches of agendas and preferences; interests are
necessary but not sufficient to explain the exclusion of Latinos and Asians—
and alternative reforms—from the educational policy arena. Nor are bureaucratic resistance arguments about characteristics of the educational community
adequate explanations of the difficulties in pursuing new educational reforms
in a multiethnic context (Henig 1995). While we find substantial variation in
the problem definitions put forward by these new school constituencies, this
also appears to be an insufficient explanation for the lack of influence and the
lag in institutional response. In many ways the institutional lags and shifts evident as cities moved beyond the desegregation agenda—the multiethnic
moment we analyze—permitted the rise of a new policy paradigm oriented
around efficiency and school-based performance standards rather than equity
concerns. As our analysis reveals, a "new educational populism" agenda replete
with market-oriented school reforms is increasingly prominent in these cities,
reflecting interests and norms rarely linked to pedagogical principles and seldom voiced by the new school constituencies (but see Hess and Leal 2001;
Pew 2004a).

Chapter 6 maps the institutional landscape in each city, including three possible scenarios for the politics of school reform as the courts became less significant institutional actors. Chapter 7 considers the implications of this comparative study, both in terms of the limits to local reform revealed by our analysis and the developmental sequence of institutional transformation in education politics. We depict a series of policy regimes, leading to the new educational populism orientation that seemed most prevalent toward the end of the time period under study. Our observations correspond to other concerns that reform ideas churn through local educational institutions but remain disconnected to the needs of new school constituencies. More responsive and effective school reform in multiethnic cities is likely only with the reframing of the concerns of these new constituencies and the restructuring of the institutional setting to accommodate these new ideas and interests.

Race, Ethnicity, and Education

R ACE AND ETHNICITY are critical elements of U.S. politics. Numerous observers and scholars understand race and ethnicity as historically central to the U.S. social and political systems—indeed, a major "dilemma" for American society (Burnham 1974; Myrdal 1944; Key 1949; Tocqueville 1958; Schmidt 2000). Although the United States is often referred to as "a nation of immigrants," scholars increasingly acknowledge that the circumstances of groups' immigration differ considerably. Not all groups came voluntarily; countries of origin have varied in both their political relations with the United States and also in the degree to which they are culturally, socially, and politically distinct from this country. This complex reality has major implications for American politics generally, and for the local politics of education especially.

Given immigration trends in the 1980s and 1990s, more and more cities became truly multiethnic during the twenty-first century, so understanding the political dynamics of such places becomes increasingly important (Ramakrishnan 2005). Two-tiered pluralism provides an analytical perspective for understanding race and ethnicity in education politics. This perspective suggests race/ethnicity is essentially a structural feature of American political life and it rejects as overly narrow the view of race/ethnicity as simply a basis of political interest. While differences in race and ethnicity certainly give rise to distinct communities of interest in education politics, we argue that race and ethnicity also infuse the institutional landscape of local education systems and are intertwined with the perceptions and the fates of education policy ideas. In the following chapters, our analysis examines the intersection of race and ethnicity with all three facets of education politics—interests, ideas, and institutions—to reveal the multiple dimensions of racial and ethnic inequality that persist in this policy arena.

The concept of two-tiered pluralism highlights the unequal positions of racial and ethnic minority groups relative to the majority group within the American pluralist system, and the implications of these different positions for group influence and policy outcomes. In an initial theoretical presentation of this broad concept, Rodney E. Hero (1992) sketched the distinct positions of different racial and ethnic minorities, particularly contrasting that of Latinos and African Americans with whites/Anglos. In this chapter, we apply the concept of two-tiered pluralism more specifically to education politics in multiethnic cities. The notion of two-tiered pluralism offers a flexible analytic framework, capable of transcending the "black/white" paradigm that has dominated scholarship and discourse on U.S. race relations and politics. Given that our focus is on multiethnic cities, we require such an alternative perspective to ground our analysis of the interests, ideas, and institutions driving school reform politics in the reality of multiethnic cities.

Our study starts with the observation that neither Latinos nor Asians fully embraced the desegregation paradigm originally advanced by African Americans in each of our cities. In Denver and Boston, Latino advocates joined lawsuits after ten to fifteen years of implementation. Bilingual education programs were added on to the definition of equal education advanced by the original cases but were pursued and administered separately from the desegregation parts of the case. The Los Angeles district included Latinos and Asians in its voluntary desegregation plan about a decade after the original lawsuits had been filed by black plaintiffs. Bilingual programs were added later as well. In San Francisco, the court denied Latinos and Asians status as plaintiffs, although the consent decree affected them by including them among the groups whose presence in specific schools would be monitored to ensure integration. As court orders to desegregate school districts were challenged and lifted in the 1980s and 1990s, a new window for education reform opened, and the marginal role of Latinos and Asians in local education policymaking became more apparent.

This chapter considers the common political challenges and experiences of blacks, Latinos, and Asians, stemming from their position in the lower tier of the two-tiered U.S. pluralist political system. It then discusses the unique place of each group within that lower tier, derived from their particular histories, cultures, and demographic composition. Awareness of such distinctions is critical, we argue, to understanding political life and education policy as it unfolded in multiethnic cities in the 1990s. We describe the distinctive context of multiethnic cities with examples from our four case cities. Finally, we present the historic context of education reform in each city, showing the paths each took toward the desegregation paradigm, and, later, away from it, as the institutional arrangements supporting this paradigm were dismantled. We argue that the study period was particularly critical for multiracial school constituencies and particularly puzzling because even as desegregation programs came to a close, Latinos and Asians struggled to define a new education agenda, much less to put their ideas into place. Although the dismantling of desegregation arrangements appeared to offer new opportunities for these new school constituencies, the subsequent years proved less auspicious. Our research indicates that the difficulties in articulating new, coherent education agendas and the lagged responsiveness of local institutional channels meant the numerical presence of new school constituencies was rarely translated into policy change.

Racial and Ethnic Minorities in Pluralist Politics

The concept of two-tiered pluralism asserts that racial and ethnic minorities generally have come to enjoy formal equality within the U.S. political system, but they do not experience substantive equality. This shift in minorities' status within the pluralistic system mirrors their status within the U.S. legal system—the difference between de jure and de facto segregation and exclusion. Today minorities experience "de jure pluralism" but de facto exclusion, because they occupy a second, and lower, tier of pluralist politics. Figure 2.1 offers a schematic representation of the concept two-tiered pluralism.

In the case of education politics, we can point to minorities' achievement of policies such as busing and bilingual education, yet other important policy issues remained largely beyond their influence, including the institutional design of school districts and education finance systems, and district-wide systemic reform initiatives. Additionally, despite the implementation of equalizing or compensatory programs for pupil assignment and bilingual education, educational outcomes for minorities improved only marginally in the 1990s, and these "special" programs were increasingly contested.

Politics in the Second Tier

Why such limits to shaping change and securing benefits? Groups who occupy the lower tier of pluralist politics face severe obstacles, in contrast to the advantages and privileges of groups in the first tier. In effect, a "mobilization of bias" exists in favor of the latter and against the former (Schattschneider 1960; Schmidt 2000). Thus, whites (especially those in the upper and middle classes) may use the political system *to maintain and enhance* their power and status, but when minorities pursue politics, they often are trying *to achieve* such status—that is, to gain a modicum of equality, to realize equal opportunity in

FIGURE 2.1 TWO-TIERED PLURALISM—A SCHEMATIC PRESENTATION

Power	Policy Arena	Stage of Policy Process
Systemic (situational+ indirect)	Developmental	Agenda Setting
Non Decision Making (intentional+ indirect)	Allocational	Policy Formulation
Anticipated Reaction (situational+ direct)		Policy Legitimation
Decision Making (intentional+ direct)	Redistributive	Policy Implementation

Anglo (white)

First Tier

Second Tier

Threshold (minorities as "recipients" of policies)

Blacks   Latinos

"Floor" of individual Rights

Sources: Overall schematic is from Hero 1992, p. 195; data on Power are from Stone 1980, on Policy Arena, from Peterson 1981, Sharp 1990; on Stage of Policy Process, from C. Jones 1984.

the first place. When whites engage in political action, their activities appear as "normal" incremental politics, in which groups express "preferences, priorities, or concerns." Policies in their interest seem to coincide with the public interest, such that explicit political mobilization may not even be necessary (Schneider and Ingram 1993, 339–41).

Minority groups, on the other hand, commonly find that exerting influence typically requires explicit political action. As they use politics to pursue equality, their inherent challenge to prevailing conditions casts them in an unfavorable light. To the general public, they are perceived as making "demands" or raising "complaints," rather than just legitimately participating. Policies in their interest seem suspect and essentially redistributive. These biases hold even when "minority" groups are a numerical majority, as is the case in multiethnic school districts.

The socioeconomic structure of most minority groups has implications for the qualities of their political engagement. Blacks and Latinos in particular have a triangular or pyramid-like socioeconomic structure, in contrast to whites' diamond-shaped structure. In other words, whereas the majority of whites hold middle-class status, the majority of blacks and Latinos fall into lower income categories. The minority middle and upper classes are numerically small (if growing), within adult populations already small relative to the white adult population. If political leadership and activities are most likely to come from the middle class, minority groups are hindered by their small size. As Clarence N. Stone, Robert K. Whelan, and William J. Murin have argued (1986), this weak position can make a minority group particularly vulnerable to the dominant group's offer of selective incentives in return for political support, to "recognition politics," and to co-optation (Virgil 1987; Wolfinger 1974). Additionally, while upper-class minorities may be able to form political coalitions with middle-class whites because of shared socioeconomic status, they also experience a distance from their own group's large lower class. This situation creates the necessity for "dual validation"—minority political officials must appeal to both minorities and to whites (cf. Stone et al. 1986; Baird 1977).

Generally, few Latinos, blacks, or Asians are among the most politically or socioeconomically advantaged in U.S. cities. In light of their limited status, and their meager economic and political resources, minority groups face a political dilemma. On the one hand, they may accept labels and support policies that confer symbolic, and perhaps some substantive, policy recognition and advantage. Examples include labels such as "minority" and "protected class," and policies such as affirmative action, desegregation, and bilingual education (cf. Schmidt 2000). Within the prevailing ideational and institutional contexts, however, these policies and labels may also signal inferior status; thus they bring stigma along with recognition and possible advantage. The other option minorities have for political engagement is to seek modest change over the long run by modifying their goals or supporting policies other groups have developed for other purposes. For example, some Latino community advocates and elected officials in Denver eventually supported state-level charter-school legislation in the 1990s, an initiative sponsored primarily by education-related nonprofit organizations and policy entrepreneurs outside of the Latino community.

Differing Positions in the Second Tier:
Blacks, Latinos, and Asians

To summarize the argument thus far, all racial and ethnic minorities face a variety of political disadvantages stemming from their position in the lower tier of pluralist politics. Meaningful political inclusion and social achievement are relatively rare for significant numbers of all such groups. But within this lower tier, the situations of blacks, Latinos, and Asians are distinct in many ways. Differences in group histories and culture, and in demographic, socioeconomic, ideological, and other characteristics influence each group's political status and prospects. As we move toward our empirical analysis of education politics in multiethnic cities, appreciating the differences among racial and ethnic minority groups is just as critical as understanding the common obstacles they face. Here we explore these differences as they stood at the time of our analysis; we also would note that although the African American political experience has been the most studied and documented, less political science research has focused on Latinos and Asians, although there is evidence that this situation is changing quickly.

African Americans

African Americans' historical legacy is distinct from that of Latinos and Asians because their arrival in this country as slaves meant that for centuries they were considered purely as property rather than as human beings. While the dominant society has perceived Latinos and Asians as a labor supply as well, and has manipulated their entrance and exit from this country through public policy, the institution of slavery experienced by Africans was the most extreme of these mechanisms. In contrast to Latinos and Asians, African Americans are "intensely and rigidly racialized in American society" (Browning, Marshall, and Tabb 2003b, 367). After the abolition of slavery, persistence of ideas about the biological inferiority of nonwhites contributed to blacks' legal exclusion from the democratic rights and privileges that white men enjoyed (Smith 1993). Numerous authors have found blacks' historic inequality to be the central dilemma within the American democratic tradition, the quintessential American moral conundrum driving cycles of political reform (e.g., Huntington 1981; Myrdal 1944; Shklar 1998). During the Civil Rights Movement in the 1960s, for example, blacks and their allies argued that all Americans should be able to participate fully in society and have the opportunity to succeed, regardless of race.

Blacks have experienced a highly unequal and disadvantaged status in this country; throughout history and continuing into the present, a significant obstacle has been negative characterizations by whites (and also by other groups) as "inferior and unfit for participation" in the civic community (Kim 1999, n. 43). The image of the black "underclass" was only a recent manifestation of arguments that blacks' pathological culture prevents them from achieving social mobility (Kim 1999, n. 43). Such negative constructions deflect attention from structural impediments to blacks' success (Kim 1999, 121; Reed 1995).

Now, blacks constitute about 13 percent of the U.S. population. In 1992, during the period of our study, blacks' unemployment rate (at 14 percent) was more than double that of whites, and their poverty rate (at 33 percent) was triple that of whites (U.S. Department of Commerce 1994). The same ratios persist. The 2000 census indicated that about 24 percent of blacks had incomes at or below the poverty level, as compared to about 8 percent of non-Hispanic whites, and about 11 percent were unemployed, compared to about 5 percent of whites. During the 1980s, the poverty rate for black children rose to 46 percent; by 2002, this figure was 32 percent. Blacks are twice as likely as whites to live in central cities, and less likely to live in suburbs (U.S. Department of Commerce 1994). They are the most residentially segregated of all racial and

ethnic minorities. This isolation negatively affects prospects for securing quality education and employment (Massey and Denton 1993).

Segregation sometimes has helped blacks achieve political representation
in district-based elections (but also see Grofman and Handley 1989). They dis-
play the greatest partisan unity among racial and ethnic minorities; in 1996,
about 70 percent identified as Democrats (McClain and Stewart 2002, 73). For
blacks, two-tiered pluralism has also had what might be called a "parallel"
dimension. Excluded by law and practice from white institutions, they developed alternative or parallel public and private institutions. For example, the
black state colleges and universities in the South, while originally created by
whites for the purpose of maintaining and reinforcing racial segregation and
inequality, have proved important for the development of a black intellectual
class and tradition. Black churches had similar implications.

Latinos
Numerous public policies have influenced Latinos' social and political status,
from the original conquest of Mexico in the mid-1880s to subsequent land
rights decisions, water rights policies, labor policies, and the nature and
enforcement of immigration policies (Barrera 1979; Moore and Pachon 1985).
But this history has not evoked the same broad normative concern as has the
inequality experienced by blacks, rooted in the institution of slavery. Political
and policy issues relating to Latinos have seemed somehow less worthy of
attention and action (Barrera 1979; Hero 1992, Chapter 3; de la Garza and
DeSipio 1996; Meier and Stewart 1991).

Latinos share with Asians a vulnerability to perceptions of "foreignness";
even for Latinos whose families arrived generations ago, citizenship in U.S.
society may be called into question informally, if not formally. For example,
Latinos' low rates of political participation relative to whites are sometimes
attributed to language differences and cultural "attachment" to countries of
origin, or to "ethnic estrangement" from American culture (cf., however, Meier
and Stewart 1991, 159–60; Pew Hispanic Center 2004b). Latinos' "loyalty" to
the United States is sometimes called into question (cf. de la Garza 1985). A
strong belief among the general population that speaking English is an important part of being an American, in a sense linked to American nationalism, even
nativism, means that those Latinos with limited English ability may be perceived as "less" American (Citrin et al. 1990; de la Garza and DeSipio 1996;
Schmidt 2000). The general perception by non-Latinos that Latinos choose not
to use English can serve as a justification for their inequality; some portion of
the black community also expresses such views. Typically, then, the dominant
society frames the Latino experience in terms of cultural and language differences. Such differences become defined as "deficiencies" to explain Latinos'
political and social disadvantage.

Latinos are a diverse group, with countries of origin including Cuba, Mexico, Puerto Rico, Central and South American countries, and Caribbean countries. With a shared language, there is some anticipation of a potential panethnic Latino identity, although the differential experiences of these groups makes this problematic (DeSipio 1996). Most Latinos live in the Southwest, but New York, Florida, Illinois, New Jersey, and Massachusetts also have significant Latino populations. The Latino population constitutes about 13 percent of the U.S. population. In 1990, about 64 percent of Latinos were born in the United States, with nearly three-quarters either native-born or naturalized citizens (U.S. Department of Commerce 1993). In 1994, during our study period, the Bureau of the Census estimated that about 40 percent of Latinos were born outside the U.S, with about half of these arriving in the U.S. between 1980 and 1990 (U.S. Department of Commerce 1995, 1993). Similar figures have been estimated from 2000 census data; about 39 percent of Latinos are estimated to be foreign-born, with about 45 percent having arrived during the 1990s (Logan 2002). There is significant variation across national origin, however. For example, about 37 percent of Mexican Americans are foreign born compared to 71 percent of Latinos of Central American descent (Logan 2002).

Latinos' socioeconomic status is slightly higher than blacks along several dimensions, with the notable exception of educational achievement. Yet statistics mask intragroup disparities. Latinos' poverty rate was 31 percent in 1993, with 41 percent of Latino children living below the poverty line; among groups, poverty rates for families ranged from 17 percent for Cubans to 35 percent for Puerto Ricans (U.S. Department of Commerce 1995). Eleven percent of Latinos were unemployed in 1994, but among Latino groups, joblessness ranged from 7 percent for Cubans to 14 percent for Puerto Ricans (U.S. Department of Commerce 1995). By 1999, 23 percent of Latino families and 34 percent of Latino children lived below the poverty line, but 44 percent of Puerto Rican children were poor, compared to 16 percent of Cuban children.

To some extent, Latinos occupy a more "mainstream" position in U.S. society than blacks (Meier and Stewart 1991). Many Latinos are neither as racially distinct from whites, nor as residentially segregated; in other words, less "social distance" divides Latinos from whites (Meier and Stewart 1991) and they are less "racialized" than African Americans (Browning, Marshall, and Tabb, 2003b). Still, Latinos have not enjoyed the same degree of political success as blacks, as indicated by the most frequently used measures, such as presence on elected governmental bodies (See Hero 1992, Chapter 5). At the local level, lower levels of residential segregation seem to have lessened Latinos' political representation (Taebel 1978; Zax 1990), but low Latino turnout rates for city elections are especially salient in contributing to their underrepresentation in local politics (Hajnal and Trounstine 2005).

Rufus P.Browning, Dale Rogers Marshall, and David H. Tabb (2003b, 367) suggest that Latinos are less likely than African Americans to see political mobilization and representation as "a preferred or even necessary means of improvement." While Latino leaders may well respond to the political opportunities presented by their growing demographic presence, Browning, Marshall, and Tabb argue that the urgency for mobilization is less than for blacks and that Latino political incorporation patterns will differ accordingly. Furthermore, Latinos are more ideologically "moderate," and more ideologically split than are blacks. With the exception of Cubans, they tend to vote Democratic, although their strength of identification with the Democratic Party does not equal that of blacks (McClain and Stewart 1998). As with Asians, partisan identities among Latinos generally strengthen in the second and third generations (Wong 2000).

Asians

Like Latinos, Asians' status as Americans is continually contested; they are often perceived as foreigners even after several generations in the U.S. Also like Latinos, fluctuations in immigration policies have shaped the Asian American experience, regulating when groups arrived and if they have been eligible to become citizens. Such policies reflected changing business needs for labor, as well as racial discrimination (See Chang 2001; Ancheta 1998). For example, the anti-Chinese exclusion movement of the 1870s was followed by an 1882 ban on Chinese immigration and a prohibition against Chinese becoming U.S. citizens. Such policies were repeatedly strengthened and expanded through the early 1900s. Indeed, restrictions on citizenship for Asian groups were not entirely lifted until 1952 (Brackman and Erie 1995). As Brackman and Erie write, "It is important to remember that today's native-born, middle-aged Asian Pacifics were born into a society that granted them citizenship but that had denied their immigrant parents the rights to naturalize, to vote, to hold public office, to qualify for civil service jobs, and even to receive federal welfare relief during the depression" (1995, 288).

Asian Americans' loyalty to the U.S. also has been subject to doubt, as illustrated most starkly by the internment of Japanese Americans during World War II. The notion of "yellow peril" has been used to warn against a variety of economic, cultural, or other alleged threats from Asian countries and Asian Americans throughout history (Kim 1999). Related to the "perpetual foreigner" status Asians face is the stereotype of Asians as the "model minority." This image rests on a characterization of Asian culture as conducive to success in American society, and idealizes Asians' limited political participation (see Ancheta 1998). Critics note that this image "assumes links to a foreign culture." Even when families have lived here for generations, they are perceived as identifying with another culture, rather than with American culture (Kim 1999). By framing Asians as "too busy getting ahead and making money to worry about politics," the model minority myth promotes an individualized explanation of social status and achievement, deflecting attention from structural constraints and opportunities, and implicitly criticizes the political action of other racial and ethnic minority groups (Kim 1999). Additionally, critics complain that this image homogenizes Asians, exaggerates their prosperity, and obscures the discriminatory treatment they continue to face (Kim 1999; also, Ancheta 1998).

Today Asians constitute about 4 percent of the U.S. population, and are in percentage terms the fastest growing racial/ethnic group in the country (from 1990 to 2000, the growth rate for all Asian Pacific Americans was 71.9 percent (UCLA 2005, 39). Two-thirds of Asian Americans were foreign-born in 1990; by 2000, about half were (U.S. Department of Commerce 1993; Logan 2001). The group we refer to as "Asian" has become increasingly diverse over the past 30 years, in part as a result of changing immigration policies. Countries of origin include China and Japan, the Philippines, Korea, Southeast and East Asian countries, India, and Pacific Island nations.[1] In contrast to Latinos, the lack of a shared language among these groups could hamper a sense of panethnicity as well as collective action efforts, although there is some evidence of bloc voting and panethnic candidate preferences in elections for both subnational and national candidates (Collet 2005; Lien 2001; UCLA 2005, 48).

The majority of Asians live in the Western United States, and 95 percent live in metropolitan areas, almost evenly split between cities and suburbs in the 1990s (U.S. Department of Commerce 1995). The Los Angeles and San Francisco metropolitan areas had the first and third, respectively, largest concentrations of Asian Pacific Americans in the United States in 2000 (UCLA 2005). In the 1990s, Asians and Latinos exhibited similar degrees of residential segregation but residential stratification was higher for Asians—they were more likely than Latinos to live in better-off neighborhoods (Timberlake 2002; see also Aguilar-San Juan 2005). The suburbanization of Asian American politics now is one of the most distinctive trends shaping their political profile (Lai 2005). The 2000 Census revealed growing concentrations of Asians in medium and smaller cities on the periphery of large Gateway Cities such as Los Angeles and San Francisco. Whereas African Americans and Latinos continue to be concentrated in central cities and to channel their political energies to these political offices, Asians in California are increasingly seeking political voice in these smaller edge cities or ethnoburbs (Li 1998).

While poverty rates for Asians were lower than those for other racial and ethnic minorities, statistics mask intragroup differences. Fourteen percent of Asians had incomes below the poverty line in 1989, but among Asian groups, the rate varied from 64 percent for Hmong and 43 percent for Cambodians to 6 and 7 percent for Filipinos and Japanese. Asians of Chinese, Korean, and Thai origin had poverty rates closest to that of whites, at 14 percent, 14 percent, and 13 percent, respectively. Similar trends were notable by 2000, when 12.4 percent of all Asian households were in poverty, with Vietnamese faring worse and Indians and Japanese faring well, in general. As a group,

Asians' unemployment rate in 1997 was estimated at about 5 percent, and had risen to about 6 percent by 2004 (U.S. Department of Commerce 1998).

Continued reliance on a black/white paradigm for political analysis is particularly detrimental to understanding Asian concerns: It leaves them "marginalized or unrecognized" (Ancheta 1998), or at best seen as an "interstitial" group and a potential "swing vote" in electoral politics (Kim and Lee 2001). Compared with blacks and Latinos, Asian levels of political activity and representation appear lower. In California in the 1990s, Asians were more likely to be U.S. citizens than Latinos, but less likely to be registered to vote (Brackman and Erie 1995). Low voter turnout rates in local elections contribute significantly to the underrepresentation of Asians and Latinos on city councils and in the mayor's office (Hajnal and Trounstine 2005). Again, Browning, Marshall, and Tabb hypothesize a distinctive political incorporation trajectory for Asians, given their less rigid racialization, high rates of suburbanization, relatively rapid economic assimilation (for some Asian groups), and the relative unlikeliness that they will see political action as the key to improving their situation (2003b, 367).

In the 1990s, Asians were characterized as "politically a population of silent Americans … underrepresented among voters and elected officeholders" (Brackman and Erie 1995). Significant voter mobilization efforts headed by the nonpartisan coalition group Vote APIA (Vote Asian and Pacific Islander American) began in 1996, with dramatic effects in subsequent elections. The 2004 elections may be a watershed for Asians' coming of age in national politics. Earlier polls found Asians most likely to be politically independent, rather than self-identified with a political party (McClain and Stewart 1998; Browning, Marshall, and Tabb, 2003b). In the 2004 elections, however, multilingual national exit polls (conducted by the Asian American Legal Defense and Education Fund AALDEF) indicated that 74 percent of Asian voters favored John Kerry over George W. Bush; since 60 percent of Asians were registered Democrats, party crossover voting was substantial (UCLA 2005, 47).[2] Language assistance and bilingual ballots and interpreters proved essential where Asian voters had limited English proficiency or were first-time voters (38 percent of those surveyed were first time voters in the AALDEF exit polls).

The Distinctive Context of Multiethnic Cities

Multiethnic cities represent a distinctive context for the unfolding of local education politics. Because such cities have significant populations of whites, Latinos, blacks, and Asians, education politics is bound to be more complex than the black/white political dynamic studied in many examples of urban scholarship. Our four cities—Boston, Denver, Los Angeles, and San Francisco—bring together groups with a diverse array of historical legacies and contemporary experiences, as described above, yet sharing a disadvantaged status relative to whites. Additionally, these four cities have notable political and economic histories that create a particular context in which racial politics plays out. Below, we sketch some of these salient features, occasionally drawing comparisons with six other cities included in the larger NSF research project, "Civic Capacity and Urban Education" (Stone et al. 2001): Four "black-led" cities—Atlanta, Baltimore, Detroit, and Washington, DC (Henig et al. 2001)—and two former "machine" cities traditionally dominated by white ethnic populations—Pittsburgh and St. Louis (Portz et al. 1999.)

Racial and Ethnic Composition

In contrast to other American cities, multiethnic cities have truly diverse populations. On average, San Francisco, Boston, Denver, and Los Angeles had 1990 populations of 50 percent white, 15 percent black, 22 percent Latino, and 12 percent Asian. The largest racial or ethnic minority group in each city varied: Latinos in Denver and Los Angeles, Asians in San Francisco, and blacks in Boston. Other sets of cities in the larger study of urban education politics had much smaller Latino and Asian populations and much larger African American populations. The four "black-led" cities averaged about 3 percent Latino and 1 percent Asian, but 67 percent black. The two "Machine" cities had about 4 percent Latinos and 1 percent Asians, but 36 percent blacks.

Demographic changes in our multiethnic cities over the past twenty years differed from those in the other cities that were part of the larger study. Of ten cities, those whose Latino populations grew the most were the multiethnic cities of San Francisco, Los Angeles, and Boston. Those with the least growth among the Asian population were the black-led cities of Atlanta, Baltimore, and Detroit. Similarly, the cities where the Latino population grew the most from 1980 to 1990, in terms of its share of the population, include the multiethnic cities of Los Angeles, Denver, and Boston. Yet the black-led, and Machine cities of St. Louis, Pittsburgh, and Detroit had the smallest changes. Trends in the black population are somewhat less straightforward. Nonetheless, the black-led cities of Detroit and Baltimore saw the highest increases in blacks' percentage of the population. Atlanta and Denver's black populations grew the least, whereas in Los Angeles and DC, blacks' share of the population declined relative to that of other groups. By 1990—and in 2000 as well—the cities with the largest black populations were the black-led cities and the multiethnic cities had the smallest black populations.

Multiethnic School Populations

Multiethnic cities also have distinctive school populations. In all four cities, students of color outnumber white students (see Table 1.1). With the exception of Boston, Latinos or Asians are the largest minority segment of the population. In Los Angeles, during our study period, more than two-thirds of the school district's seven hundred thousand–student population was Latino, 14 percent of the students were black, and 7 percent were Asian. In San Francisco, during this same period, Asians were the largest racial/ethnic group at 44 percent, with Latinos the second largest at 21 percent. Denver's school population was approaching 50 percent Latino in 1996, growing from 41 percent in 1990. In that year, 20 percent of the student body was black. In Boston, African Americans made up 48 percent of the school population, with Latinos at 23 percent. This was nearly the mirror opposite of Denver's student body, except that Boston's Asian student enrollment, at 8 percent, was larger than Denver's 3 percent. During the 1990s, these patterns persisted. By 2004, Latinos made up the majority of students in the school districts of Denver and Los Angeles; Asians and Latinos were the largest groups in San Francisco, and Latinos and black students were the largest groups in Boston. Over time, the size of the white student population declined in all four districts.

Governmental Setting

Local political legacies in these multiethnic cities, and recent interventions by state governments in local affairs, influence the prospects for minorities' political participation and influence in the education arena. The cities vary somewhat in reform histories. Los Angeles has a strong reform tradition while Denver, Boston, and San Francisco have elements of federalist/pluralist regimes (Hero 1990; DeLeon 1992; Portz et al. 1999). The Sunbelt and Western cities did not have the history of unreformed government structures dominated by white ethnics, as is found in Boston, nor did they experience the political and social conditions related to these structures. Western cities were early adopters of progressive reforms that separated "politics" from the administration of general city services, with management by a professional civil service. Progressive reforms also took care to insulate schools from city politics.

The absence of political machines dominated by white ethnics, and the promise to serve city residents' needs based on professional, technical criteria and standards, might seem to have offered an openness and responsiveness to minority groups along with other city residents. But scholarship on reform governments, and our field research in these Western cities suggests the opposite (e.g., Judd and Swanstrom 1994). In the more reformed cities, minority communities perceived the entrenched reform tradition of responsible government as diminishing government's responsiveness to their needs. But in Boston, a more traditional "machine" city, minorities also have struggled to achieve and maintain basic representation in city politics (Nelson 1999).

American cities historically supported their schools through property tax collections. Although property taxes are still important sources of school revenues, the school finance story is not so simple anymore. Even the statement that "property taxes are key pieces of the school finance puzzle" obscures the complexity of raising and collecting those taxes when states and school districts are regulated by citizen initiatives. State tax limitations and legislation, along with citizen-led ballot initiatives, constrain the resource base and governing capacity of local decision makers in each of our cities. The states in which the four cities are located—California, Colorado, and Massachusetts—have, and have frequently used, the initiative process, often with important implications for education. California's property tax limitation measure, Proposition 13 (1978) is the most famous and is commonly considered the most important in that it triggered something of a "tax revolt" in the American states. California also enacted a property tax limit in 1996 and a general tax limit on local governments and districts in 1986. In 1980, Massachusetts passed Proposition 2 1/2, a measure to limit local taxes while also rejecting an initiative to increase community shares of local education costs. A 1986 initiative established a general measure to limit state revenue tax increases, followed by a measure in 1998 that cut state income taxes (Piper 2001).

Colorado enacted the TABOR ("Taxpayers' Bill of Rights") amendment to its constitution in 1992, which constrained revenue increases to population and inflation growth, and required voter approval for proposed increases beyond that level. This meant that school districts could not increase their "mill rate"— their property tax rates—without voter approval. The 2003 DPS mill levy of 36.967 is above the state average of 34.51 (Donnell-Kay Foundation 2003): Property taxpayers in Denver pay roughly four times more property tax to the school district on similarly valued properties than residents in the wealthier community of Aspen, where the school mill levy is only 8.946 (Donnell-Kay Foundation 2003, 22). A decade earlier, Colorado had adopted the Gallagher amendment, which effectively reduced residential property taxes by harnessing property tax assessment rates. While TABOR limited the ability of the state legislature to compensate for declining local education funding, the combined effects of TABOR and Gallagher, along with state equalization requirements imposed by the 1988 and 1994 School Finance Acts, led to a reversal by 2005 of the historical ratio of 60 percent of local education funding coming from local tax revenues to 60 percent now coming from state tax revenues (Frank 2005; Teske 2005).

Colorado is seen as having "the most restrictive fiscal limits in the nation" (National Council of State Legislatures 2005); as a result of these limitations it is one of the wealthiest states in the country but its tax effort for K–12 education—the percent of income devoted to education—puts the state at the bottom in national rankings. Perhaps to circumvent some of the restrictions imposed by these earlier taxpayer revolts, statewide voters passed Amendment 23 in 2000 directing the state legislature to annually increase K–12 funding by "inflation + 1 percent" up to 2011.[3] But the interaction of TABOR's revenue limits, Gallagher property tax constraints, and a weak economy in the late

1990s resulted in Amendment 23 funding becoming the ceiling rather than the floor for legislative school funding efforts (Great Education Colorado).

State governments also intervened directly in local education reform during this period, mandating curriculum and testing tools, authorizing charter schools, and in some cases adopting other decentralizing measures. The Massachusetts legislature adopted a reform package in 1993 providing new roles for superintendents and principals, authorizing charter schools, expanding school choice across districts, mandating statewide testing and a common core of learning, and designing a new formula to improve the equalization of resources across districts (Portz 1996). That same year, the Colorado legislature passed charter school legislation and adopted statewide education standards and testing requirements. The California legislature also developed curricular frameworks and assessment tools.

Prior to the 1980s and 1990s, state intervention often indicated opposition to racial desegregation of local schools. In Colorado, tensions surrounding school desegregation in Denver prompted passage of a 1974 state constitutional amendment requiring voter approval of any annexations to the city. This contributed to the inelasticity of Denver's economic base, and protected the suburban white population from involvement in busing. That year, state voters approved a constitutional amendment prohibiting busing and assignment of students to schools for "the purpose of racial balance." In California, a 1980 state constitutional amendment limited mandatory integration. In Massachusetts, however, the 1965 Massachusetts General Court's Racial Imbalance Law required that all cities in Massachusetts begin to eliminate the dual public school system (Nelson 1999).

Economic Base

If investment in education were simply a function of economics, there would be reason for optimism about prospects for education in these multiethnic cities. Denver, Los Angeles, and San Francisco developed largely in the post–World War II, or postindustrial, era (cf. Elkin 1987). Boston achieved postindustrial standing in the last few decades. While the cities' economic bases vary (Los Angeles had a significant industrial base, Boston and San Francisco are finance and educational centers, and Denver suffered in the 1980s from its dependence on the oil industry but diversified with telecommunications and biotechnology sectors), they are more similar than different. Although each city suffered fiscal setbacks and revenue shortages, each is located in a relatively strong regional economy, and is well positioned within the emerging global economy. San Francisco, Boston, and Los Angeles are key arenas for foreign investment and trade, and Denver's global links are enhanced through cargo and passenger traffic at its international airport, which was opened in 1995.

TABLE 2.1 REVENUE SOURCES 2004

SCHOOL DISTRICT	FEDERAL (%)	LOCAL	STATE
Boston	10	58	32
Denver	11	55	34
Los Angeles	12	22	66
San Francisco	12	59	29

Source: Constructed by Hero from data provided by National Center for Education Statistics.

With state equalization of school funding in some places, a local economic base becomes somewhat less salient to local school funding although economic conditions still shape the day-to-day hardships many children face in getting an education.[4] As Table 2.1 shows, in three of our four cities, local sources of revenue make up more than half of the school districts' revenue stream—in San Francisco, local sources make up nearly 60 percent of district funds. State funds make up about a third of districts' revenues, with the exception of Los Angeles, where state funds contribute two-thirds of the district's revenues. In all four cases, federal funds make up only about 10 to 12 percent of school funding. The complex and often contradictory constraints on tax and expenditure decisions noted above are now often as significant as the sources of education funding in determining what is possible for school reform (e.g., see Teske 2005).

Civic Capacity

To some scholars, policy changes appear to be contingent on the capacity of stakeholders within a community to mobilize across sectors for educational change—reflecting the civic capacity in a community (Stone 1998; Council of Great City Schools 1997). While the concept of civic capacity has certain commonalities with "social capital" (Putnam 2000) there are important differences. "Social capital concerns behavior that is largely interpersonal and private.... By contrast, civic capacity centers on activities that are squarely in the public arena and involve governance institutions and major group representatives" (Stone et al. 2001, 5–6). When talking about a large public arena [in contrast to such inclinations as skills, social trust, and reciprocity, associated with social capital] "habits of cooperation that develop in small and close meetings do not necessarily come into play" (Stone et al. 2001, 5–6).

From the civic capacity perspective, then, educational reform entails group mobilization and joint action based on shared concerns about educational problems and a commitment to collective problem solving. The greater the civic capacity in a community—greater cross-sector mobilization and shared understandings—the greater the likelihood of educational reform. In other

CHAPTER 2

TABLE 2.2 CIVIC CAPACITY AND REFORM INITIATIVES

	DENVER	LOS ANGELES	SAN FRANCISCO	BOSTON
Civic Capacity Rank	9	3	11	2
Infrastructure of Support Reforms	7	11	8.5	11
Internal Reforms	10	12.5	7.5	11.5
Overall Reforms	17	23.5	14.5	22.51

Source: Data from Stone 1998, 256, 260.

Note: The civic capacity rankings reflect the extent to which various groups are involved in educational improvement efforts: the higher the rank, the more extensive the collective roles of government, business, teachers', school administrators', and parents' groups in cross-sector efforts to promote school improvement. The rankings reflect the efforts of these cities relative to the eleven cities in the NSF project on Civic Capacity and Urban Reform; the highest rank is 1, the lowest is 11. Infrastructure of support scores reflects assessments of extra school efforts to prepare students to learn and to support school efforts. Internal reforms scores assess efforts to change internal school operations, which includes site-based management, parent participation, use of evaluation and research in education decisions, and use of assessment measures. Overall reform score totals these two ratings into a comprehensive score. In the NSF project, the rank order correlations of civic capacity and each reform score was relatively high: Infrastructure of support (0.83), Internal Reforms (0.71), and Overall reforms (0.81).

analyses of school reform (Stone 1998), the four cities compared here varied dramatically on civic capacity during the study period.

Boston ranked high on civic capacity, thanks to a broad coalition of stakeholders including the business sector, parents' groups, and teachers' unions. Los Angeles was similar in the extensiveness of the school reform coalition; in both Boston and Los Angeles this coalition was mobilized from the top down although dominated by business initiatives and less inclusive of parent groups in Los Angeles. Boston also stood out for engaging a broad range of groups in sustained discourse and action. In the other cities, even when an array of groups was mobilized, activities tended to be more episodic and disjointed and cooperation more elusive unless compelled by external actors. Denver and San Francisco ranked lower in civic capacity; in both instances, court orders dominated the educational policy arena for long periods of time. This may well have been at the expense of developing greater civic capacity among local actors (Jones, Portz, and Stein 1997). In Denver, the state government also intervened extensively in local education decisions; many local actors in Denver and San Francisco claimed that these external initiatives undermined local initiatives although others saw this as excuses for inaction (see Stone 1998, 258).

There is some evidence that greater civic capacity is associated with school reform efforts. In the larger NSF project, the rank order correlations between civic capacity and reform initiatives ranged from 0.71 for Internal Reforms to 0.83 for Infrastructure of Support. Denver and San Francisco deviated from this larger pattern, however: Their reform scores were higher than anticipated, given their relatively low civic capacity scores. In both cases, significant reforms could again be attributed to the effects of state and court actors. For example, a "reconstitution" process was imposed by the court on selected poorly performing San Francisco schools, and in Denver the state government pushed significant reforms onto the district. Thus these cities became involved in educational reform despite local groups' lack of mobilization around shared concerns.

These findings suggest a complex relationship between civic capacity and school reform because in the absence of civic capacity, reform still occurs. Jones, Portz, and Stein (1997) see the relationship as a double helix, with an outside loop of support from noneducators linked to an inside loop of support from professional educators concerned with educational performance (Jones, Portz, and Stein 1997; Stone 1998). Where leaders link inside and outside players, we find more civic capacity and cooperation around reform initiatives although the nature and terms of the linkages are often contested. In San Francisco, Boston, and Denver, in particular, the double helix was marked by court or state-government intervention providing positive incentives to structure new education "markets" within the public system. By establishing goals and providing negative incentives to guard against undesired outcomes, such as racial imbalances, and monitoring results, public officials and educators maintained an authoritative role in these restructuring efforts. But they also became more dependent on the cooperation and self-interest of other actors at the local and state level and noneducators in the external loop.

The Historical Context of Education Reform

The landscape of the multiethnic city is distinctive: Racial and ethnic minorities in such places find themselves in a population particularly fragmented, where the most numerous groups seem to be the least powerful. The historical context of educational reform experiences—the path toward and then away from court-ordered desegregation—is critical to understanding the contours of Latino and Asian marginalization in contemporary educational policymaking (see Figure 1.1).[5]

In our four cities, the 1960s and 1970s marked African Americans' challenge to the dominant policy paradigm in the education arena, which valued the specialized expertise of professional educators. Through social action and legal strategies, African Americans confronted education experts' control of the schools. They used new symbols, evoked alternative values, and shifted the arena of education politics from central administration to the courts. Their new paradigm defined the policy problem as unequal opportunity to education rooted in segregation, and proposed the solution of racial integration.

To some extent, African Americans were successful: Court-ordered desegregation became the policy paradigm shaping the educational agenda in these cities in the 1980s and often through much of the 1990s. But eventually judges lifted court orders and, more generally, support for this paradigm eroded, even among African Americans. No coherent policy paradigms for education

emanating from minority groups themselves had replaced court-ordered desegregation in the four cities we study. The most prominent policy orientations
were based in notions of market efficiency, accountability, and consumer
choice but with scant attention to the structural constraints on choice or the
distributional consequences of new institutional arrangements. Most important
for our purposes, reforms stemming from this choice-based orientation did not
match the concerns of the multiethnic school constituencies in these cities.

Denver
The Denver Public School District (DPS) operated under a federal court
desegregation order from 1973 to 1995. In *Keyes v. School District #1*, a class-
action lawsuit filed in 1969 by eight black families, the court found that DPS
had deliberately segregated schools in Northeast Denver not through direct
segregation but through manipulation of school boundary lines, through new
school construction, through an open enrollment plan, and through teacher
assignment. The judge ordered busing to desegregate Northeast Denver
schools (Stevens 1994), and by 1974, nearly a quarter of the district's students
were bused for the purpose of integration.

For fifteen years, blacks played the major role in monitoring desegregation
compliance in Denver, even though Latinos represented a larger share of the
student population and had been defined in the *Keyes* decision as a distinct
group in relation to issues of segregation. Over the years, DPS instituted
reforms aside from busing, including magnet schools, to comply with the court
order. About ten years after the ruling, when the district requested release
from the court order, the Congress of Hispanic Educators became involved as
a plaintiff. The federal judge ruled that the district was failing to meet the
needs of bilingual students and retained the court order. An agreement
between the district and the Congress led to guidelines for the creation of a
bilingual program.

In 1995, DPS was successful in its effort to be released from court supervision of desegregation efforts. At that time, the federal judge proclaimed that
"the Denver now before this court is very different from what it was when
this lawsuit began" in 1969. While he released the city from court-ordered
desegregation, the judge continued court oversight of the district's bilingual
education program.

Los Angeles
The Los Angeles Unified School District (LAUSD) is unusual in that it
includes parts of 27 other cities.[6] Beginning with a 1970 ruling by the California
Superior Court decreeing that each school in the LAUSD have the same ethnic enrollment as the district at large, struggles over desegregation have
embroiled the Board of Education, every level of the court system, minority-
group organizations, and city and state voters.

When the Los Angeles Board of Education appealed the initial court ruling, the NAACP filed a desegregation suit in federal court. In 1976, the
California Supreme Court upheld the 1970 decision, but granted the Los
Angeles Superior Court the authority to approve an integration plan in
compliance with the ruling and with a relaxed school enrollment standard.
The school board's efforts to expand the desegregation plan in 1980 prompted
voter approval of a state constitutional amendment to limit mandatory integration and ban busing. As a result, the LAUSD integration program was voluntary and relied on magnet schools.

These voluntary initiatives were and continue to be complicated by the
high degree of segregated neighborhoods in Los Angeles; in contrast to
statewide trends of declining neighborhood segregation in 2000, Los Angeles
had more segregated neighborhoods than any other racially diverse city in the
state, with 70 percent having Latino majorities (Public Policy Institute of
California 2002). In the 1970s, the Los Angeles school district was 58 percent
white, 20 percent African American, 18 percent Latino, and 4 percent Asian.
By the 1990s, close to 90 percent of LAUSD students were students of color,
primarily Latino. A 1994 report found that 73 percent of Latino students
attended schools where fewer than 10 percent of the students were white
(Usansky 1994).

San Francisco

Until their repeal in 1947, California laws allowed segregation of Asian and
Mexican children in public schools. By the 1960s, African American groups
and other civic organizations pressed officials to address de facto segregation
in San Francisco schools. The NAACP and black plaintiffs filed suit in 1970,
and again in 1978. The second lawsuit, filed in federal court, charged the
state and San Franciso Unified School District (SFUSD) with underrepresentation of African Americans among teachers and administrators, segregation of
both students and faculty from specific racial groups, and unequal access to
academic and after-school programs. In 1983, the parties agreed to a consent
decree stipulating the district's two primary goals as racial integration and academic achievement.

The decree made San Francisco a distinctive case: All schools had to
include at least four ethnic groups with no one group exceeding 45 percent of
the school's enrollment. In addition, it also specified system-wide remedies
that included the reorganization of several schools serving black students
where test scores were consistently below average. This reorganization
process, "reconstitution," authorized the Superintendent to select administrators and teachers at targeted schools, chosen for their innovative organizational
and curricular plans, to enhance academic achievement.

In 1992, the federal court evaluated the progress of the desegregation and
school achievement plans, and their continued appropriateness for San

52 CHAPTER 2

Francisco, given its changing demographic base (see Orfield et al. 1992). When the consent decree was created, African American students were the largest minority group at 24 percent of the student body. The panel concluded that desegregation had been achieved but that the SFUSD fell short of achieving the consent decree's goal of academic achievement: "We conclude that the District has not realized the goals of academic achievement for the overwhelming majority of African American and Hispanic students in the critical areas of educational attainment, dropouts, special education placement, and suspensions from school" (Orfield et al. 1992, 1).

Boston

Boston historically features ethnic enclaves and social segregation (Aguilar-San Juan 2005; Portz et al. 1999). To some observers, race relations in Boston are among the worst in the nation (Nelson 1999). Education politics in Boston are a prime arena for activists of color; they also offer a window into the dynamics of city politics (see Nelson 2005). Growing discontent with continued segregation in schools throughout the 1960s featured marches by Martin Luther King Jr. from Roxbury to Boston Commons and escalating pressures on the School Committee from the NAACP and other black activists. Finally, in 1972, when black plaintiffs sued to end segregation in Boston schools, they threw the local political system and school board into crisis.[7] The reaction of whites to court-ordered busing in 1974 included widespread resistance and violence; to some observers, Mayor Kevin White's refusal to intervene in support of blacks during this crisis and his insistence that the elected School Committee, not the mayor, was responsible for carrying out these policies seemed inconsistent with his previous efforts in support of blacks (Nelson 1999). Under the leadership of its chair, Louise Day Hicks, the School Committee publicly opposed school desegregation as well. Although he came into politics as a leader of the anti-busing struggles in South Boston, White's successor, Ray Flynn, supported the federal court rulings on desegregation when he took office in the early 1980s.

During fifteen years of court-ordered desegregation, the federal court issued orders ranging from mandatory busing, to teacher and student assignments, to school partnerships with business, to the creation of magnet schools. As part of the 1974 court order, racial-ethnic councils for parents were established in every school to ensure communication and dialogue on problems with potentially racial dimensions. A Citywide Parents Advisory Council (CPC) was established to monitor the desegregation process and assist the school-based councils. In 1991, the Latino parents association El Comité joined the black plaintiffs as parties to the case. The CPC had been charged with inattention to involvement of parents of bilingual and special needs children in its activities. By 1994, 17 percent of Boston public school students were in bilingual programs with instruction in nine languages.

Court orders also involved compliance with the state's special education law; since 1976, six separate court orders guided the school system's actions in this area. With the broad definition of special needs in the 1972 special education law, 21 percent of all students are in special needs programs; special education captures about 30 percent of the school system budget (Portz 1996).

In 1982, the court turned monitoring responsibilities over to the State Board of Education, and in 1989, the court approved a controlled-choice plan to replace busing. In 1990, the judge issued his final orders on racial guidelines for school district employment. The controlled choice plan put elementary and middle schools in attendance zones and allowed parents to prioritize school choices within their zone. Student assignments are made in accordance with parental choices and racial guidelines to maintain integrated schools (Portz 1994, 21). With implementation of controlled-choice, the district began to experiment with site-based management.

In 1974, white students constituted about 52 percent of Boston's public school enrollment; by 1995, they were less than 20 percent, and overall public school enrollment dropped by one-third during the same period. By 1999 when the School Committee voted to drop race as a factor in school assignment, only 15 percent of public school children were white.

The Legacy of the Desegregation Paradigm

Several observations on the marginalization of new school constituencies emerge from tracking these events. The historical context reminds us that although they may share some material interests, Latino, Asian, and African American groups historically are situated in different positions of influence within key decision structures. Although Latino and Asian students were numerically larger groups at the time of the court orders in Denver and San Francisco, the plaintiffs in the desegregation cases were African Americans. Historically, Latinos and Asians were not fully included in the institutional changes attendant to desegregation suits. In some cases, this judicial exclusion was explicit and deliberate. To the extent that postsegregation institutions were designed to respond to African Americans' needs and priorities, they often seemed less responsive to the concerns and agendas of other minority groups. As a result, African Americans may appear "overrepresented" in teaching and administrative positions relative to the African American school population in each city. Even to some African American intellectuals, this dominance in personnel and on programs is viewed as a major barrier to ongoing educational reform (Orr 1992; Rich 1996).

The paradoxical and unintended consequences of court interventions stand out. In each of our cities, the desegregation process sowed the seeds for many of the organizations and initiatives that characterized education reform activities in the 1980s and 1990s. It also created stalemates and policy lags. For example, according to one observer, the Boston Public School system had been "in crisis management mode since desegregation" (quoted in Portz 1996). On the other hand, another argues there would have been "no genuine efforts to improve the schools without a court order" (Portz 1996). Similar sentiments were voiced in Denver and San Francisco. That is, the courts provided the direction for educational change by requiring it to occur. In the absence of court orders, there was little evidence of sufficient capacity or will to address segregated schools and initiate voluntary reforms. But court intervention also shifted the arena for discourse and policymaking from a community setting of negotiation and coalition building to a legal context of judicial procedures and decisions (Jones, Portz, and Stein 1997). Ironically, local education became more integrated and equitable, but the prospects for community mobilizing around future reforms eroded.

Past reform struggles constrained later efforts. Previous reforms stemming from desegregation contributed to subsequent collective action difficulties within and across ethnic constituencies. Latinos often self-identified as white in census counts, for example, and courts generally defined them as white "for educational purposes," with some exceptions (see *Keyes* 1973). Indeed, when the courts did respond to Latino interests, they were defined in terms of "language" and addressed through bilingual education programs rather than broader, better-funded approaches focused on achievement. Court orders created institutional channels that were open to some types of demands and group identities but not others; redefining group identities and demands to respond to changing understandings of problems became especially difficult when certain claims were institutionalized. Latinos received the "add-on" of bilingual education to court orders, but little else.

Rhetorical capital is critical. The legacy of the struggle for desegregation demonstrates that groups need a stock of rhetorical capital—a collection of symbols, metaphors, stories, and images—that allows them to frame their issues in ways ensuring agenda access. The success of African Americans in advocating their policy paradigm stemmed not only from their mobilization as a civil rights movement, but also from their ability to draw on symbols and cultural values of social justice and equity. In a sense, this language vaulted the educational concerns of African Americans onto the agendas in the top tier of pluralist politics. For Latinos and Asians, similar efforts were more readily interpreted as "special interests." For policy entrepreneurs from Latino and Asian communities to be successful in breaking the stalemate on educational reform, they would have to have found policy images that framed the dilemmas faced by their children in ways that resonated with core societal values. Lack of rhetorical capital posed a barrier to the emergence of a policy paradigm sensitive to the self-defined needs of new school constituencies and continued to constrain Latinos and Asians to the second tier of influence.

Given these implications of the desegregation struggles, it is not surprising that our field research found some observers and participants in education politics characterizing the African Americans' civil rights movement as successful in securing electoral and bureaucratic access for them, but as constraining the political opportunity structure to other groups. In particular, Latinos and Asians felt that other groups controlled the terms of their marginal incorporation into these structures. On the other hand, Browning, Marshall, and Tabb suggest their political incorporation will be distinct from African American patterns, with less urgency, more fragmentation, and more amenable to issue-oriented coalitions (2003b). Given the salience and shared values of educational achievement for their children, education issues would appear to be one of the greatest opportunities for Latinos and Asians to mobilize and form multiethnic and even multiracial coalitions.

Yet this did not happen in our four cities. Any potential coalitions advocating for recognition of multiethnic school needs were swamped by a wave of school reform proposals promoted by policy entrepreneurs looking to national constituencies. As the desegregation paradigm eroded in these four cities, school reform agendas increasingly featured initiatives centered on choice, competition, and accountability—all divorced from direct concerns with multiethnic student needs.

Nevertheless, it is possible these market-based reforms might offer these previously excluded groups a chance for greater influence on school decisions as well as a means for closing the racial-ethnic educational achievement gap still persisting after desegregation efforts. Our review in the following chapter of key education reforms in the four cities suggests the design of these reforms meant they did neither.

## CHAPTER THREE

Local School Reform Agendas: Changing the Rules of the Game

URING THE 1990s, courts ceased mandating desegregation initiatives in San Francisco, Denver, and Boston; in Los Angeles, the courts allowed the school district to develop a voluntary desegregation plan in the 1980s. Our field research centered on these critical periods as communities emerged from local desegregation struggles to search for new school reform agendas. As these local policy agendas shifted, "the rules of the game" changed and groups perceived different sets of gains and losses in the educational policy arena. Since Latino and Asian groups were not visible, active players in school reform coalitions in most cities, shifting rules brought unknown consequences for them. To better understand the consequences of these local reform agendas, we trace the development of new reform initiatives as they unfolded in Boston, Denver, Los Angeles, and San Francisco and assess how changing the rules of the game in local education affected new school constituencies.

School reforms are context specific: National reform initiatives such as charter schools or site-based management take on distinctively local meanings and designs when implemented. Or, as Larry Cuban puts it, "Schools change reforms as much as reforms change schools" (1998, 455). These reform initiatives, therefore, are moving targets evolving over time and space rather than static programs that mean the same thing always and everywhere. Also, not all members of racial and ethnic groups share the same understandings of these reforms or necessarily anticipate similar consequences. To claim that some reform will benefit or harm Latinos or Asians or blacks or whites is to overlook the multiple identities and situations within each group; a simple argument about distributional consequences of school reforms is unwarranted. Notably, views that these new constituencies hold on school reform are not stable: Over the last decade, for example, some Latino organizations have moved from ambivalence about charter schools to advocacy of small charter schools that support bilingual, culturally grounded education for Latino students.[1] Thus the following snapshots capture the historical moments in these four cities as they struggled with and moved beyond court orders and integration agendas. By sketching out the key reform issues, we highlight the competing ideas and critical stakeholders in each city, their fears and hopes for reform. In subsequent chapters, we illustrate how these ideas were channeled by local institutional arrangements to shape distinctive school reform agendas.

Reform Agendas and Democratic Performance

By 2003, whites and African Americans had become less optimistic than Latinos about public schools. Fewer whites (25 percent) and African Americans (31 percent) reported that schools had improved over the last five years, compared to Latinos (45 percent). But nearly half of whites surveyed say that schools attended primarily by Latinos and African Americans are comparable to schools attended primarily by whites (Pew Hispanic Center 2004).

So, not surprisingly, views on school reforms also vary substantially by race and ethnicity. During our study period, for example, 59 percent of respondents to a 1999 national survey agreed more should be done to integrate schools. However, 90 percent of African Americans agreed, compared to 54 percent of whites (publicagenda.org), and while 44 percent of African Americans were willing to transfer students away from neighborhood schools to achieve this goal, only 10 percent of whites agreed. Similarly, Hispanics are more likely (38 percent) than whites (13 percent) or blacks (29 percent) to say discrimination against Hispanics/Latinos is a major problem in schools (Pew Hispanic Center 2004). By 2004, most Americans ranked laws to help blacks and minorities as low on the list of legislative priorities for Congress and the White House: 16 percent ranked it as "extremely important" and 31 percent as "very important." However, 44 percent ranked education as "extremely important" and 42 percent as "very important" (Public Agenda 2004). Thus even seemingly widely held views about schools and school reform are likely to obscure important racial and ethnic differences in citizens' viewpoints. This becomes even starker when specific reforms are at stake. Our focus, therefore, is not on public opinion but on the reform packages—or solution sets—that dominated education policy debates in each community during our study period.

Local agendas are made of solution sets. These shared understandings of education problems and appropriate solutions (Jones and Bachelor 1993), along with tendencies to apply standard policy solutions to new problems, are common features of decision processes. As particular understandings of the education problems facing a city become accepted, and are tied to particular solutions, alternative problem definitions and solutions become less salient. Accepted solution sets dominate decision making not just because they reflect shared understandings, but also because they are implemented through organizational arrangements, routines, and decision rules that become standardized over time. Changing the rules of the game—institutional change—is at the heart of every reform. From this perspective, group influence derives from the context of local decision-making processes rather than primarily from group resources or other factors exclusive to the group (Immergut 1992, 66).

Because solution sets limit consideration of alternative problem definitions and solutions, they will affect the relative "weight" different groups have in education politics. There are differential opportunities for resisting or promoting new initiatives. Over time, the "heavy hand of history" makes it difficult to respond to new circumstances and decision making becomes less flexible and responsive. Latino leaders, for example, characterized the Latino educational landscape as characterized by "missed opportunities in early childhood education, unsound educational treatments in elementary and secondary schools, and barriers to college." In blaming "Federal bureaucrats," they emphasized the tendency to continue with old programs in the face of new constituencies and needs (Yzaguirre 2002). This sluggish response from public institutions underscores the need to incorporate democratic performance criteria into our assessment of local school reform processes and proposals. That is, we need to consider the extent to which democratic processes can identify problems and direct attention and solutions to the most pressing issues facing it.

Policy Change and Local Policy Agendas

Not surprisingly, the emergence of new solution sets—here, education reforms—is itself problematic (Kingdon 1995; Baumgartner and Jones 1993). But if we heed E. E. Schattschneider's (1960) reminders of the mobilization of bias attendant to solving educational problems, we want to move beyond reform "scorecards" for cities to ask how these new policy agendas will affect new school constituencies. The politics of problem definition become especially significant if we find that different racial/ethnic groups define "the problem with schools" differently from conventional assumptions—and possibly even from one another—and thus seek different solutions.

Old Solution Sets and New School Constituencies

For each city our evidence indicates a wide range of "stories" about "the problem" with schools and appropriate solutions to those problems. But in each city we also find the persistence of a historical policy paradigm centered on desegregation. Not that the solution of desegregation necessarily remains a priority but, as Bryan D. Jones and Lynn Bachelor (1993, 207) put it, these understandings of education problems and solutions have been embedded or codified "in the bureaucratic structure of government."

As a consequence, school reforms that alter the institutional setting itself face substantial barriers. Court-ordered desegregation was lifted at different points in Denver, Los Angeles, Boston, and San Francisco. Increasing social diversity in all these cities also was eroding the desegregation paradigm. But there remained a lag in adapting to new multiethnic realities. No new systemic reforms stressing racial equity issues were advanced to take the place of the desegregation paradigm. Instead, partial reforms were churned through the school systems in rapid succession in these cities, reflecting the momentary advantage of reform coalitions at the local and state level around particular solution sets. In this fluid context, and in the absence of alternative solution sets that would highlight the concerns of new school constituencies, the consequences of partial reforms for new school constituencies became significant.

Churning Educational Reforms

There is no shortage of reform ideas and reform activity in education circles. There are literally hundreds of state-level task forces examining new educational initiatives and a large field of reform networks, such as the Coalition for Essential Schools and the Center for Education Reform, advocating particular initiatives. Evaluations of different strategies appear on a nearly monthly basis, generating a rush of attention to the latest conclusion on "what works" in public schools. These strategies and studies overwhelm the ability of practitioners and analysts to consider much less to incorporate reforms.

To some critics these waves of reform are part of the problem, in that reforms are rarely fully implemented before the next wave arrives (Hess 1998). The unsteady equilibrium of many partially implemented reforms may even serve the political and organizational needs of school administrators (McDermott 1997). In this context, it is not surprising that systemic change is infrequent and that responses to new school constituencies are inadequate. This seemingly unstable and turbulent environment allows new solutions to be considered but, over time, can make the education system itself increasingly vulnerable to additional disruptive institutional reform efforts (Hess 1998; McDermott 1997). This reform instability ultimately can erode public authority and the legitimacy of the public school system. For Latino and Asian constituencies, it means that reforms are broached but these are not necessarily the reforms they might advocate or prefer.

In this volatile environment, local school reforms are layered and overlapping. Given the high turnover rate for school superintendents, it is not unusual to find new reform initiatives brought in by new superintendents before previous reforms have had a chance to take hold. Assessing the effectiveness of any particular reform becomes difficult, and it is likely that contradictory reforms may be operating simultaneously in the school system. To Paul T. Hill, Christine Campbell, and James Harvey (2000, 138), reform efforts are often not well aligned. On the other hand, such redundancy and layering may be strategic: One outcome of a greater emphasis on testing and accountability may be an increased interest in choice options among parents whose children and schools are labeled as failing.[2] In Denver, increased demands for parental involvement followed the end of busing and the introduction of standardized testing. "It came with publication of the test scores," said Pam Martinez of the activist Padres Unidos. "Parents are suddenly keenly aware of how many kids aren't proficient in reading, writing, math and science. It's scary" (Kreck 2001, 1A).

Frustration and concern with the lack of meaningful change and the seeming inertia of public school systems is widespread. Nowhere is this more acute than among parents of color: Millions of dollars flow into reform initiatives, old programs are cut to support new efforts, and yet little improvement in their children's performance is evident. In our interviews we continually heard troubled accounts of the mismatch between the reform agendas in a city and parents of color's perceptions of their children's needs. In some cases, this is a question of emphasis: Fanfare and dollars are directed to large, visible, "innovative" programs that show the district is involved in the latest initiatives, while the day-to-day programs many parents see as crucial—school-to-work transition programs, bilingual education, early childhood education, targeted science and math programs—gain little public attention and fewer dollars. In other cases, there is outright suspicion and skepticism about the intentions and likely beneficiaries of reform initiatives. This is especially so for institutional reforms promising to restructure public schools.

Four Reform Strategies and their Consequences for Democratic Practice

To varying degrees, all four cities embraced reforms—solution sets—in the 1990s that promised to change the rules of the game in education policymaking. With one exception, they failed to address equity concerns and none responded directly to the new multiethnic constituencies in their schools. These partial reforms exemplify the churning, layering, and overlapping of reforms that frustrate and exasperate those seeking more fundamental reforms. Two reforms addressed the scale and locus of education policy authority: Site-based decision making and school reconstitution. Two others extended that policy authority beyond the traditional public education sector to new suppliers of public education: Charter schools and partnership arrangements. All of our cities were actively involved in some version of charter schools and site-based management; there was more variable involvement in partnerships and only San Francisco fully experimented with school reconstitution although it was selectively used in Denver as well.

To activists and parents of color, the consequences these restructuring initiatives would have for their voice in educational decisions were not obvious; nor did various racial and ethnic constituencies necessarily perceive these consequences in the same way. These differences clearly complicated the capacity to generate cooperation around reform alternatives. While we do not attempt to evaluate the effectiveness of each reform, we are interested in thinking about and comparing for whom these reforms work, under what conditions, and on whose terms (Wells and Scott 1999). Several of these reforms shared an underlying understanding of education as a commodity in a competitive market. As such, they signaled the emerging new educational populism solution set although this was not yet a coherent or comprehensive agenda; indeed, we emphasize the disconnect between many reforms as they became layered and overlapping at the local level.

As we tell the stories of local struggles over school reform, our special concern is with the implications these reforms have for problem solving in democratic settings. We focus on two possible tensions inherent in these school reforms: Do these initiatives provide greater school-based control over priority setting while abdicating central authority needed to prevent system-wide resegregation? Does broader participation in school decisions come at the cost of increased veto points in policymaking and greater exit options for some participants, with less voice for parents in decisions about their children's education? (see Table 3.1).

School-based Control vs. Resegregation

Challenges to hierarchical controls are common elements in education reform arguments (Henig et al. 1994; Elmore 1991). The "one size fits all" mentality of centralized control over priority setting and regulation of performance is seen as stifling flexibility and innovation at the school level. In response, numerous decentralization strategies aim to enhance flexibility and accountability by

---

TABLE 3.1 SCHOOL REFORMS AND NEW SCHOOL CONSTITUENCIES

	SITE-BASED MANAGEMENT	CHARTER SCHOOLS	PARTNERSHIPS
Consequence: More Control Over Priorities	Yes	Yes	Some
More Veto Points	Yes	Some	Yes
More Exit Options	Yes	Some	Yes
Less Voice	Some	Some	Yes

expanding the decisions made at the school level. Decentralized control also aims to differentiate and better "market" individual schools. However as Terry M. Moe (1994) points out, the problem may be the administrative management paradigm rather than bureaucracy itself. That is, centralization remains necessary in some domains; more authoritative management with stronger support could be more likely to improve educational quality than a generic decentralization response. Weakening central management, particularly replacing administrators with committees and nonprofit organizations, may increase the power of private consultants and contractors with specialized knowledge rather than increasing the power of parents (Moe 1994). In the absence of specific mechanisms to ensure a diverse school, it may also contribute indirectly to resegregation at the school level.

More Participation vs. More Veto Points and Exit Options

Gaining the support of parents, teachers, business, social agencies, and other critical actors is essential to successfully restructuring public schools. Yet the new mechanisms for gaining this cooperation often make change more difficult because they extend the decision chains—the sequence of affirmative decisions necessary for action—to more institutional arenas and to more actors (Immergut 1992). In doing so, they expand the number of veto points involved in policy formulation. In itself, this makes cooperation more difficult because each veto point reflects areas of strategic uncertainty in the decision process with distinctive political configurations and different rules for reaching decisions and transferring decisions to the next arena (Immergut 1992). These concerns are especially germane in site-based management and partnership initiatives. More veto points also increase the opportunities to exit. Some individuals or groups can affect policy outcomes more than others by threatening to withdraw from participation if their needs are not addressed.

Changing the Rules of the Game

Site-based Management: Devolving Policy Authority

Site-based management schemes devolving decisions to the school level have cycled through schools for decades. In practice, school-based decision makers rarely gain influence over a wide range of nonroutine decisions; they are especially unlikely to enjoy control over budgets or personnel. Nor do they often move beyond advisory roles and into substantive decision making (Malen, Ogawa, and Kranz 1990; Hill, Campbell, et al. 2000; Hill 1995). Site-based reforms are often established as ends in themselves and relatively divorced from real school governance. Nevertheless, these are recurrent and attractive reform options; they are on the agenda in each of the four cities but their policy roots differ, as do their actual structures.

Denver

Denver's collaborative decision-making process, or CDM, was instituted as part of a compromise during local labor negotiations. In 1991 the Denver Classroom Teachers Association (DCTA) and the District administration were stalemated in contract negotiations. Then-governor Roy Romer (a Democrat) invoked an obscure 1918 state law to justify his intervention in the dispute. One of the major outcomes of the negotiated agreement was the creation of CDMs presumably to help assure parent/citizen involvement and, at the same time, to bring about more "site-based management," particularly on hiring decisions. More specifically, their stated purpose is "to more effectively manage direct service resources," with the idea that school funding decisions would be tied to student achievement through School Improvement Plans (Cross-City Campaign 2001).

Colorado has a strong local-control tradition in education but the CDMs shifted authority from the local district to local stakeholders. All 115 Denver schools established CDMs composed of four teachers, four parents, a business representative, a nonteaching school employee, and the principal at each school; a bid by DCTA to add a union member to each team was rejected in favor of adding the fourth parent (Bingham 1994). Their peers elected the staff members and parents. These teams were given authority to design instructional programs, organize the school and classrooms, establish budget priorities, determine teacher work rules, and organize and assign staff time. The committees were to operate by consensus, either unanimous or majority decisions that all agreed to implement. Principals had veto powers although they did not use them frequently.

CDMs brought groups to the table who were often at odds with each other and with school administrators over issues of autonomy, principal and teacher assignment, and curriculum choice. Thus CDMs functioned to enforce coalitions that appeared unable to sustain cohesion and cooperation without such an external structure. Given their political legacy, CDMs had little local support and were perceived to have only weak support from DPS (Hernandez 1994).[3]

As a consequence of the CDM arrangement, teachers had to argue their case at the school level, rather than be represented in central administration by the union. Business participation was seen as essential, yet remained problematic; at one point, the business representatives on the CDMs had the highest turnover rate and their participation was weak in other respects as well. Cuts in staff resources continually threatened CDM effectiveness and collaborative potential. While the contract creating CDMs stipulated provision of CDM training, staff resources were more vulnerable to fiscal pressures. Without, or even with, such support, CDMs became "one more thing" principals had to accommodate, as one respondent put it.

Los Angeles

Somewhat parallel to Denver's experience, site-based management was included in a contract that ended the 1989 teachers union strike in Los Angeles. It provided for a three-year transition but there were never sufficient funds for teacher and parent training; furthermore, there were difficulties in gaining district and state waivers to allow school-based control. It took off, however, in 1993 when the Board of Education approved the Los Angeles Educational Alliance for Restructuring Now (LEARN) reform proposals, including measures to shift decision-making authority to schools and hold teachers and principals accountable for school performance (the LEARN initiative is detailed below). The proposals would give schools control over 85 percent of their budget, the freedom to develop their own plans, and would hold them accountable for student achievement. By 1994, 84 schools had some form of site-based management, up to 705 by 2001. The stated purpose was to improve student achievement, budget flexibility, and fiscal accountability (Cross-City Campaign 2001). Schools featured governance councils, school site councils, and categorical advisory councils comprised of the principal, teachers, and parents. To some, school-based management arrangements proliferated at the expense of the power of the primarily African American administrators. There was also apprehension that increased parent participation in school governance would exacerbate existing tensions between the mostly Anglo teachers and the mostly Latino parents. Some parent activists complained that LEARN failed to deliver on its promised parent training to complement its intensive teacher-retraining program.

San Francisco

To the extent that site-based management occurred in the San Fransisco Unified School District (SFUSD), it resulted directly from the 1983 Consent Decree. School-based decision making was promoted by the district, within the guidelines established by the consent decree for those schools targeted for reconstitution. Luis R. Fraga and Bari A. Ehrlichson (1994) argue that education professionals continued to dominate education policymaking in San Francisco, with the exception of reconstituted schools (see below). Assistance for reconstituted schools came from the central administration; however, school principals, teachers, parents, and students were allowed to develop new relationships that aimed toward a more inclusive management of these schools.

Boston

Boston's site-based management efforts were rooted in a long history of school councils established during the troubled desegregation process. In 1989, beginning with a few volunteer schools, Boston began to experiment with site-based management as an option in the teachers union contract. The School-Based Management/Shared Decision-Making (SBM/SDM) program accelerated with the 1993 Massachusetts Education Reform Act mandating advisory school councils of parents, teachers, and the principal. But Boston's legacy of school councils provided a foundation for a stronger role: In Boston's program, councils had significant authority and responsibility to manage the operation of their schools. As part of teachers union contracts in 1993 and 1994, SBMs became mandatory for all 117 schools in the system; in contrast to the earlier initiative, schools received twenty-five dollars per pupil as an incentive to carry out the SBM program and support services for councils were established (Portz 1994, 23).

By 1994/95, SBM/SDMs were implemented on a system-wide basis, with the support and contractual agreement of the Boston Schools Committee, the Boston Teachers union and the Superintendent of Schools. The major components included election of School-Site Council members to include teachers, parents, and administrators, professional development support of School-Site Council members, and shared decision making for most school decisions. By 1995/96, this effort involved 120 schools, 63,000 students, and School-Site Council members including 536 teachers, 120 staff members, and 880 parents. With the adoption of SBM/SDM, a number of schools claimed an increase in test scores (CGCS 1996).

Site-based Management and Democratic Practice

Decentralizing decision authority to the school level prompted some participants in education politics to worry that the lack of centralized monitoring would be harmful to education outcomes. In Denver, the DCTA union emphasized this issue of central control in their 1994 strike; teachers worried that work conditions would not be standardized, and that teachers were not adequately heard in the new CDM structures, particularly since principals had veto powers. Ill-defined and underfunded "de-centering" processes in Denver also created conflicts between DPS and the school teams over resource allocation. And to many, they were primarily symbolic efforts. One prominent local administrator in Denver charged:

> I think CDMs are rhetoric. Governance doesn't make changes in classrooms ... they don't say what they want the processes to do ... they just say they want the processes. Then they say: What kind of processes should the CDM be involved in? They say: All of them. Then somebody says: No, not that. Maybe it's easier to talk process because process appears to be more neutral. You can keep people busy on process. There is no product being demanded through this process. None.

Site-based management initiatives also established a new decision chain that shifted veto points; they thus privileged some groups and some strategies by altering the opportunities to influence and overturn decisions. In Denver, decisions on issues such as bilingual education previously were made within the DPS bureaucracy—in concert with the court order and in consultation with the Hispanic Education Advisory Council (HEAC)—and ultimately approved by the school board for implementation by DPS through directives to schools. Given the historic lack of Hispanic representation on the school board and the independence of the school board from the elected representatives of the city council, the only recourse for Latino groups to influence or challenge bilingual policy decisions was through the HEAC or at public hearings held by the school board prior to reaching a decision. This proved unsatisfactory; as noted below, many Latino leaders disagreed with the DPS interpretation of the court order on bilingual education, but were powerless to challenge DPS directives to schools on assigning students as well as qualifying and funding teachers. Each of the veto points in the previous system existed in an arena dominated by education professionals, board-appointed Latino advisors, or board members with no territorial constituencies.

Site-based management was not necessarily an improvement. Given the varying interests represented in CDMs, rather than the concentration of common interests within DPS, agreement became more difficult and less stable. It also was subject to resource-based oversight by DPS, political intervention from district-based council members, and the unspecified roles and informal vetoes of existing groups such as HEACs (Hispanic Education Advisory Council), PTSA (Parent Teacher Student Association), SIACs (School Improvement Accountability Council), and other neighborhood-based groups. Although the CDMs were granted significant autonomy, their effectiveness was limited by this potential divisiveness and the continual possibility of intervention of the board and the DPS administration.

Site-based management schemes also underscored the exit options available to those whose participation and support was essential in reaching school-based decisions. In Denver, the CDMs appeared to allow all participants to threaten to withdraw; they exemplified the argument that majority decision rules produce unstable accords since such decisions are vulnerable to being overthrown by newly constructed majorities with alternative proposals (Immergut 1992, 64). In reality, CDMs limited this cycling of preferences and restricted choices by giving school principals explicit veto powers over CDM decisions. As the DCTA union head put it, "the effectiveness of the committees is determined by the effectiveness of the principal. If the principal doesn't buy in, the principal can control" (Bingham 1994, 10A). Veto powers allowed the principal to compensate for the unstable decisions likely from the multiple interests represented on the CDM, although they did not improve the ability to reach decisions.

Reconstituting Schools: Restructuring Policy Authority

In the 1983 Consent Decree in San Francisco, unlike in most other desegregation plans, the court linked desegregation with academic achievement. The physical desegregation of students alone was not sufficient to demonstrate compliance with the court's directives. If the academic achievement of substantial segments of the student population, particularly African Americans and Latinos, was not also enhanced, the SFUSD would not be in compliance with the consent decree (Fraga et al. 1998). By coupling desegregation efforts to academic achievement of targeted student groups, the consent decree compelled San Francisco to address equity issues.

The Bayview–Hunters Point neighborhood of San Francisco, long known for its segregated African American community as well as for poor test scores at each of its schools, was the focus of the academic improvement sections of the 1983 Consent Decree (Consent Decree 1983). Critical to the efforts to improve the schools in Bayview–Hunters Point was the requirement that the District "*reconstitute* the staff of the ... schools to facilitate the new educational programs" (Consent Decree 1983, 17). As Hill, Campbell, and Harvey (2000, 169) note, this was "the ultimate intervention": All existing principals were replaced, substantial resources were available to work toward higher expectations and positive race relations, the teachers union contract was suspended and the new principals were given the opportunity to recruit nationwide.

In 1992, a court-appointed panel of experts evaluated the progress of the desegregation and school achievement plan and considered the plan's appropriateness for the city given its changing demographic base. This panel concluded that the consent decree had "largely achieved" the Decree's desegregation goals. However, "it was less sanguine" about the Decree's second goal relating to academic achievement, concluding "the District has not realized the goals for academic achievement for the overwhelming majority of African American and Hispanic students in the critical areas of educational attainment, dropouts, special education placement, and suspensions from school" (Orfield et al. 1992, 1).

Nevertheless, the original efforts in the Bayview–Hunters Point area made a difference. The reconstitution of schools resulted in African American students earning higher test scores, even though statistics on free lunch availability indicated that their level of disadvantage was comparable to African American students in other parts of the city. The panel concluded that even though other schools received a significant amount of supplemental funds, "achievement data show[ed] that money by itself often [had] little impact" and that "there [was] no proof in San Francisco that the provision of large budgets to fund school level plans, without the reconstitution and staff developments that distinguished [schools in Bayview–Hunters Point] ... produce[d] any academic benefits for the victims of segregation" (Orfield 1992, 35, 47). The success of these reconstitution efforts led the panel to recommend similar plans at other San Francisco schools. In the 1990s, ten schools were reconstituted and fourteen more placed on academic probation (Whitmire 1997). Around six hundred of the district's four thousand teachers and three hundred assistants were reassigned (Wood 1997).

Although not directly attributable to reconstitution, math and reading test scores in San Francisco rose after 1992; students began to score above the national average, with black and Latino student scores lagging behind those of Asians and whites but still improving steadily (Wood 1997). The 1993 provisions strongly recommended that special efforts be made to enhance the academic achievement of both groups of students.[4] The superintendent saw reconstitution as an important element in this improvement but also credited a district-wide teacher training program focused on math and literacy, the city's class-size reduction initiatives, and voter support for over two hundred million dollars in school bond issues since 1993 (Wood 1997).

To administrators in other cities, reconstitution was a tool—and a threat—that could be used selectively to orient schools to performance-based measures. In 1995, Denver replaced the majority of teachers at two low-performing elementary schools in a modified reconstitution effort. In a twist on reconstitution, a low-performing Denver middle school was forced in 2004 by a new state law to convert to a charter school, and the principal was transferred out (Sherry 2004). Although no urban district yet matches San Francisco's record, reconstituted schools exist in Cleveland, San Antonio, Chicago, Baltimore, and Prince George's County, Maryland (Whitmire 1997).

Reconstitution and Democratic Practice

In a distinctive way, school reconstitution reforms provided mechanisms aimed at preventing the negative effects of resegregation; they may, however, limit attention to these concerns to those schools with well-organized groups able to demand it. In San Francisco, the court—rather than local officials—exercised central oversight. Through the court's focus on the academic attainment of African American and Latino students, the needs of these communities for greater opportunities in formal education were met—at least in certain schools. This occurred, however, largely without the consistent and sustained oversight of leaders of these communities. In a sense, the court took over the role of this indigenous leadership by serving as a watchdog of the school system. These communities' educational needs were being met, to a degree, as a result of reconstitution, but it did not affect all segments of these communities equally. Reconstitution also, to a substantial degree, formally omitted any significant role for leaders of Latino and Asian American communities.

Charter Schools: Providing Alternative Public Education

The charter school movement has many roots (see Johnson and Medler 2000; Medler 2004). Albert Shanker, former president of the American Federation of Teachers, is often given credit as one of the originators of the charter school concept. To Shanker, they offered a counter to the accountability/assessment standards movements gaining steam (Shanker 1988a, 1988b). To other liberals also critical of the standards movement, charter schools (Nathan 1996) and even vouchers (Jencks 1970) promised new solutions to problems of educational inequalities. The charter schools movement offered an umbrella solution for critics of the standards movement, which was seeking a way to pursue more "bottom-up" approaches to school reform. These critics included those interested in small schools, those pursuing a school reform design centered on coherent pedagogies and curricular approaches undermined by increased testing, and those seeing charter schools as a mechanism for advancing other types of education reforms.[5]

But despite the appeal to reform advocates, national surveys consistently identify citizens' widespread lack of knowledge about charter schools and vouchers: Nearly two-thirds of Latinos, whites, and African Americans in the Pew Hispanic Center's 2004 national survey did not know enough about these reforms to have an opinion. Of those offering opinions, 25 percent of Latinos, and similar proportions of African Americans and whites supported charter schools operating according to state standards. Similarly, 46 percent of Latinos, 39 percent of whites, and 40 percent of African Americans say they do not know enough about vouchers to have an opinion. Of those expressing opinions, 42 percent of Latinos, 35 percent of whites, and 39 percent of African Americans would support vouchers, although these figures decline sharply if vouchers would mean less funding for public schools.

The more familiar understanding of charter schools is that it is a response to the contention that the institutional design of public schools limits student choice and parental control, stifles accountability, and lowers performance standards (Finn et al. 2000; Moe 2001). While public funds and regulations continue to shape these alternative projects, they operate outside the formal public education sector and under the aegis of local groups. They alter the institutional design of schools as well as shift the scale of control over budgets, teaching, and curriculum. There are "strong" and "weak" versions of charter school legislation: Stronger laws determine the number of charter schools, the ease of getting a charter, the degree of autonomy, the nature and type of oversight, and whether charter schools are fully funded on a per-student basis (CER 2001; Hill and Bonan 1991).

Our four cities are in states with "strong" charter school legislation: As of August 1998, California was second only to Arizona in the number of charter schools opened (130); together, California, Colorado, and Massachusetts were home to nearly one-third (204) of the 781 charter schools in the country (CER 1998b);[6] the total number of public schools differs in each state, of course. The local school board (in Colorado and in Massachusetts' pilot district schools) or a state agency or board of education (in California and the Massachusetts state charter school program) must grant the charter for the school to operate for a set number of years, but its control extends no further.

Thus the schools remain publicly financed and regulated, but their governance is more autonomous and responsive to parent and student direction. By allowing district funds to follow students moving from public schools to charter schools, the intent is to increase the financial incentives for conventional public schools to improve. In Colorado, charter schools received no startup funds, but do receive at least 80 percent of the average funds a district spends on each student; Massachusetts and California allow full district funding to follow students to charter schools. As Douglas J. Lamdin and Michael Mintrom (1997, 232) note, these unrestrictive full-funding policies "are the supply-side equivalent of a voucher and would thus have potentially similar consequences." In addition, the California Charter School Revolving Loan Fund provides interest free loans of up to two hundred fifty thousand dollars to help charter schools with startup costs. Capital costs are one of the most troublesome problems for charter schools; California's fund (approximately $5.5 million in 1999) pools federal funds to the state for charter schools with other funds garnered through the annual budget process.

In Colorado and California, charter schools have legal status as schools within the local school district; in Massachusetts, charter schools are generally legally independent of the school district with the exception of some select schools. In each case, school management is held responsible for producing the student achievement as promised in their contract or "charter" with the state; failure can result in losing the right to operate. As designed, the charter school experiment is intended to allow incremental, innovative changes within the public school system for "active choosers" (Elmore 1991); it allows adjustments, including termination, to be made as more information is gathered.

As of 2005, 40 states had enacted charter school legislation; about 400 new charter schools had opened for the 2004/2005 school year, bringing the total number of charters in the United States to about 3,400 (CER 2005). Since most charters are granted for three to five years, with differing degrees of funding, autonomy, and operating scope, systematic evidence on their effectiveness is scarce. A growing number of state studies and national evaluations now document the characteristics of charter schools, along with contested efforts at measuring their effectiveness on student performance and school district performance. There is some preliminary evidence that more charter schools are established to serve students of color and students with special needs than initially anticipated, although this varies significantly by state (U.S. Department of Education 1998, 1999, 2000, 2001; U.S. Department of

Education 2001; CER 2001).[7] Their fiscal impacts on other public schools is also variable: As Rofes (1998) points out, districts with continuing increases in new enrollments are less likely to feel the fiscal pinch of students lost to charter schools and, therefore, the anticipated impacts of charter schools on other public schools are weakened.

There is some evidence of charter schools' "ripple effect." That is, in some places, competition for students and dollars has brought innovation and improvement in the district. Boston showed "moderate" responsiveness, for example, by launching its own in-district pilot school program when state charter schools were introduced. The ability of charter schools to function as laboratories generating innovations and diffusing them to district schools varies: Denver's DPS-sponsored charter school was aimed at doing so but there are no formal means for transfer of ideas and programs; Boston's City on a Hill charter school may fare better, thanks to a federal grant to support collaboration among charter and district teachers (Hassel 1998, 15). Indeed, in states with a wide variety of choice options—such as Colorado and Massachusetts—it is difficult to sort out the contributions of specific initiatives on school districts (Rofes 1998, 18).

Denver

Colorado and California were among the early experimenters with the charter school concept first put forward in Minnesota in 1991. Although Colorado voters rejected school voucher initiatives in the early 1990s, there was strong and growing support for experimenting with alternative public education approaches minimizing the "publicness" of school operations. Charter schools were the prime example of such initiatives: In the Colorado context, charter schools were perceived as an alternative to outright privatization. To supporters, they promised to be "a new kind of public school" maximizing student choice, parental options, and competitive performance standards. To detractors, they resembled "backdoor voucher proposals" that will divert system funds for the benefit of a few selected students. While state enabling legislation required charter schools to be open to all students, critics saw the need for transportation, the demands for parent volunteer time, the admissions interview procedures, and the high information costs of the process as creating "an educational Bosnia," a dual-school system that sorted out students by socioeconomic status (Bingham 1994, 16).

The Colorado path to charter school reforms was contested more by professional educators than by parents of color. Following voters' defeat of school vouchers in 1992, a policy analyst in the state Department of Education acted as the political entrepreneur promoting charter schools (Elmore 1991; Mintrom 2000). He tapped into the national charter school movement and the local discontent with public education evidenced by the voucher vote by designing legislation based on the Minnesota program and pulling together a coalition (Hirsch 1993). The 1993 legislative struggle over charter schools in the General Assembly pitted the state's two teachers unions, state education associations, and school administrators—particularly from Denver—against a bipartisan coalition of conservative and generally nonurban legislators and state department of education officials, along with the Democratic governor Roy Romer, and the Colorado Children's Campaign, backed by the Denver-based media. A Latino organization, the Latin American Research and Service Association (LARASA), mobilized state and local Latino organizations to consider the proposed legislation; although troubled by the potential long-term effects on the public education system, they decided not to oppose the bill.[8]

Legislative critics managed to limit the initial scope of charter schools by initially capping them at fifty (the cap was lifted as of 1997) and to specify that special emphasis should be given to students who are "at risk" due to physical, emotional, socioeconomic, or cultural factors (Hirsch 1993). Within a year of legislative enactment, fourteen charter schools were operating in Colorado; by 1998, fifty charter schools were open and ten more approved (CER 1998b). By 2005, ninety-three charters served the state. Local school districts' reluctance to support charter schools and their control over authorization and scope of charter schools impeded faster growth. Thirteen of the original fifty schools were designated for students at risk of not succeeding because of "physical, emotional, socioeconomic, or cultural factors" (CER 2005). Charter school founders across the state have formed the Colorado League for Charter Schools.

Boston

The 1993 state education reform act in Massachusetts included provisions for a state-supported charter school program. Republican Governor William Weld created the Executive Office of Education to coordinate state efforts; it sponsored charter school conferences, provided technical assistance to charter school sponsors, and assigned three of its eighteen employees to work on charter school initiatives (Rabrenovic 1995). In contrast to the Colorado approach, the more autonomous Commonwealth charter schools were authorized by state officials with no approval necessary from local school committees. For the less autonomous conversions from public to charter schools at the district level, the local school committee, local teachers union, and the state board must approve. Also in contrast to Denver, charter schools received funding from the local school district at the same per student levels as other district schools. From 1993 to 1995, twenty-five schools were granted charters, the legal maximum; according to the legislation, no more than five could be located in Boston. Legislation passed in 2000 brought the maximum to seventy-two state-approved charter schools; by 2005, fifty charters were operating in the state.

One of the largest charter schools in the country is in Boston, the Boston Renaissance Charter School, founded by the Edison Project in partnership with the Horace Mann Foundation. The school ended its relationship with Edison in 2002 and began to run independently. With substantial state support, the school gained a lease on a vacant state-owned building downtown; the state also helped the school secure a twelve-million-dollar loan for repairs and was charging below-market rent. The plan was to have 630 students in grades K–5 and to eventually reach 1,265 students in grades K–12 (Rabrenovic 1995). The Edison Project's objectives were to create a model school blueprint that could be transferred to other public schools while generating profits for investors in the project. Pedagogically, the emphasis was on computer skills, foreign language training, and longer school days. By 2005, 1,425 students attended Renaissance from grades pre-K through 8.

A second version of charter schools—pilot schools—emerged in 1994 from Boston teachers union contract negotiations. These pilot schools were within-district charter schools: They were proposed by groups working with BPS staff and approved by the local school committee. Approval criteria included the prospects for replicating or transferring pilot school innovations to other schools in the district. Pilot schools were relatively free from union and central office regulations; in return for this autonomy, they received only a lump sum budget from the school system and, as in Colorado, must document meeting their performance goals. John Portz (1994, 22) reports that seventeen proposals for pilot schools were received in 1994 and six were chosen to begin in 1995/96.

In Boston, the school administration preferred the pilot schools program to the state charter schools initiative. Indeed, many saw pilot schools as public schools' response to the introduction of charter schools. The local control was greater (including oversight by the Boston Teachers Union) and the costs to the local district were fixed. In contrast, the success of the state charter school program imposed real costs on the remaining schools in the district. One estimate is that Boston schools would lose nearly $7.5 million to state-supported charter schools (Rabrenovic 1995); this meant a loss of funds for local initiatives, including pilot schools.[9]

Los Angeles

Although California initially (1992) capped the number of charter schools at one hundred and limited them to ten in any district, the State Board of Education exceeded that cap by granting charters on a case-by-case basis until 125 charter schools were in operation (CER 1998a). The cap is now lifted; by 2001 California had 358 charter schools. This large number is partly attributable to conversions; the state law allows existing schools to convert to charter status if a majority of the teachers approve. A 1994 law mandated that all California school districts establish an open enrollment policy although transportation is not provided for students attending nonneighborhood schools.

The Vaughn Next Century Learning Center in the LAUSD was an early charter school in Los Angeles, opening in 1992 after struggles with the school board over funding and with the teachers union over health benefits (CER 1998a). Five years after opening, it served 1,140 students; nearly 95 percent are Hispanic and 83 percent have limited proficiency in English (CER 1998a). In 1995, Vaughn received the state education department's California School Award and in 1997 was named one of thirty-four National Blue Ribbon Schools by the U.S. Department of Education. In 1998, Vaughn reported scores that were twice that of comparable schools in the area. The school now claims that student performance is close to the national median in math and language, that English proficiency has tripled, and that its budget controls have allowed it to reinvest in facilities, reduce class size, and hire new teachers (CER 1998a).

San Francisco

There is a dearth of charter schools (six) in San Francisco, but the city featured the state's first startup charter school, Leadership High School. Funded by private and philanthropic support, the school served inner-city students with a program developed with the assistance of the Bay Area Coalition of Equitable Schools (BayCES). Approximately 27 percent of the students are Latino, 23 percent are African American, 20 percent are Asian, and 18 percent are white. Private funding allowed it to spend eighteen hundred dollars more per student than the state average. With small classes and an emphasis on leadership and service—students must contribute thirty-five hours of community service a year—nearly every Leadership graduate goes on to college. Five years after its founding in 1997, Leadership showed the third-highest high school test scores in the district; on the 2001 statewide Academic Performance Index, Leadership received the highest possible score—a 10—when compared to schools with similar student populations.

Charter Schools and Democratic Practice

In cities with court-ordered desegregation and busing programs, many middle-class families carried out the exit threat by putting their children in private schools or moving to suburban school districts. With the end of busing, this threat persisted and became even more salient as cities tried to attract these families back into public schools. Charter schools represent one such method.

Even with the shift to neighborhood schools in Denver, for example, 64 percent of respondents said they would send their children to private schools rather than DPS if they could afford it (Illescas 1998). Charter school initiatives and, to some extent, site-based management efforts amplified the significance of exit or nonparticipation options by certain groups, including students of color (Wells and Scott 1999). The availability of the exit option for middle-class families was a continuing incentive for administrators to direct resources to accommodate these interests. Increases in school violence exacerbated these exit threats in every urban school district. Given the declining share of white children in the student populations of most urban districts and the slim margin of middle-class families remaining in the public school system, public officials have directed substantial resources to responding to the threat of exit by these families through charter schools and other initiatives.

Partnership Arrangements: Extending Policy Authority

The ascendance of partnerships and nonprofit organizations reflected the shift in public discourse and policy paradigms in the 1980s to decentralization, privatization, and efficiency. This privatization rhetoric encouraged receptivity to business leadership and nonbureaucratic, nonprofit organizations and granted more legitimacy to new arrangements and values (cf. Powell 1987). Business leadership and participation is considered essential in most aspects of local policymaking but it has been weak and disjointed in most local educational arenas. Interviews in our four cities suggested this as well. This contrasts with the more visible role business leaders play in state and national educational reform initiatives. Clarence N. Stone (1998, 257) attributes the difference to the need at the local level for sustained engagement with concrete and contentious policy choices, rather than the broad, often symbolic, business support rallied for state and national legislation. And as noted previously, business sectors vary in their dependence on human capital resources as well as in their capacity and motivation to work with the varied and complex set of stakeholders involved in local educational issues. Thus, the involvement of business in local education policymaking is variable: In Boston, it was broad and institutionalized in a number of long-standing cross-sector coalitions; in Los Angeles, it was institutionalized in LEARN but with little history of sustained collaboration to support it; and in Denver and San Francisco, business involvement was modest and episodic.

Although business involvement is crucial to reform success, the inclusion of parents, teachers, educators, and other community-based groups also is critical. While teachers and educators are often organized into unions for collective bargaining purposes, other stakeholders increasingly organize as nonprofit organizations. Nonprofits' quasipublic and quasimarket status appear to offer greater prospects for legitimacy gained through the public's confidence that they are applying their expertise in the public interest and that they are accessible to citizen voice (Maynard-Moody 1989, 141).

Greater roles in education for nonprofits do not necessarily come at the expense of local governments. These intermediary organizations offer advantages to local officials. Local governments potentially can increase their effectiveness by legitimating and coordinating the work of nonprofit organizations. They not only act as a buffer for local governments, but they also

provide significant staff resources. In contrast to the bureaucratic and politi-
cized structures of the school district, the organizational structures of these
groups are more able to focus and persist in following through on school reforms.
This quality of stability stems, in part, from their greater insulation from both
economic competition and political pressures (Smith and Lipsky 1993).

Denver

Overall there were no persistent—formal or informal—change-oriented cross-
sector coalitions shaping Denver education politics. Denver was characterized
as having many leaders directly involved in issues; although reforms will not
work without such leaders, these leaders were generally individuals with repu-
tations for effectiveness and commitment, rather than leaders of organizations
that could be mobilized for education goals. One consultant identified roughly
ten to twelve people in Denver as critical to the success of any educational
venture; they form an interlocking network across DPS, corporations, foundations, state education associations, and state political sectors, but do not
include community leaders. The school bureaucracy remained ambivalent
about education restructuring; there was ferment at the teacher and midad-
ministrative levels, but the overall response was slow and reactive. The education subsystem—professionals and insiders alike—was fragmented; it was
unable to present a coherent core of resistance to external pressures for
change, yet it remained unable to articulate alternative reform strategies. The
high turnover of superintendents during and beyond the study period contributed to this lack of coherence.

Business groups in Denver are highly organized and effective in promoting
downtown redevelopment and megaprojects, such as the Denver International
Airport, the Rockies baseball stadium (Coors Field), and the Denver Ocean
Journey aquarium. But this mobilization and capacity for cooperation did not
transfer to the human capital arena. The business community generally was
seen as "disengaged" from public school issues. Involvement from business on
a system-wide scale was relatively absent; while individual business people may
find their status lends them credibility and legitimacy in educational forums,
their failure to "bring" their business network or corporate connections to bear
in significant or enduring ways meant that broader civic capacity was not
achieved. While business groups are organized on a city level, the most powerful have a metropolitan-wide focus on economic development, perhaps
weakening their concerns about the city public schools.

While business leaders contended that the business community was concerned with education issues, they also confessed that they were not well
orchestrated and lacked "the Generals" to provide leadership. Coordination
became more difficult because of the lack of authoritative mechanisms and the
fluctuating cast of players on each issue, although there were no demands for

new mechanisms. Indeed, one foundation official pointed out that nobody was in a sufficiently authoritative position to make them.

In the absence of cross-sector coalitions and partnerships, nonprofit organizations stepped in to fill this leadership gap. The reliance on nonprofit organizations in Denver also increased because of restrictive tax and expenditure limitations imposed by Colorado voters through the initiative process (the TABOR initiative, "Taxpayers' Bill of Rights") in 1992. While nonprofit organizations have been prominent in Denver across issue areas, they became vital actors in education in the 1990s; these groups provided a means for circumventing the fiscal limits on the district and overcoming the political constraints on promoting systemic reforms. Furthermore, they were one of the few mechanisms in Denver for bringing key players and stakeholders to the table.

The major nonprofit players included the Piton Foundation, Citizens for Quality Schools, The Hunt Alternative Fund, the Public Education Coalition, the Colorado Partnership for Educational Renewal, the Colorado Alliance of Business, and the school district's own foundation formed to receive revenues outside the TABOR restrictions.[10] In 1992, the Piton Foundation changed from a grant-making foundation to an operating foundation in order to become more directly involved in its investment in education reform and poverty reduction. Denver also was the site for several national programs in which local organizations partnered with major national foundations. The Piton Foundation, for example, partnered with the Ford Foundation on its Community Development Project targeting neighborhood revitalization; it also collaborated with the Rockefeller Foundation on the Denver Poverty Project—which included public education as a major agenda issue—as well as on the Community Planning and Action Program.

While this long-standing history of nonprofit involvement was important, nonprofit organizations blossomed with the educational reforms of the 1990s. This was especially so for those reforms initiated by the state government; in many cases, nonprofit organizations were advocates for reforms devolving authority and resources from DPS to school levels. In an event indicative of the growing importance of nonprofit organizations, the breakdown of contract negotiations between the district and the teachers union in 1990 brought the Citizens for Quality Schools (CQS) to the negotiating table. CQS claimed that nobody spoke for the parents' and citizens' interests in avoiding a strike and promoting broader education values. They allied with the governor in negotiating the terms of the new contract, one that included site-based management and collaborative decision making that included parents. As a result, CQS began to move from an independent advocacy group to a collaborative partner in educational reform.

Los Angeles

Partnership arrangements were essential in Los Angeles.[11] Progressive Era reforms seeking to rationalize government succeeded in fragmenting authority to the point that Los Angeles lacked a political structure capable of "focusing complete energies and talents" toward any goal, particularly a goal from which side payments cannot be squeezed (Guerra and Cohen 1994).

With over seven hundred governments in Los Angeles County—many with the power to tax and make public policy—the local government of Los Angeles is highly fragmented across geographic and functional jurisdictions. This dispersion of political power reflects the Progressive reformers' attempt to separate politics from governance. As V. O. Key observed, however, "In a granulated political structure of this kind with thousands of points of authority, there is no point at which accountability can be enforced" (1949, 307). Consequently, many matters are not addressed because it is impossible to secure the collaboration of all those whose involvement is needed. To the extent that the decentralization of authority is overcome, collaboration is ad hoc, often with compromises that promise "something to everybody" in order to get measures accepted (Banfield and Wilson 1963, 111).

In addition to this institutional fragmentation, economic trends left a rather porous civic elite structure in Los Angeles, as in Denver. In contrast to the 1950s and 1960s when an elite business group, the Committee of 25, dominated the electoral and civic arenas, Los Angeles (like Denver) lacks the homegrown corporations and headquarters that support such leadership. This relative lack of "old families and old money" opened up leadership positions to those with enough new money and initiative to push their agendas into prominence (Purdum 2000, A10). But it also made such leadership contingent on the ability to mobilize support issue by issue. Thus, educational reform required the mobilization of both public authority and civic will. The effective manipulation of political symbols and the formation of alliances were important components of the education reform battleground in the city.

Educational reforms in Los Angeles were promoted during our study period by LEARN, then the latest effort (1990) at creating a broad-based coalition in support of educational reform. LEARN was a 501(c)(3) organization: Business leaders, education administrators, teachers, foundations, and community advocacy groups were part of this coalition; parents' organizations played a minor role (Stone 1998, 256). The five founding members included Robert Wycoff, the CEO of ARCO, Richard Riordan, Mayor from 1993 to 2001, and other representatives of Los Angeles' old guard civic and corporate elite. With Wycoff as LEARN Chairman, the group went on to enlist other corporate leaders by articulating the link between education and regional economic development.

From the beginning, LEARN saw educational reform as a *political* task. In Los Angeles this meant bringing a broad set of interests to the table; representatives of the three largest minority communities joined the Executive Working Group, as did representatives of the California Business Roundtable, the LAUSD Superintendent, and the President of the teachers union (later adding the President of the LAUSD Board of Education and leadership of the service employees union). The Working Group created a Council of Trustees encompassing hundreds of community representatives to work on reform plans. As LEARN's material put it, "Our 625 trustees represent nearly every kind of advocacy organization which exists in Los Angeles ... Our mission is to forge a community wide consensus of how our schools should work and get these reforms implemented."

Despite LEARN's rhetoric, the process of drafting the reform plan was "a new level of Dante's Inferno." According to a top LEARN official:

Long, hard hours and hours and hours of meeting into the night. People threatening to walk and then they know for our kids we must stay ... And then, all this going on in the midst of (the April 1992) civil unrest ... the ethnic problems in this community and the misunderstandings and the real division ... that are not yet healed, and it was a tremendous challenge.

LEARN raised over three million dollars from private sources and foundations to begin implementation of its programs. In the first year of implementation, thirty-five schools signed on as LEARN schools. Fifty-four additional schools—fewer than LEARN hoped for—signed on for 1994/95. LEARN sought implementation of its reforms at all Los Angeles Unified schools by 1997/98, although by 1998/99, only 43 percent had signed on (LEARN Collection). Maintaining broad support was an ongoing challenge for LEARN's staff. In assessing LEARN's prospects for continued success, a top LEARN official observed in 1994, "I think that the success of our operation so far is that we have kept all stakeholders by and large believing that this has a real fair chance of substantially and dramatically changing the environment.... It's a very impressive accomplishment, but it could collapse tomorrow."

In 2001, LEARN merged with the Los Angeles Annenberg Metropolitan Project (LAAMP) which had been working to create stable "school families," clusters of one high school and its feeder schools with coordinated policies and programs. LAAMP was governed by a board of business executives and university administrators. This merger became the Los Angeles County Alliance for Student Achievement. It then morphed into the Alliance for College-Ready Public Schools, a nonprofit charter school–management corporation that launched its first charter in 2004. It aimed to create "a network of excellent small high-performing 9–12 and K–8 public schools in historically underachieving, low income, overcrowded communities in Los Angeles that will significantly outperform other public schools in preparing students to enter and succeed in college" (Alliance 2005). The Alliance is governed by a board consisting primarily of corporate executives, with some education specialists and civil-rights attorneys as well. Robert Wycoff, the founder of LEARN serves as a senior advisor. Meanwhile in 2004, LAUSD Superintendent Roy Romer (former Governor of Colorado) had moved away from LEARN's approach of individualized school plans to a system-wide approach, allowing the LEARN model to operate only in the district's highest performing schools (Archer 2004).

Part of LEARN's original reform package included reorganization of the school district away from central bureaucratic control by implementing school-based management. To others, including suburban community leaders, true decentralization would require breaking up the school district itself. When the City Council approved a Los Angeles Unified reapportionment plan in 1992, taking away a Board seat from the Valley and creating a new district in the largely Latino Eastside, the Valley Chamber of Commerce vowed to renew their efforts to dismantle the District. In August 1995, then Governor Pete Wilson facilitated some efforts by signing a bill lowering the number of necessary signatures for a petition and eliminating the veto power of the LAUSD. By 1996, a *Los Angeles Times* poll revealed that 51 percent of the respondents favored dismantling the district in order to gain smaller classes, local control, and improved quality. The strongest opposition to the breakup came from Latinos, African Americans, and residents of South Los Angeles. A secession referendum in November 2002 failed.

San Francisco

Sharing some of the same Progressive tradition and state political culture as Los Angeles, San Francisco is also characterized by fragmented government structures and limited citywide leadership.[12] As DeLeon notes, the downtown business elite lacks coherence and consensus but the antigrowth, progressive coalition dominating local politics fails to articulate a broad governing agenda (1992, 7–8). A Business Advisory Committee organized to support public schools only formed in 2002 but subsequently was instrumental in passage of bonds and ballot initiatives channeling city funds to the school district. The Committee is frank about its economic interests in better schools.

In contrast to Los Angeles, partnership arrangements and nonprofit organizations were not central to efforts to change the rules of the game for education in San Francisco. The politics of hyperpluralism that characterize the city and county of San Francisco generally (Wirt 1974) were also present in educational politics and policymaking but in modified form. There were a number of different actors affecting education but not nearly as many well-organized, consistent players in the politics of education as there are in much of the city's general politics. Education displayed the same lack of an inclusive, integrated leadership from diverse interests.

In contrast to Denver, community foundations were not involved in education reform in any systematic way. The Irvine Foundation and the San Francisco Foundation made modest grants to the school district but did not spearhead new initiatives. Fraga and Ehrlichson (1994) argue that if effective school reform in any city depends significantly on developing a cross-sector civic capacity to identify schools as an important policy issue—along with a broad-based strategy to address educational issues and collaborative arrangements to implement reforms—San Francisco should not be successful in any reform effort. They rated the level of civic capacity in the city/county jurisdiction as very low.

In a sense, the Federal District Court compensated for this lack of leadership and partnerships. Important changes took place in the SFUSD through the court's efforts at reconstitution. Through the consent decree, the court itself tried to build a coalition of interests to work together in promoting school reform. The comprehensiveness of the consent decree suggested that the Court's logic was one which to a substantial degree sought to compensate for the lack of inclusive, integrated leadership in educational policy in the community overall. But this raised serious questions for future reforms in San Francisco: Fraga and Ehrlichson (1994) wondered whether such court-dominated leadership was in the long term interests of San Francisco and especially its public school students who were, in fact, completely dependent on the courts for any significant innovations in educational policy. That is, it is possible that the court's actions in promoting reform may serve to further inhibit civic capacity from developing because the court was such a strong leader.

Boston

Boston is nationally famous for its educational partnership arrangements. Portz (1994) identified three major cross-sector education reform coalitions in Boston: The Boston Compact, the Boston Plan for Excellence, and the Citywide Educational Coalition. Business leaders played important roles in each but were especially visible in the Boston Compact. The Compact began in 1982, eight years after the court desegregation order; its signatories recommit every five years. Compact III was signed in January 1994, and Compact IV in 2000. The signatories also included higher education, labor, city government, and public school leaders; the Compact is distinguished from other partnership arrangements by its utilization of committees to oversee implementation of agreements and its use of measurable standards to evaluate the performance of partners in reaching Compact goals. These goals included supporting schools in improving educational performance but also encouraging businesses and colleges to offer employment and higher education opportunities to Boston public school graduates (Glazer 1993). Goals for the fourth Compact included meeting higher standards, increasing opportunities for college and career success, and recruiting and preparing the next generation of teachers and principals (Boston Compact 2000).

Framing education issues as a question of workplace development linked the schools and local businesses (Jones et al. 1997). Many businesses not only were active in the Compact but also in forty business-school partnerships involving direct interactions on operating issues and, often, donations of equipment and executive time. In contrast, the Citywide Education Coalition, started in 1973, acted as an advocate by sponsoring public forums on education issues and providing information on the school system. It did not sponsor or operate programs but provided a citizen voice for its broad-based membership of educators, businesses, foundations, banks, and community-based organizations.

The Boston Plan for Excellence is an especially important cross-sector partnership working directly with the school system on whole-school reform and teacher coaching models. It embarked on extensive fundraising in the mid-1990s to support its reform initiatives, targeting private foundations for multi-million-dollar support.

Although the density and sustainability of these cross-sector partnerships supporting school reform is distinctive, business involvement rarely meant an emphasis on racial integration. Many of the African American parents, activists, and lawyers involved in the heated and protracted desegregation lawsuit and busing endeavors grew discouraged and disappointed over time in the lack of improvement in African American children's education. By the early 1980s, the promise of better quality education and more choice over which schools their children could go to made the promises of the Boston Compact and the Plan more appealing than continued court struggles (Jones et al. 1997).

Partnerships and Democratic Practice

Not surprisingly, greater reliance on partnerships and nonprofit organizations loosens central controls but also introduces a number of unanticipated consequences. From the reformers' perspective, relying on new nonprofit entities circumvents the routinized and ongoing practices of established organizations and agencies. But nonprofits also may serve as means for furthering the influence of local leaders, particularly by deflecting the energies and attention of those who may have otherwise mounted more direct challenges to extant power structures (cf. Salamon and Ahneier 1994).

The ability of parents groups and racial and ethnic minority groups to sustain their participation in these partnerships, especially in the face of protracted negotiations, becomes problematic. Furthermore, these arrangements and organizations may not reach all issues or penetrate all schools. Some respondents thought that true school reform would require ongoing, close involvement and funding, and they doubted that nonprofit organizations could sustain such an effort. As one Denver respondent said, "The nonprofits have the vision and the intention, but don't always have the resources."

Greater reliance on partnerships and nonprofit organizations also may affect how minorities form coalitions and present demands for policy change. As nonprofit organizations gain favor for implementing educational reforms, they shape how groups consider priorities; many nonprofit organizations are sensitive to the needs for visible, reasonably quick program benefits that allow them to build track records and accountability with sponsoring organizations. To the extent that nonprofit organizations capture major external funding sources, these priorities become dominant. With resource constraints and institutional configurations favoring nonprofit organizations, it is difficult for groups with other priorities and broad-based membership to sustain participation. This underscores the interactive effects of institutional configurations and social capital (Putnam 1993; Smith 1994). In the long run, this relatively benign implementation strategy can starve local areas of the social capital necessary for building cooperation and trust by hampering group maintenance and coalition stability (Smith 1994). In this sense, the nonprofit "solution" may create further dilemmas for disadvantaged groups who are not central participants in nonprofits.

More pragmatically, reliance on third-party organizations for implementation may make achievement of program purposes less certain, may exacerbate the leakage of program benefits, and make generation of political support more problematic. But to their advocates, these indirect, less visible, less administratively complex tools may spur less opposition, exhibit fewer visible costs, and promise greater administrative ease with fewer side effects and greater emphasis on performance standards than more conventional direct government intervention (Salamon 1981, 269).

Reforms expanding the number of veto points may also have the unintended consequence of hampering policy learning within the district. Bringing in more nonprofit organizations and more CDMs in Denver, for example, transformed the system from the rather tightly coupled DPS administrative unit to a more loosely coupled system. In a loosely coupled system, the barriers to learning center on the viability of the networks linking groups together rather than lack of information or resistance to change assumed to permeate bureaucracies (Henig 1995).

The very notions of civic capacity, partnerships, and cross-sector coalitions imply more complex decision processes. Bringing together stakeholders from different sectors and seeking common grounds for cooperation in itself increases the number of veto points possible. Yet the nature of the problems faced in urban public schools demands collaborative efforts. As one respondent in San Francisco saw it, there was an

epidemic [of] violence by youth, against youth. It is catastrophic proportions; it is a major concern of parents. Some of the programs that
he [Superintendent Rojas] is trying to implement involve collaboration between all of the different city departments and private agencies. It is the only way that makes any sense.

Every partnership and coalition struggled to overcome these potential vetoes
and find a mechanism for reaching agreement. In large, informal coalitions,
such as LEARN, members could depart if their preferences were not met. In
more formal arrangements, such as the Boston Compact, negotiations over
sticking points continued until all parties were satisfied and willing to sign on.
In 1994, for example, reauthorization of the Compact was delayed until agreement was reached on extending site-based management to all schools (Portz
1994). In San Francisco, when then-Superintendent Rojas launched interagency initiatives, these required formal collaboration among agencies, as did
the city program to combat school violence.

Reform Initiatives and New School
Constituencies: Privileging Frames and
Organizational Structures

Although there are many reservations about the implications of these school
reform initiatives for new school constituencies as well as for democratic practice, one of the most significant concerns is that some frames are privileged at
the expense of others. Since public institutions are limited in the ability to
address multiple social problems (Hilgartner and Bosk 1988), a prevailing
approach to reform often emerges and displaces other options. Increasingly,
issue frames based on market assumptions and emphasizing "choice" challenge
issue frames centered on equity and resource shortage priorities. Framing the
education problem as a matter of more choice and competition rather than
greater equity and more resources has profound political and distributional
consequences.[13]

Privileging Choice

The word "choice" has an "all-American ring to it" (Cookson 1992, 92) and proponents of school choice note that "choice is a self-contained reform with its
own rationale and justification" (Chubb and Moe 1990, 217). It is difficult for
other institutional reforms that focus on nonmarket solutions—that is, creating
enhanced formal (bureaucratic) linkages between public institutions and private organizations or court supervised school reconstitution, as in San

Francisco (Fraga et al. 1995, 1998)—to defend their rationales against the symbols and values conjured by the "choice" rhetoric.

As noted previously, we characterize choice and market-like issue frames as "the New Educational Populism," a paradigm reflecting interests and norms distant from those of the new school constituencies. This frame also elides the staggering fiscal disparities between wealthy districts able to spend three to four times more per child than poor school districts.[14] In the absence of efforts to restore an issue frame that highlights the inequities built into our education system by the tax structure, zoning regulations, and housing patterns, the "choice" frame and New Educational Populism persists.

Choice-related reforms are often promoted by policy entrepreneurs able to capitalize on the waning appeal of the old symbols and stories, and the new anxieties, to change how people think about education problems (cf. Weiss 1989; Mintrom 2000). State interventions, such as the site-based management efforts, standards-based outcome assessment procedures, charter schools, and other privatization alternatives found in our cities displaced existing definitions and ways of doing things and thus affected basic features of the educational system. According to critics of such reforms, the concern is not so much that these are the wrong solutions, but that they are solving the wrong problems (cf. Dunn 1994).

Furthermore, these partial issue frames have significant consequences. With the lifting of court orders, the "problem" of education in Denver, Los Angeles, and Boston gave priority to issue frames emphasizing increased school choice. A competing problem definition, one increasingly championed by Latino and other minority groups, stressed *disparities* in student achievement and resegregation within schools. Given the limited "carrying capacities" of public institutions (Hilgartner and Bosk 1988), the ascendance of alternative problem definitions—such as students' civil rights, resegregation, or economic integration—is perceived as a threat to the values of choice, accountability, and parental involvement. As an African American school board member in Denver put it, the emphasis on parental involvement in minority communities means attempting "to empower a group of people who feel disenfranchised" and alienated from the school system (Stevens 1994, 2B). And as is clear in other cities, it often placed demands on groups with the fewest resources available to respond (Henig et al. 1999).

Slighting Bilingual Concerns

Choice-based issue frames obscured other agendas, such as bilingual education. Issues of language and culture continue to fragment new school constituencies. Overall, national surveys report strong sentiment supporting teaching of English to immigrant children, but Latinos (88 percent) are more likely than blacks (79 percent) or whites (57 percent) to stress the importance of also retaining native languages (Pew Hispanic Center 2004, 6).

In 1994, about fifteen thousand of Denver's sixty-three thousand students had limited English skills; about ten thousand of these were Spanish speakers and the others spoke seventy-three different languages. In the bilingual programs stemming from the 1984 court decree requiring adequate programs, Spanish-speaking students must receive core academic subjects in Spanish in a classroom with a bilingual teacher. Latino parents charged that the district never adequately carried out this plan. But they also disagreed on the best tack. Some sanctioned a long-term bilingual program as a means of retaining a native language and culture. Others saw this as a form of resegregation, particularly when other options were available but not encouraged for Spanish speaking children.

To many Latinos, the need for attracting and retaining qualified bilingual teachers was at the heart of the problem. Of equal concern was the perception that bilingual programs were used by paraprofessionals and new teachers as stepping-stones to regular classroom assignments after the three-year probationary teaching term. DPS' revised bilingual program—emphasizing three years of native language instruction and then exclusive English instruction—continues to be considered unacceptable by the U.S. Department of Education's Office of Civil Rights.

If and when the district is freed from court supervision on this count, bilingual programs could become subject to school-level decisions, although the federal funds for bilingual education affect choices toward lengthier retention. Under site-based management, local groups then would have a stronger voice in how Spanish-speaking children are taught and how teachers are allocated to bilingual courses. These new arrangements would allow parents to structure choices about how their children learn. But this is contingent on their ability to mobilize and to formulate alternative programs; in Denver, Latino parent participation in schools is historically low, due in part, some believe, to monolingual Spanish-speaking families. In addition, about 10 percent of the school population is estimated to be children of undocumented immigrants; estimates for Los Angeles are similar (Illescas 1999a). These features are likely to constrain Latino voice in collaborative decision-making bodies in the near future, even in schools with predominantly Latino student populations.

Ronald Schmidt Sr. (2000) notes that many Latino activists have moved away from demands that bilingual education promote Latino culture. Indeed, Kenneth Meier and Joseph Stewart Jr. (1991) report a decline in Mexican American assignment to bilingual education classes in Texas once Latinos gained power in local politics because these classes were often perceived as dumping grounds for Latino students. To the extent that disputes over language policies are about contested identities, as Schmidt suggests, it is not surprising that bilingual education debates reach beyond the schoolyard or the domain of school-based committees. California's Proposition 227, passed in 1998 by a 61 percent margin and was labeled as "English for the Children," replaced bilingual programs for English learners in the state's public schools with English-only instruction and modest one-year bilingual transition plans. The initiative campaign featured overt anti-immigrant rhetoric as well as references to ethnic nationalism and threatened American identity. Exit polls revealed Anglos supported the measure by 67 percent and Asians by 57 percent; Latinos and African Americans, in contrast, opposed it by 63 percent and 52 percent respectively (*LA Times* 1996).

In Colorado and Massachusetts, as in California, advocates of English-language-only strategies are also turning to the ballot box to dismantle bilingual education. These initiative efforts are linked organizationally and financially through support from entrepreneur Ronald Unz; they also feature similar initiative language and campaign tactics. In 2002, voters in Colorado defeated an initiative similar to 227 that would have limited bilingual education to one year (instead of the current program of a three-year transition). In Massachusetts, state support for bilingual education began in 1971 with Chapter 71A, the Transitional Bilingual Education Act, which mandated separate and extensive bilingual classes for non-English speakers. By the late 1990s, nearly 15 percent of Boston public school students were enrolled in bilingual classes offered in over eleven different languages; the costs were escalating beyond any state or federal compensation. When Unz brought his initiative to replace the three-year transitional programs with a quick one-year immersion program, Massachusetts voters approved by 70 percent, with "large majorities in Boston's immigrant areas" (States' Impact 2006, 79).

Slighting Economic Integration Agendas

Although there is little likelihood that an integration agenda featuring race or ethnicity will gain support, there is growing attention to the prospects for economic integration, another nascent issue frame obscured by the choice or market paradigm. In the face of the racial and ethnic resegregation of many schools after the lifting of court orders, some local groups are debating the value of economic integration of schools and classrooms. In Denver, the Piton Foundation sponsored an analysis of DPS test scores, which revealed that low-income students did better in schools where less than 50 percent of the students were poor, and more affluent students did no worse (Piton 2002). The advantages of these mixes stem not from the actual physical composition of the classroom but from the likelihood that the nature of teaching and learning is different in different socioeconomic settings—particularly the extent to which poor and minority students learn "higher order" analytic skills (Ucelli 2001).

Although economic integration is less likely to be achieved through student-assignment mechanisms, it does put renewed emphasis on initiatives that attract a mix of students, such as magnet schools and structured charter schools, as well as strategies linking schools with different socioeconomic characteristics.

Privileged Organizational Structures

One of the less obvious aspects of this new educational politics arena is the changing universe of organizations involved in promoting and protesting different policy alternatives. As Table 3.2 reveals, the parents and children most affected by educational policies are more likely to be organized as traditional membership-based voluntary associations. In these groups, members and their dues are the major assets available to the organization; their influence stems from their ability to claim legitimacy and representativeness. Not surprisingly, their impacts increasingly are dwarfed by more professional groups, including nonprofits, who rely on "wallets" or contributions rather than members as a resource base (Skocpol 2004). These organizations are staffed by salaried workers rather than volunteers; their resources include not only the contributions they receive and the income they generate (and their tax-exempt status, in the case of nonprofits), but also their ability to produce information and analysis needed by policymakers. As noted in Chapter 1, these strategic resources are sometimes less tangible, but especially powerful, in the politics of ideas surrounding school reform.. These organizations are likely to be more sustainable over time than voluntary associations; they become woven into the fabric of local politics, producing ideas and often services and programs as well. Many, of course, champion reforms to improve education for all children but relatively few focus on the racial-ethnic achievement gap.

Many of these professional organizations and nonprofits also participate in cross-sector coalitions, further enhancing their influence. These cross-sector alliances, as discussed above, contribute to the institutional density supporting school innovations; they can also operate as a barrier to less familiar ideas and interests who may find it difficult to penetrate the façade of expertise and influence projected by such coalitions. Although our larger project examined whether such cross-sector ties generated "civic capacity" and increased the prospects for innovation, it is clear that there is no direct relationship: Cities that ranked relatively high on civic capacity did not necessarily rank high on school reforms. The ability of these cross-sector alliances in Boston, for example, to support and guide school reform is evident, but it is not without its critics (Nelson 2005). What is notable here is that the new landscape of school reform in multiethnic cities further weakens the voices of new school constituencies by privileging organizational forms and practices that are based on professional expertise rather than parental concerns.

TABLE 3.2 GROUPS AND STAKEHOLDERS IN LOCAL SCHOOL REFORM

	MEMBERSHIP BASED	NONPROFITS	PROFESSIONAL ASSOCIATIONS	PARTNERSHIPS/CROSS-SECTOR ALLIANCEs
BOSTON	Citywide Parents Advisory Council Black Parents Committee El Comité Critical Friends Boston Parents Organizing Network Walk 2 School Work 4 Quality Schools Citizens United for Charter Public Schools Boston	Boston Foundation Boston's Children First Boston Partners in Education	Boston Teachers Union Teacher Union Reform Network Lawyers' Committee for Civil Rights/Boston Bar Association	Boston Compact Boston Plan for Excellence Citywide Educational Coalition Private Industry Council
DENVER	Padres Unidos Jovenes Unidos Hispanic League Metropolitan Organizations for People (MOP) PTSA Black Ministerial Alliance Black Alliance for Educational Options Finding Common Ground	Colorado Children's Campaign Latin American Research and Service Association (LARASA) Congress of Hispanic Educators Colorado League for Charter Schools Colorado Education Association Denver Kids Hunt Alternative Fund Piton Foundation DPS Foundation Donnell-Kay Foundation Citizens for Quality Schools (CQS) Alliance for Quality Education The Hunt Alternative Fund Public Education Coalition (PEC) Colorado Alliance of Business	DCTA: Denver Classroom Teachers Association Denver Chamber of Commerce	Colorado Partnership for Educational Renewal

TABLE 3.2 GROUPS AND STAKEHOLDERS IN LOCAL SCHOOL REFORM (*continued*)

	MEMBERSHIP BASED	NONPROFITS	PROFESSIONAL ASSOCIATIONS	PARTNERSHIPS/CROSS-SECTOR ALLIANCEs
LOS ANGELES	Mexican American Political Association	Latino Urban Forum MALDEF Korean American Federation	United Teachers Los Angeles (UTLA) Associated Administrators of Los Angeles Service Employees Union LA Chamber of Commerce California Business Roundtable California Teachers Association	LEARN Alliance for College-Ready Public Schools Los Angeles Educational Partnership (LAEP)
SAN FRANSISCO	Chinese American Voters Committee Chinese American Democratic Club Parents for Public Schools SF Black Leadership Forum SFSOS SF PTA	Bay Area Coalition for Equitable Schools MALDEF The Irvine Foundation San Francisco Foundation Chinese American Voters Education Committee San Francisco Education Fund	Hispanic Chamber of Commerce CA Teachers Association	Multicultural Education Training and Advocacy (META) United Educators of SF Lawyers' Committee for Civil Rights

The Reform Dilemma

Changing the rules of the game through site-based management, charter schools, reconstitution, and partnerships with business and nonprofit organizations occurred to varying degrees in our four cities. These sorts of reforms corresponded to the rhetoric of choice and markets, but introduced the potential of negative distributional consequences for numerically dominant, but politically weak, school constituencies. While there was a shared sense of the need for improvement in education, and support for moving the system away from educator-led policy toward parent-community involvement, there was also a lack of agreement across constituencies on how to do this and the full or "real" implications of doing so. Lack of common frameworks meant few cooperative reform efforts took hold in these cities despite the universal preference for improved educational performance.

This may seem surprising since the "decentralization" elements of systemic reforms are portrayed as a means of providing more context-sensitive resources and services that respond to the needs of particular groups and neighborhoods. They are also depicted as reflecting the growing interest in customizing education for individual needs through choice strategies, although there is substantial divergence on where and how these decisions are to be made. But to many parents of color, the reforms introduced by the state and the courts further weakened their voice in educational policymaking and enhanced the exit options available to white middle-class families. Furthermore, in this fragmented context it was difficult to get meaningful information on reform successes since the success stories themselves are volatile and ambiguous.[15]

We suggest that the limits to reform stemmed from the failure to work out the different, often competing, interpretations of policy alternatives and their distributional consequences. Even though school-level reform was evident in these cities, there was little systemic reform gained from scaling-up smaller successes to the system-level because of these competing goals and priorities (Paris 1995, 187). Ideational and institutional factors exacerbated the difficulty that Stone (1998, 261) attributes to intergroup tensions and conflicts in material interests.

In reform contexts characterized by diverse populations, it is important that we recognize race and ethnicity as more than interest-group features of the local setting, but also as having ideational and institutional dimensions. The different worldviews stemming from diverse social experiences and the distributional consequences associated with different institutional configurations both contribute to an increasingly complex educational policy arena. Now that we have traced the status of education reform in our four cities, and contemplated the threats to democratic and equal outcomes that specific reforms embody, we ask why these particular reforms dominate local agendas even though they may not meet the needs of new school constituencies.

Interests and Education Reform
in Multiethnic Cities

N INTEREST-BASED perspective is a natural starting point for our
analysis of the school reform puzzle. To understand why the concerns
of new school constituencies are not reflected in school-reform agendas, we focus first on an analysis of the interests involved. The belief that
interests matter—usually interpreted to refer to self-interested and purpo-
sive pursuit of material goals, social status, and power as a central force in politics—is the most common orientation to the study of politics in the United
States. This approach highlights the relevance of material resources as both
bases of political influence and incentives for maintaining group action and
cohesion. A closely related view, the pluralist interpretation, argues that patterns of interest group interaction, such as competition, conflict, cooperation,
and coalition building, are the core factors in understanding politics. And pluralism is probably the leading perspective on American politics (see Chapter
2). Most often, the basis for interest group formation and activity is economic
interest; groups support or oppose public policies depending on their expected
impact on groups' material interests. Typically, analyses treat politics as competition over "who wins and who loses" or as "who gets what,when, and how"
and usually explain outcomes in terms of comparative levels of resource across
groups, or comparative mobilization and use of resources.

There is much that is attractive and intuitively plausible about interest-
based interpretations that lead to their acceptance. They are consistent with
the ideas of major thinkers in American politics. James Madison's *Federalist 10*
asserted the importance of factions, or interest groups, in politics and society,
arguing that factions were inevitable, and were rooted in unequal financial

resources. Thus, to assume that self interest and material resources play a major role in political outcomes simply makes a great deal of sense. Moreover, the nature of interests and resources seems more immediately understandable, and perhaps more measurable, than other analytical perspectives grounded in more ostensibly abstract notions—such as ideas and institutions. For example, one can more readily measure or quantify the membership size, financial contributions, and economic characteristics of a group, while precisely measuring an idea or an institution and imputing specific impacts to them are more inherently elusive.

As we argue here, an interest-based analysis of school reform highlights the complex relationship of resources, influence, and educational policy outcomes in multiethnic cities. But ultimately a purely interest-based approach raises as many questions as it answers. Ethnic and racial minority groups, for example, cannot be considered only or perhaps even primarily as economically motivated interest groups; it appears that interest group–based approaches and pluralist assumptions "about group origins and self-interest maximization motives" may be less relevant in analyzing identity politics and distinctive issues such as education (Clarke et al. 1995, 206). Furthermore, the relationships between groups in the multiethnic politics of education are often more complicated than either conflict or cooperation. Finally an interest-based analysis points to seemingly counterintuitive results when groups appear to be acting against their interests.

An Interest-based Analysis of Education Politics

This chapter examines education politics from the standpoint of the dominant paradigm, an interest-based analytical perspective (see, for example, Marquez 1993; Hero 1992; McClain and Stewart 1998). In doing so, the chapter makes certain assumptions. It assumes, of course, that the interest-based framework is applicable to education policy issues and to group concerns about those issues. While the framework may be applicable within limits, it should be noted that education policy might be particularly elusive and complex: For instance, it may simultaneously have aspects of developmental, redistributive, and regulatory policy (Peterson 1981; cf. Clarke et al. 1995). The ambiguous divisibility of education as a public and private good makes analysis more complicated. Moreover, as a matter of human—rather than physical—capital, education has a host of characteristics and ambiguities that limit the applicability of interest-based analyses. And all these points must be considered within the complex reality of multiethnic politics.

Another assumption is that racial/ethnic groups are a major part of the interest-based story. This seems appropriate in that much of the legal and related political and policy debates about education—including equality and the quality of education—have been argued largely in racial/ethnic terms (Hochschild 1984; Myrdal 1944). The "American Dilemma" of race (and ethnicity) has been strikingly evident in the education arena. For example, many of the major Supreme Court decisions concerning equality—including the landmark case of *Brown v. Board of Education* (1954) and a number of court cases leading up to and subsequent to *Brown*—focused on education policy and institutions. "Equality of opportunity" has been called the "lynchpin of American society" (Hochschild 1984, 202), and education has commonly been viewed as the key to equality of opportunity. Thus it is hardly accidental that education has been at the center of equality of opportunity concerns. Similarly, it is not surprising that racial/ethnic groups have focused on education politics and policies because of education's (presumed) connection to "life chances," social status, and a host of other aspects of individual and group well-being. However, each of the several minority groups considered here has experienced education problems and policies somewhat differently and therefore views them differently.

A further complicating factor is that it is not clear that racial/ethnic groups—individually or collectively—necessarily think of themselves as "interest groups." And while focusing heavily on racial/ethnic groups, we neither mean to imply that they are the only groups of importance, nor that identity is their only or primary motivation. Many group concerns are also economically driven, generated by socioeconomic status. Teachers' unions and business interests often come into play. These caveats noted, however, we do maintain that racial/ethnic groups are central to understanding education politics and policy.

The goal, then, is to understand how the presence and circumstances of multiple racial/ethnic groups within cities—with varying interests, concerns, and policy situations—shapes education politics. We first look at the interest group landscape and the education policy context that we anticipate would affect how groups perceive policies.

New School Constituencies: Influence and Outcomes

The concept of two-tiered pluralism and more recent research on "social diversity"—varying racial/ethnic composition and configurations within political systems—are critical to understanding political processes and outcomes in the United States. (Hero 1998; Hero and Tolbert 1996). In research utilizing those concepts to date, however, blacks, Latinos, and Asians were grouped together as "minority groups" rather than studied separately. The increasingly multiethnic and socially diverse nature of the United States, most notable in city and school district settings, makes clear the limits of lumping these groups together and implies the need for further, more specific assessment.

To distinguish the situations of these new school configurations in the second tier, we delineate their political influence and educational status. Figure 4.1 diagrams the levels of political influence and the educational outcomes of each of four major blacks, whites, Latinos, and Asians groups in San Francisco, Boston, Denver, and Los Angeles. By "levels of political influence" we mean the extent to which a group is or has been consistently and significantly represented or included (see Browning, Marshall, and Tabb 1984) in formal, decision-making processes of the school district or city government. Groups achieve political incorporation when their members become integrated into the governing coalition of a political jurisdiction. Representation is thus seen as a necessary, but not sufficient, condition for substantive influence. Among the indicators of political influence are the percentages and the "parity ratios" of a group in such formal positions as the legislative body, that is, the school board; administrators; teachers and staff; and/or those on other important decision-making or advisory bodies that affect relevant policies (cf. Browning, Marshall, and Tabb 1984; Meier and Stewart 1991). Indicators of educational outcomes or achievement include graduation rates, dropout rates, suspension rates, scores on standardized tests, and the like.

We draw on various sources of evidence on national and local patterns of groups' political influence and education policy—including our archival and interview research in each city—to place the groups in Figure 4.1. Notably, the four major groups fall into different cells in the figure. This evidence provides both an intriguing picture and a puzzle to be explained; in this chapter the explanation emphasizes an interest-based interpretation.

Not surprisingly, Figure 4.1 suggests that whites tend to do relatively well on both dimensions and, on the whole, have the "optimal" placement. This contrasts most directly with Latinos, who tend to have low—commonly the lowest—educational outcomes and rather low levels of political influence, which is considered the "worst case" scenario. African Americans and Asians both have in-between or "high/low" situations, but the specific patterns differ in important ways. African Americans tend to have substantial political presence and influence in education policy arenas, but they have low education outcomes. Asians tend to have high education outcomes but generally do not appear to have extensive political clout, at least as typically measured in studies of urban government (cf. Brackman and Erie 1995; Kim 1999). Competing or compatible interests shape potential patterns of competition, patterns of cooperation, and other kinds of relationships between groups. Also shaping these relationships are issues and policy debates—or ideas—and particular structural factors and procedures—institutions. Before we consider the roles of

FIGURE 4.1 EDUCATIONAL ACHIEVEMENT AND POLITICAL INFLUENCE

POLITICAL INFLUENCE	EDUCATIONAL ACHIEVEMENT	
	Low	High
High	Blacks	Whites
Low	Latinos	Asians

ideas and institutions, we will "unpack" the patterns sketched in Figure 4.1 and draw out some of the implications.

Indexes of Representation and Underrepresentation

Assessing the political influence of groups in urban political systems is not a simple task. Research on Latinos and U.S. politics has grown dramatically over the last decade or so, but remains somewhat sparse; research on Asians and local politics is yet more scant but growing. Research on blacks is rather more extensive than on other minority groups, but a large number of issues have not been fully explored.

Figure 4.1 suggests that Latinos and Asians tend to have a low degree of political influence, while whites and African Americans tend to have a relatively higher rate of influence. Indeed, the lack of or gap in Latino political influence is the starting point for much political science research (see, e.g., Garcia and de la Garza 1977; Browning, Marshall, and Tabb 1984; Hero 1992). In one of the earliest studies of Latinos (specifically, Chicanos or Mexican Americans) and the U.S. political system, F. Chris Garcia and Rodolfo O. de la Garza (1977) found that Latinos were very weak politically and, while not directly addressed but readily deducible, weaker than blacks, and dramatically weaker than whites. Rufus P. Browning, Dale Rogers Marshall, and David H. Tabb's major study (1984) of the "Struggle of Blacks and Hispanics for Equality in Urban Politics" found that Hispanics typically lagged substantially behind blacks in their political incorporation and the policy responsiveness achieved in the ten northern California cities examined; San Francisco was one of those cities. Subsequent analyses (see, Browning, Marshall, and Tabb 1995) of cities with substantial African American and Latino populations typically find blacks to be substantially more politically influential than Latinos, with whites strongest of all. Indeed, Raphael Sonenshein's analyses of Los Angeles (1993, 1997) argue that city politics can be largely understood "in black and white," clearly implying the political weakness of Latinos and of other racial/ethnic minority groups within the city's political system (also see Regalado 1988).[1] Another large study, focusing on school districts—and specifically districts with substantial Latino populations—came to conclusions about Latino political influence in education politics consistent with our assessment: Among the findings in Kenneth Meier and Joseph Stewart Jr.'s study of "the politics of Hispanic education" is that "Hispanics do not have the same political clout that Blacks do" (1991, 156–58).

Until recently, the situation of Asians has been less studied and less well understood by political scientists than that of other groups (but see Lien 2001; Chang 2001; Kim 2002). Asian Pacific politics has been characterized as "politics by other means" (Brackman and Erie 1995). That is, rather than the traditional, direct electoral routes of voting and office holding, indirect influence through individualized efforts as well as interest group lobbying, targeted campaign contributions, litigation, and protest have been common. However extensive the impact of this indirect influence, most scholarship suggests that Asians "have been highly underrepresented among voters and elected officeholders" and this tends to be the case at all levels of U.S. politics. Political mobilization appears to be hindered, in part, by linguistic and socioeconomic differences among groups classified as "Asian." And as noted in Chapter 2, Browning, Marshall, and Tabb ask whether political action is as compelling for Asians as for African Americans (2003b).

While data on minority presence in cities and student bodies were discussed earlier (Chapter 2), they bear repeating, especially in relation to indicators of representation in important official positions. Evidence in Table 4.1 from Denver, San Francisco, Los Angeles, and Boston on school board membership, administrators, and teachers supports the assessments suggested in Figure 4.1. There is a clear and rather consistent pattern that Latinos are underrepresented and otherwise have relatively little political influence in these multiethnic settings. In contrast, white political power appears strong and enduring, while that of blacks is relatively strong in terms of representation and the perceptions of various observers that blacks have significant influence. Boston appears to deviate from the patterns of representation just noted; as we detail below, minority representation in Boston may be as much a function of white indifference as "real" minority power, or "strong" political incorporation in Browning, Marshall, and Tabb's terms (2003b, 358).

Numbers and ratios concerning school board membership and top-level administrators need to be viewed cautiously because the small total numbers mean the addition or subtraction of one person can dramatically alter the ratios. The teacher ratios are based on relatively large numbers and are thus less affected by small numerical changes. While some specific data are presented below, the broad picture evident in and across cities is relatively clear. With minor exceptions, the patterns suggested in Figure 4.1 are supported.

Denver

The Denver Public Schools system had a Latino student population of about 42 percent during the early 1990s, which increased to over 55 percent by the end of the decade. But similar percentages are not found in various aspects of school district governance and administration. For example, there were no Latino members on the Denver School Board in the early 1990s; one Latino member gained a seat on the seven-member board in 1995 and another by the end of the decade. More recently, two Latinos are now on the Denver school board; this increase is notable but should be kept in perspective relative to the burgeoning Latino student body. Asians also had no members on the school board during the 1990s; in some contrast to Latinos, however, Asian students are a much smaller proportion of students, about 4 percent.

TABLE 4.1 REPRESENTATION AND UNDERREPRESENTATION INDEXES

SCHOOL BOARD REPRESENTATION *Index*

	Black	Hispanic	Asian
Boston	64	139	189
Denver	143	0	0
LA	(missing)	117/130	26/40
SF	78	78	66

TEACHERS REPRESENTATION *Index*

	Black	Hispanic	Asian
Boston	58/108	37/70	46/67
Denver	43/70	31/55	39/51
LA	114/98	20	30
SF	59/99	38/57	38/57

TOP TEN ADMINISTRATORS *(percent)*, 1993

	Black	Hispanic	Asian
Boston	50°	0	0
Denver	10	30	0
LA	20		
SF	(missing)		

Note: *Index* indicates the number represents a ratio relative to the student population. For example, the 31 index for Denver's Teacher Representation index for Hispanics indicates that the ratio of the percent of Hispanic teachers relative to the percent of Hispanics students equals 31 percent. On the other hand, the *percent* indicates the simple percentage of the top ten administrative positions held by members from a particular racial/ethnic background. Thus, for example, in Boston Blacks hold five of the top ten positions; the asterisk (°) indicates this is the only instance where a group's percentage of top ten administrators is equal to or above parity.

Blacks fare better in terms of representation on the school board compared to the proportion of students. Blacks comprised about 20 percent of the student body in Denver schools, but their proportion of school board members typically has been twice that. Recent data indicate a small decline in that earlier pattern. Similarly, the white membership on the school board has been two to three times the proportion of white students of 34 percent.

The situation of these four racial/ethnic groups in Denver was similar regarding presence among teachers and among administrators in the 1990s. A teacher representation ratio (of percent Latino teachers/Latinos in student body) indicates an index of 0.55 (i.e., 45 percent underrepresentation) for Latinos. The ratio for Asians was similar. Blacks also had a substantially smaller proportion among teachers as they did among students, although it was higher than that for Latinos and Asians (the ratio for blacks is 0.70). This underrepresentation among teachers evident for Latinos, Asians, and Blacks implies that whites are "overrepresented."

The pattern for higher-level administrators is somewhat less clear. However, most of the evidence suggests a pattern similar to that found for school board membership and teachers. Few Latinos or Asians had served in high-level administrative positions in the Denver school district and no Latino had served as superintendent; both Asians and Latinos had a weak presence in these administrative positions.

Blacks appeared better represented among administrators, but still less than what might be expected relative to their numbers and proportion in the student body. Notably, a black woman served as superintendent for several years in the early 1990s. Overall, whites held and have held higher proportions of administrative positions.

Boston

Until 1992, Boston had an elected school board; after that, the Mayor of Boston appointed the members. Evidence indicates that Latinos and Asians had substantial representation on the Boston School Committee relative to their student-body numbers. Indeed, for both groups the proportions were higher on the school committee than in the student body. Meier and Stewart (1991, 113) found that "appointive systems actually produce better representation than elective systems such as at-large or district elections." In some contrast, blacks and whites had fewer members on the school committee than would be expected. Blacks have less presence on the school committee than their percentage among students, as did whites. However, the Boston situation was more complex than indicated by these data.

John Portz (1994) argued, "Many Bostonians do not consider the public school 'their own.' In fact, fewer than 20 percent of households in the city have children in the public schools." He adds that some of the major divisions in the city have "an important racial character" and that

> students in the Boston Public Schools are predominately children of color, while the entire population of the city remains predominately White. Thus ... 81 percent of students are of African-American, Asian, or Hispanic heritage, yet persons of color account for only 41 percent of the city's overall population. Not only are there more school-age children in families of color, but also many White school-age students attend private schools. In fact, approximately 90 percent of African-American, Asian, and Hispanic elementary and high school students in Boston attend public schools, whereas for White school children the comparable measure is approximately 50 percent (1994, 3).

Portz further claims that "Boston is becoming a city split between adult White neighborhoods, politically active but with limited involvement in public schools, and neighborhoods of color, with children in schools but limited political standing" (1994, 3). The Boston situation at the time underscored the complexity of racial/ethnic politics in education, and directs attention to the importance of such factors as the ability and decision to "opt out" of public schools.

Data from Boston on groups' presence among teachers and administrators are consistent with Portz's assertion and our general assessment of groups' political influence. Blacks comprised a slightly higher proportion among teachers than they did among the student body of the Boston schools. Whites comprised 63 percent of teachers, and only 25 percent of the student body. The "teacher representation index" for Hispanics and for Asians suggests underrepresentation of about a third for each group. The pattern for high-level administrators was similar. Boston had had numerous high-level white and black administrators but virtually no Hispanic and Asian high-level administrators. Although blacks in Boston were the only group in our four cities to achieve a measure of parity (Table 4.1) in the Administrator ranks, their tenure as Superintendents, for example, had been fraught with political manipulation (Nelson 1999, 86).

Los Angeles

Los Angeles was and remains clearly a majority-minority school district; Latinos comprised over 66 percent of the students in the Los Angeles Unified School District (LAUSD) in the 1990s; 14.4 percent were African American, 7.3 percent were Asian, Filipino, or Pacific Islander, and 0.3 percent were American Indian or Alaska Native. The white enrollment was about 12 percent. Recent evidence suggests Latino *under*representation on the school board relative to percentages in the student body is large; the parity ratio is approximately 0.20. Latinos had the clearest underrepresentation among teachers, constituting about 16 percent of teachers, but over two-thirds of the students. The percentage of Asian teachers was about equal to that of Asians in the student body, while both blacks and whites constituted larger proportions of teachers than of students; blacks comprised 17 percent of teachers (and 14 percent of students) and whites 58 percent of teachers (and 12 percent of students). Among the top-level administrators, Latinos were, again, very much underrepresented, while Asians, blacks, and whites had proportions among administrators above, or well above, the percentages in the student body. In addition, blacks had served as school superintendents in Los Angeles.

Reflecting their large population size, yet weak political influence, Latinos' role in Los Angeles school politics and education reform has been called "The Case of the Sleeping Giant." Mara Cohen and Fernando Guerra state, "Latinos are among those who debated, demanded, and now are implementing school reform, but the impetus, broad contours, and strategy" of the major reform efforts has "emanated from members of LA's traditional civic leaders—a set of corporate, Anglo elites" (1995, 1). These elites were said to represent an old-guard of LA's civic-minded elite as opposed to a newer breed of business leaders for whom public spiritedness was less important than profit seeking. Up until the 1960s, according to Rodolfo Acuna, California was "a leader in per capita expenditures on education. But as the Latino and minority populations grew, and as the baby-boomers got older, California's commitment to excellence waned" (quoted in Cohen and Guerra 1995, 5). However, the Los Angeles Education Alliance for Restructuring Now (LEARN), the leading education reform effort in Los Angeles in the early 1990s, had some success in redefining public education as an issue affecting everyone in Los Angeles and education restructuring as a win-win endeavor, capable of supplanting previous cleavages (Guerra and Cohen 1994). While education reform efforts appeared well intentioned and concerned about inclusiveness, the nature and extent of Latinos' influence appeared limited; other racial/ethnic groups appear better situated politically.

San Francisco

San Francisco is somewhat unique in that Asians are the largest single group in the schools. Furthermore, there is diversity among the Asian groups, with sizeable groups of Chinese, Japanese, Filipinos, and others. Despite their size and other factors that might suggest substantial political influence, Asians seemed to have less influence than might be expected, although some groups were more influential than others. The variation stemmed from different group histories, length of time in the United States, language, and related issues.

Asian and Hispanic representation on the school board had not been as high as the percentages among students; in both instances the ratios indicated underrepresentation of about one-third. Black representation has also been less than parity, but not to the same extent as Latinos and Asians. In short, these "minority" groups have commonly had smaller presence on the school board than their percentages among students. This also suggests that whites' representation on the school board was greater than their presence in the student body.

The patterns of teacher racial composition generally parallel those of the school board. The ratio of black teachers was comparable to the ratio of black students. However, Asians and Hispanics comprise a substantially lesser proportion of teachers than students. Again, the patterns of underrepresentation imply that whites have greater representation among teachers relative to the proportion of white students. Notably, two recent school superintendents have been Latino; more recently, an African American woman held the position, but she has since resigned.

Educational Outcomes

Interest group interpretations bring attention not only to levels of political influence, but also to the concerns or grievances leading groups to mobilize.

Thus, the educational outcomes for these groups are a second factor considered in Figure 4.1. While evidence from national-level data does not speak
directly to the issue of present outcomes in the school districts, it is broadly
suggestive. The percentage of whites (age 25 or more) who are high-school
graduates is 84 percent (McClain and Stewart 1998, 30); for Asians it is 82 percent. About 68 percent of blacks are high school graduates. By a substantial
margin Latinos have the lowest percent of high school graduates at 53 percent
(as a whole); the percent among Cuban Americans, the highest subgroup
among the Hispanic populations, is 62 percent (McClain and Stewart 1998, 30;
also see Meier and Stewart 1991, 40).

Similarly, Meier and Stewart's analyses indicate low education outcomes
for Latinos and blacks. For example, the dropout, suspension, and expulsion
rates for Latinos were significantly higher than for whites, while the assignment to gifted and talented classes and the graduation rates were significantly
lower in the school districts studied (Meier and Stewart 1991, 130–37). In a
parallel study focusing on school districts with large black populations Kenneth
Meier, Joseph Stewart Jr., and Robert E. England (1989) also found strong evidence of very poor relative outcomes of blacks compared to whites. Hence,
these two major studies find that Latinos and blacks have very low education
outcomes compared to whites. Most research continues to document this racial
and ethnic "achievement gap" relative to educational outcomes for whites and
Asians (Pew Hispanic Center 2004a; Hendrie 2004).

Denver

As in many large-city public school systems, students in the Denver Public
Schools tend to score below national averages on standardized tests.
However, the patterns vary considerably between racial/ethnic groups in
Denver. On reading and math tests, Latinos typically score the lowest of the
four racial/ethnic groups. (American Indians also tend to score very low—often
about the same as Hispanics.) Blacks tend to be the second lowest. Whites and
Asians have the highest outcomes, although there is considerable variation
between the two depending on what specific indicator is used. For example,
Asians tend to do better on math and less well on reading while the situation is
reversed for whites.

Another major concern in Denver—especially strong among Latinos and
blacks—is very high dropout rates. While the appropriate measures and specific numbers are disputed, it is clear that Hispanics and blacks have dropout
rates dramatically higher than do whites and Asians.

Boston

Minority educational achievement is low in Boston. According to John Portz
(1994, 18), students of color in the Boston schools "fare quite poorly on standardized tests. In the 1992–93 Metropolitan Achievement Tests, for example,

the median score for 12th grade African Americans on the reading test was the 32nd percentile, whereas the median for White 12th graders was the 67th percentile. In the Latino community, a 1991 study highlighted the dropout rate among Latino students and the ill-equipped nature of the schools to respond to curricula and other needs" of this population.

Los Angeles

Latinos and blacks have relatively low education outcomes in the LAUSD. For example, both Latinos and blacks have dropout rates that are 40 percent or more above that of whites. In contrast, the dropout rate for Asians is dramatically lower than that for Latinos and blacks, and is even lower than that of whites (California Department of Education, Profile of District 1995–96).

San Francisco

The consent decree in San Francisco developed a set of system-wide remedies that included the reorganization of several schools serving black students. These schools were identified based on their history of consistently producing students who did not achieve at mean levels of academic performance. Also, the 1993 Consent Decree—which revisited the earlier agreement—specified that both African Americans and Latino students were underserved by the SFUSD. In comparisons of achievement scores across all schools in the district, it was noted that the average academic achievement of these two groups was well below the district-wide average. Evidence showed that Asians in the San Francisco schools on the whole did very well on indicators of educational achievement. Following the initiatives promoted by the consent decree, students of color in the reconstituted schools improved their academic achievement scores, though they remained below district averages.

Explaining Patterns of Political Influence

If we think political influence may affect the degree of educational success for new school constituencies, what might explain these variations in levels or patterns of political influence and outcomes? Here we consider a number of factors commonly emphasized in interest-based interpretations of politics.

Groups and Resources

Group Size

Group size or population is often taken as an important political resource. The assumption is that larger group membership, in relative or absolute terms, can translate into political clout because of the technically majoritarian nature of the U.S. political system, particularly its electoral structures. Hence, other things being equal, the larger a group, the greater its potential for political influence and impact. In each of the four cities, numbers alone would lead us to expect that the minority groups would be influential. But there is reason to question the assumption that population size necessarily leads to political influence.

First, while the size of the minority groups among the student body within the schools may be large, they constitute a smaller proportion of the general population. Blacks and Latinos typically comprise about twice the proportion of students as they do of the general population. The large size and policy "needs" often associated with minority populations may actually weaken the group, rather than make it more politically influential, in part because they are seen more as "dependents" requiring "redistributive" policies. Also, a substantial body of research indicates that larger minority populations may actually be weaker because they are more likely to be seen as a threat to the political and economic well being of others (see, e.g., Key 1949; Giles and Buckner 1993). In short, population size may well be a double-edged sword; it can be detrimental to a group's political influence.

In any case, size in and of itself is not enough; the importance of group size is a function of levels of participation in politics. Considerable evidence suggests that Latinos and Asians are much less likely to participate in politics, specifically to register and to vote, than are whites and blacks. Paula D. McClain and Joseph Stewart Jr. (1998, 77), for instance, provide evidence from a 1992 national sample indicating that 70 percent of the whites and 64 percent of the black voting age population are registered to vote. In contrast, 35 percent of Hispanics and 31 percent of Asians were registered; where many members of these communities are recent immigrants and ineligible to vote, their political voice is weakened further. When one examines only citizens, Hispanic and Asian registration rates rise to 55 percent and 49 percent respectively (McClain and Stewart 2002, 83). The differences between whites and blacks, on the one hand, and Latinos and Asians on the other, was also apparent in actual voting, not just registration. Sixty-four percent of whites and 54 percent of blacks actually voted; 29 percent of Latinos and 27 percent of Asians actually voted. In 1998, among Hispanic and Asian citizens, about a third of each group reported voting (McClain and Stewart 2002, 83); as noted previously, low turnout in city elections is associated with substantial reductions in representation in local government (Hajnal and Trounstine 2005). Various other research provides similar findings (see, e.g., Hero and Campbell 1996; Brackman and Erie 1995; Browning, Marshall, and Tabb, 2003a). Thus, if electoral participation patterns in these cities and school districts parallel these general patterns, Figure 4.1 begins to become more understandable.

Cohesion and Organization

Group cohesion helps to convert sheer numbers into political influence and to articulate the concerns that groups have, assuming that there is some consensus.

The cohesion of the various groups is not easy to summarize, but certain patterns exist. Blacks tend to be seen as reasonably cohesive and when there is disagreement among blacks they are perceived as being able to work out differences behind the scenes. At the same time, our interviews suggested that blacks' views of education differed somewhat by generation. The "older generation," the "veterans" of the civil rights era, seemed more resistant to abandoning court-ordered desegregation while the younger blacks seemed less wedded to busing and more focused on improving educational achievement. Thus, some factors may weaken black cohesion, at least marginally.

Interviews suggest that Latinos as a group appear to be fragmented and not consistently engaged. Some observers see Hispanic involvement in school politics as episodic and crisis-oriented. In Denver, for instance, the "Hispanic community" was often referred to as important, but interviewees commonly had difficulty citing a major Latino organization that was continually active and important. Several organizations thought of themselves as spokespersons for the Latino population; but a number of persons we interviewed, both within, and outside, the Hispanic population did not always recognize these individuals or the role of these organizations. Furthermore, the specific goals and the preferred approaches of various Latino activists differed.

Asian groups may also be diverse and, hence, not highly cohesive. For example, in San Francisco and Los Angeles the "Asian" group is divided among populations of Chinese, Japanese, Filipino, and Korean descent. In Denver, Hmong and Korean immigration had contributed to further expansion of the Asian community. The relations between these groups are not always close, and their experiences also differ along several dimensions, including social class, generation, distinct social and political experiences in the United States, and other factors. There may also be fragmentation within groups based on political ideology or simply on the best approaches to achieving certain goals. For example, in San Francisco, two groups representing the Chinese American population took different positions on access to the elite high school. And Harold Brackman and Steven Erie (1995, 289–98) describe a variety of factors leading to Asian intragroup divisions, and tensions between other minority groups in Los Angeles.

Social Status

A group's social status may be both cause and consequence of political influence; here we stress the former while acknowledging the latter. Social status is important because it is commonly linked to the group's perceived "legitimacy" and "deservedness." In important ways, a group's status is "socially constructed" and has implications for the extent and nature of policy attention (Ingram and Schneider 1993).

Scholarly work on the "social construction of target populations" (Ingram and Schneider 1993) argues that groups' social constructions are determined by whether the group is seen as (a) weak or strong, and (b) as positive or negative.

Groups that are strong and perceived positively are "Advantaged." Those that are strong and perceived negatively are "Contenders." Groups seen as politically weak but viewed positively are "Dependents," and those that are weak and viewed negatively are "Deviants." The interaction of power and social construction leads to "a distinctive pattern in the allocation of benefits and burdens to the different types of target groups" (Ingram and Schneider 1993, 337). According to the Ingram and Schneider framework, benefits and burdens will be over- or undersubscribed, depending on groups' social construction, or social status. The patterns in Figure 4.1 parallel this framework and speak particularly to the social status, and more generally to the broader configuration, developed in our broader interpretation.

Whites are among the "Advantaged," having the strongest political power and a positive construction, as well as the highest group "social status" overall. Thus, some have argued that magnet programs and gifted/talented programs have been developed and implemented in such a way as to placate advantaged groups, particularly in that such groups often get greater access to such programs (cf. Meier and Stewart 1991). Nonetheless, whites, perhaps especially in large urban school districts, may not be satisfied with schools and therefore seek to create or maintain policies toward those ends or exercise the "exit option," moving to suburban and/or private schools.

Figure 4.1 suggests that blacks, Latinos, and Asians are all somewhat "*disadvantaged*" in education politics. It is often the case that blacks and/or Latinos have borne the brunt of busing. The central point is that Latinos and blacks typically have lower social status to draw upon as a resource in the political arena. Whites generally have higher social status, while the situation for Asians is somewhat ambiguous, although, on the whole, it appears higher than for Latinos and blacks. Claire Jean Kim (1999) has argued that even while Asians do well economically they are nonetheless seen as "different," particularly in being contrasted with blacks but also relative to white Americans.

Socioeconomic Resources

Interest group analyses suggest that groups with greater socioeconomic and financial resources are typically more likely to have political influence. Meier and Stewart (1991), for example, found that where Latinos had higher levels of income and education, the degree of "second generation discrimination" in education outcomes was significantly diminished. Higher education and income is associated with a greater sense of political efficacy and other characteristics associated with more political involvement and influence.

Recognizing that there is substantial intragroup variation, on the whole the patterns of racial/ethnic group socioeconomic status (based on national-level data) during the study period were as follows (McClain and Stewart 1998, 30–33). Whites had the highest percentage of high-school graduates, high median family incomes, and the lowest rates of poverty. Asians had the highest levels of median family income ($42,245), higher than whites ($33,335), and their percentage of high-school graduates among those twenty-five or older (81.8) approached that of whites (84.1). While Asians are often viewed as a "model minority" this masked considerable variation between groups.

Latinos' and blacks' socioeconomic status, and related socioeconomic resources, appeared much weaker than those of whites and Asians. Blacks' median family income ($21,548) was much lower than that of whites and Asians, as was Latinos' ($22,859). Latinos had the lowest percentage of high-school graduates (53.1); for blacks it was about 68 percent. The Latino situation may be more complicated than the raw data suggest, however. Variation by groups—which are in turn shaped by factors such as recentness of immigration, language, and other factors—also affect patterns.

Group Goals

Group influence is also shaped by the nature of specific policy goals and what is entailed in achieving them—whether what they seek essentially is consistent with, or challenges the status quo. Groups defending established positions and programs are generally more successful in that they have tradition and sunk costs on their side. In addition, the structures and processes of policymaking in the United States tend to be complicated and cumbersome, providing numerous "veto points" for those wishing to maintain established relations and policies, further dampening the likelihood of major policy change. Finally, if policy change is seen as redistributive, that is, seriously altering existing patterns of policy benefits away from the better-off and toward the less well-off, they are also more likely to bring resistance.

It appears that whites—and to some degree blacks as well—with their influence on desegregation plans, have achieved some education policy goals. The situation for Latinos and Asians is less clear. Bilingual policies, which Latinos have often supported, are seen as redistributive in part, but they may also be seen as simply distributive, as a useful tool for encouraging assimilation. Asians have been less likely to push for distinct policies; instead, they tend to stress access to the highest quality existing programs.

Potential for Coalitions

Interest-based approaches stress the internal resources of groups. But another important dimension is the potential for coalitions among various racial/ethnic groups. Multiethnic cities present distinct, but increasingly common, problems for mobilizing "civic capacity" to effect education reform (cf. Browning, Marshall, and Tabb 1984, 2003a; Meier and Stewart 1990b, 1991). A central question is whether cooperation or competition would be anticipated between the various groups (e.g., Kim and Lee 2001; Kim 2004). The empirical evidence on cities provides mixed findings, however. And few studies have explicitly or extensively considered these dynamics in the politics of *education* reform, particularly in multiethnic settings.

Browning, Marshall, and Tabb's major study (1984) of ten northern California cities (which included San Francisco) found complex relationships between whites, blacks, and Hispanics. Coalitions with white liberals appeared essential for black and Latino political success. The study also refers to several cases where blacks and Latinos were not mutually supportive, for example:

> It would not be accurate to conclude that blacks generally supported the political aspirations of Hispanics. Some black activists regarded Hispanics as whites who were achieving political influence ... on the coattails of the black mobilization movement (Browning, Marshall, and Tabb 1984, 2003a, 124).

Browning, Marshall, and Tabb also note other evidence of competition. Even when blacks and Latinos supported similar policies and coalitions, "relationships between the groups sometimes remained highly competitive" (Browning, Marshall, and Tabb 1984, 2003a, 124). Their later work (2003a) underscores these competitive relations and the difficulties of forming multiethnic or multiracial coalitions.

McClain and Karnig (1990) and McClain (1993) examined municipal employment outcomes for blacks and Hispanics in forty-nine cities with at least 10 percent black and 10 percent Hispanic populations. McClain and Karnig state: "When either Blacks or Hispanics gain politically, they do so at the expense of Whites. Political competition between Blacks and Hispanics is evident only when controls for White political outcomes are introduced. This suggests that as Black and Hispanic political successes increase, political competition may be triggered, especially as fewer Whites reside in minority-dominated cities" (542).

In a follow-up study, McClain (1993) found that black and Hispanic municipal employment outcomes "vary negatively with White municipal employment but not with each other. Still, evidence also indicates that competition in municipal employment does appear as the size of the Black work force increases. Additionally, in cities with Black majorities or pluralities, Hispanics seem to fare less well in municipal employment outcomes, while in cities in which Hispanics are a majority or plurality, the consequences for blacks are more diffuse" (399). In short, the formation of coalitions is rather more complex than is often assumed.

What factors affect these intergroup relations? While interest-based analyses generally point to competition or compatibility of economic interests, the direct applicability to education politics is not as clear. Meier and Stewart (1991), and others who study the politics of education, consider other dimensions. In analyzing elections to school boards, Meier and Stewart argue that "social distance"—the extent to which groups perceive themselves as more or less "close-to" or similar to other groups in social class, economic status, race, and so on—is critical in influencing electoral coalitions. They note other research (Dyer, Vedlitz, and Worchel 1989) indicating that both blacks and Latinos perceive themselves as being closer to whites than to each other. On the other hand, they suggest that whites often perceive closer social similarity to Latinos than blacks. Other things being equal, then, Latino/white political coalitions might be expected. However, as Meier and Stewart (126) note,

> This logic holds if all other things are equal. *Political effectiveness* and *group size* may be two things that are not equal. Blacks appear to have greater political success than Latinos because they are more cohesive, more likely to vote, and more likely to use political action. The potential effectiveness of coalition partners might mitigate against the general preference for Anglo-Latino rather than Anglo-Black coalitions. Similarly if Blacks are more numerous than Latinos, they might provide coalitions over Latinos especially if Anglos are not unified.

Thus, political power factors may significantly alter social distance factors. Angelo Falcon (1988, 184, 176) points out important differences in the perceptions of blacks and Latinos (Puerto Ricans) in New York City that stem, in large part, from different historical experiences. His points are broadly relevant: "The effects of the black experience with slavery in the United States compared to the Latino colonial experience are critical to any understanding of many of the current values and perceptions of each group ... While American blacks have developed a distinctive heritage after close to four hundred years in the United States, Latinos come from culturally and/or politically foreign countries. Compared to the black rootedness in the U.S. experience, albeit in a subordinate relationship, Latinos have a more tenuous relationship". That is why some have suggested that the black relationship is subordinate (or subcultural) while the Latino situation may be thought of as bicultural (Hero 1992, 200); the two situations produce somewhat different political dynamics. When Asians are part of the mix, the dynamics are likely to be yet more complicated.

In their studies of education policy outcomes, Meier and Stewart (1991) find that higher Latino educational successes, that is, lesser second-generation discrimination, sometimes occurs where there are substantial black populations. That is, blacks, rather than Latinos, may become the targets for discriminatory outcomes. This, Meier and Stewart suggest, presumably results from social distance factors. Social distance may also be related to "ideological distance," but that linkage is not typically stressed in the research.

While highly insightful, much of the previous research does not speak directly to broader issues of systemic education reform. Nor are Asians accounted for in most analyses of local politics. When we consider the involvement of whites, Latinos, Asians, and blacks in complex school reform politics, we anticipate substantially more complicated and different issues than those involved in electoral coalitions.

Shifting Configurations in School Reform

Much of the research on racial/ethnic politics assumes a situation of either conflict or cooperation. That, in turn, seems to stem from the assumptions of a "power over" rather than a "power to" relationship (Stone 1989). We find ample evidence of competition and conflict over policies, group status, and a host of other dimensions. At the same time, we think these "dualist" assumptions are overly limiting because they do not capture the full complexity of potential relationships, especially in the multiethnic politics of education.

Tacit Noncooperation or Negotiation

Where there is basic agreement on substantive policy (ends) but disagreement on methods (means) there is often a situation of "tacit noncooperation" or independence. Thus, groups may not be in direct conflict, but simply "go their own way" much of the time. Where there is disagreement on ends and agreement on means, there tends to be ongoing discussion, or negotiation, seeking to establish mutually acceptable policies. This may lead to "distributive politics" where the substantive differences are not resolved, and policy outcomes where "there's a little something for everyone." This may help explain why education politics is often characterized by "reform by addition," that is, with numerous policies ("side-payments") adopted but little in the way of broad-based, fundamental reform. For example, desegregation, magnet schools, charter schools, bilingual education, and other reforms all occur within a larger economic and social structure that changes incrementally at most.

Configurations within the Four Cities

As complicated as the situation is, it is yet more complex where there are numerous groups—as in these four multiethnic cities. That complexity makes analysis tremendously difficult; but it also makes the effort especially important. Various comments from interviewees underscore this point.

In Denver, one observer noted the "need to know one's A, B, C's—Asians, Blacks, Chicanos," to begin to fully understand education politics in the district. Of these groups, blacks have had the most impact in shaping education policies. They were the initiators of the major legal actions that brought a federal desegregation order in the early 1970s, and have continued to be visible and major players. For example, blacks not only had maintained substantial and consistent presence on the school board, but they had also served as school board presidents. The same could not be said for Hispanics and Asians.

Hispanics became significant political players in Denver education politics later than blacks, primarily through the requirements for bilingual education programs. Latinos, who had become far and away the largest group in Denver's schools, had generally lagged in terms of their presence on the school board and have often been seen as not having a consistent, ongoing presence in school politics. The Asian influence, beyond that suggested by the data presented earlier, was unclear; none of those we interviewed spoke about the Asian group as being politically influential. All three groups had some institutionalized presence, however, through Advisory Committees that were required by the court order; though the impact of that institutionalized presence was not evident in the research we conducted.

A major source of black influence in Denver was seen as rooted, in significant part, from an interchurch organization, the Black Ministerial Alliance. In contrast, a Latino activist observed that "the Hispanic community [did] not have a group like the ministerial alliance to help keep them together; ... [Hispanic] groups crop up around issues that are grass roots organized, but really about the most they can do is influence individual issues." In fact, Latino community advocates noted a number of efforts and collaborations between Latino organizations at specific schools with large Hispanic student enrollment, but were unable to point to citywide interorganizational initiatives.

Racial/ethnic issues make their way into many levels of education politics in Denver. According to a Latino activist, an issue that has been and continues to be important is that

> minority non-Anglo kids, multi-ethnic kids, were not succeeding in the Denver Public Schools.... And so really as an ongoing source of conflict the issues surrounding ethnicity are the A number one. It really pervades the entire system, from the Superintendent's office, down to a first-day kindergartner, and a first-day custodian.

These issues were also said to affect relationships within schools. A white respondent claimed that "It influences everything that goes on in the school. It sets up kids to be able to call Anglo teachers racists, or Hispanic teachers racists, or ... a Hispanic kid calling a Black teacher racist. It sets up kids to ... follow after adults." Not all interviewees saw the situation quite so starkly. There were perceptions of group conflict, but also of separate paths with features of noncooperation or independence, as well as perceptions of some degree of general cooperation.

Much of the time, in all the cities, when we asked about "how well those involved in education politics work together" the answer was typically somewhat complex, but usually suggested lack of coordination or consensus. But neither cooperation nor conflict was necessarily the only or the most common characterization. Latinos, for example, had been less supportive of busing as a solution to problems, commonly favoring more direct attention to outcomes, that is, achievement and schools sensitive to cultural concerns. Blacks, on the

other hand, had generally been more directly supportive of desegregation, seeing it as symbolic of blacks' political influence and as a way of assuring compliance with policy goals. Over time, however, the black community became
somewhat more divided over desegregation versus educational achievement as
the major policy goal.

One Latino activist in San Francisco also suggested that cooperation and
conflict were not the only patterns. In talking about all community groups,
including, but not limited to, racial/ethnic groups, he said:

> I think a lot of the community-based groups [are] going down the
> same road. We have similar goals ... but seldom do we see our paths
> merging together. We're kind of all going down parallel streets. And
> once in awhile there'll be people coming together and collaborating.
> But I still see a lot of individual programs.

Boston has been described as a "tribal city" based on race, ethnicity, and
geography (Portz 1994, 16). Racial and ethnic groups were extraordinarily het-
erogeneous and diverse: African Americans are eclipsed by migrations of Cape
Verdeans and West Indians, for example. The education politics here often
produced conflict, as was most evident in the hostile reaction to the original
busing orders. Separateness and segmentation, often reinforced by residential
segregation, was a common response; this included, for example, whites attending private schools or moving out of the district. Conflicts between African
Americans and Latinos were rooted in competition for public and private
funds, especially for development projects (Nelson 1999). The rapid increase
in the Latino population occurring at the time exacerbated these divisions.
When the administration of Mayor Thomas Menino replaced black school
committee members with appointed Latino school committee members,
resulting in less African American political influence, the tensions between
these groups increased further (Nelson 1999).

Observers in Los Angeles commonly noted tension between the several
groups. Various affluent white communities and the related homeowners associations were seen as "driving municipal government" and having "disproportionate clout." At the same time there was a perception of competition
between blacks and Latinos. As a Latino activist stated, certain policies were

> stacked in favor of Blacks and that it's our turn and it ought to be
> stacked in favor of us; we are the majority now. The Blacks are saying
> 'no,' we earned this, we have the right. [So there is tension] between
> this emerging Latino majority and the shrinking black population that
> is very frustrated and feeling under siege.

Luis R. Fraga and Bari A. Erlichson (1994) wrote that, "The most significant
cleavages in educational politics in San Francisco are on the basis of racial and

ethnic divisions" (27). However, even with substantial ethnic diversity in school enrollment, the desegregation lawsuit insured the interests of African American students were always present but gave no standing to other ethnic groups until the 1993 Consent Decree noted both Latinos' and blacks' lagging achievement (Fraga and Erlichson 1994). But the situation was even more complicated.

According to a white official, the "community is a lot of small pieces." The black community is somewhat fragmented on issues and does not seem to have a unified voice. Asians are seen as far from monolithic, comprised of various groups. The Southeast Asian groups have certain language problems or concerns that distinguish them from others, but they did not appear politically influential. For example, it was perceived that the Vietnamese "haven't organized yet." Even within the Chinese population there were major differences between the older, more established populations and the new immigrants, the latter often having language concerns and related policy problems distinct from the former and, in some ways, similar to those faced by poor Latinos. And there were at least two major factions among the Chinese in terms of support for, or opposition to, affirmative action. This manifested itself regarding the access of Chinese students to the "elite" public schools, among other issues. But participation often did not occur through group activities as such; it often occurred individually. The official said:

> You don't find middle-class parents [involved through groups with the schools] because they know how to work the system, [and] by and large, because their kids go to . . . all the high achievement schools. But Chinese immigrant parents . . . express the sense of not feeling empowered.

The Hispanic community in San Francisco was seen as fragmented. According to one respondent, "It [is] primarily from Central America. There are 17 countries, and they all go their own way. There isn't really someone who can speak for them. MALDEF (the Mexican American Legal Defense and Education Fund) comes up from time-to-time. The Hispanic Chamber of Commerce does exist; it speaks for the Latino business community. [But, overall, the Hispanic community] is really in fractions."

Are Interests Enough?

Overall, in the school districts we studied, Latinos were about twice as large (in numbers) as they were in the corresponding city's population, but half as politically influential in school politics as in city politics—and their influence in the latter settings was not especially high either. Representational "parity," which is seldom found for minorities, does not directly translate into proportional policy outcomes. In this setting, then, descriptive representation and status politics are especially important but may actually undermine or obscure the quest for the more elusive goals of policy resolution and substantive change.

Recent evidence on the four school districts shows patterns of continued growth in the multiethnic compositions among students; the patterns of (under)representation are not especially different from those we found in the 1990s. According to data from the Harvard Civil Rights project, in 2000/01 Latinos comprised 71 percent of students in the LAUSD, 53 percent in Denver Public Schools, and over 27 percent in Boston (Frankenberg, Lee, and Orfield 2003). In Boston, blacks continue to be the largest group, comprising almost half the student body, and the Latino population is over a quarter of the students. The percentage of blacks in Denver, Los Angeles, and San Francisco is substantial, but considerably smaller than the Latino population in these cities. In San Francisco, Asians continue as the largest group—over a third— and Latinos are a quarter, but the percentages of Asian students in Denver, Los Angeles, and Boston are relatively small.

Despite growing diversity of the school-age population, there has been "an overwhelming trend toward school district *resegregation*" (Frankenberg, Lee, and Orfield 2003, 53, emphasis added). "Exposure" measures between racial/ethnic groups in the four cities, where lower scores mean less exposure, that is, more separation or segregation, were as follows. The exposure of Latino and of black students to white students in Los Angeles was 6.1 and 8.0, respectively. In Boston, the comparable numbers were 12.8 and 11.2, and in Denver they were 14.6 and 19.4. (Exposure indicators for Asians were not provided in the study.) Data on residential segregation in San Francisco indicates low exposure scores of Latinos and blacks to white residents, 10.7 and 5.6; exposure of whites with Asian residents was somewhat higher, 30 percent (Lewis Mumford Center). A consistent pattern in the four cities studied is an increasing school and residential segregation of Latinos (Lewis Mumford Center).

While the composition of the student bodies is increasingly multiethnic, the percentage of Latinos, blacks, and Asians on the school boards has changed little since the 1990s. In each of our cities, the electoral structure of the school boards has been open to challenge; since 1992, Boston's School Committee has been appointed by the mayor. Since 1979, Los Angeles' seven-member board is elected by districts and San Francisco's seven-member board continues to be elected at large. Since 1992, five of Denver's seven-member board are elected by district and two are at-large. For Latinos, at large systems appear to dampen representation on boards, with a ripple effect then associated with smaller shares of Latino administrators and teachers in the system (Leal et al. 2004). Kenneth Meier and others (2005) find similar effects, linking electoral systems to variations both in representation on school boards and in substantive policy outcomes. Data from 2004 indicate that the degree of descriptive representation and related parity scores of school board membership has increased modestly at most, even as the proportion of Latino and Asian students in public schools increased rapidly.[2]

Interest-based analysis helps reveal the material resources and group organizational traits shaping the successes and failures of ethnic and racial minorities in education politics. However, as suggested in this chapter it is quite clear that "interests" are significantly more ambiguous, fragmented, and difficult for minority groups to articulate and pursue; this seems especially so in the education policy arena. Groups may not similarly perceive or react in the same way to specific, "objective" circumstances, even though they may be both situated in the second tier of pluralist influence. Thus, members of the same group may have different perceptions and ideas—problem definitions, satisfactory resolutions—about education issues, and institutional factors will make these approaches to problem solving more or less plausible. It is not only resources and interests that are important, but perceptions, proposed solutions, and the broader context also matter in explaining the situation of racial/ethnic groups in education politics. It is therefore necessary to consider other analytic perspective to more fully understand the politics of educational change during the critical juncture of the 1990s. To those issues we now turn.

## CHAPTER FIVE

Ideas and Education Reform
in Multiethnic Cities

A S CHAPTER 4 ILLUSTRATES, analyzing the economic and political resources of racial and ethnic groups is a natural starting point for understanding their varying situations in the education arena. For example, factors such as voting rates, group cohesiveness, and socioeconomic status do partially explain why Latinos have less influence on the education system than blacks, even though both groups have an interest in the system. But such analysis falls short of fully explaining why minorities generally have made greater inroads in city politics than in education politics, especially given both their greater representation among school constituencies compared to city constituencies, and also the urgent need to raise their children's achievement levels in urban school districts. An interest-based analysis also leads us to expect collaboration across minority groups, given this shared stake in improving the education system. In the cities we studied, however, we saw little collaboration of this kind.

The insufficiency of an interest-based analysis of education politics in multiethnic cities stems from the absence of a theoretical approach to studying politics that incorporates race in a central, structural way. As we described in Chapter 2, the diverse racial groups present in these cities cannot be treated as "just" other interests. Rather, translating resources into political influence is more problematic for racial and ethnic minorities than it is for traditional interest groups, such as producer groups or large membership organizations. This is so because minority groups are faced with distinctive barriers: their unique historical experiences; their positions within local social, economic, and political structures; and their relationship to the majority group within a two-tiered pluralism structure. We have argued that to better understand the political situation of racial minorities in education politics, we need to look at the roles of ideas and institutions.

This chapter proposes that analyzing the role of ideas sheds light on dimensions of urban education politics that a focus on interests alone overlooks. A focus on ideas means acknowledging the socially constructed nature of problems, and the presence of "multiple realities" (Berger and Luckmann 1967; Croucher 1997; Edelman 1988; Rochefort and Cobb 1994; Yanow 1995). That is, groups situated differently within the context of education politics are expected to interpret education issues differently. For example, something one group sees as inefficiency, another may see as promoting fairness, and something one group interprets as a strategy of empowerment, another may see as a strategy of exclusion.

In part, the presence of multiple realities reflects the inherent complexity of the social world and of policy problems. Since any policy issue, including education, emerges from a web of causal relationships and interactions, and is connected to a variety of other issues both directly and indirectly, contrasting interpretations of "the problem" will inevitably emerge and can be defended with reference to "the facts." While some scholars criticize the relativism and indeterminacy of this approach to studying political life, we maintain that the presence of multiple realities and social constructions cannot be eliminated from the analysis, only ignored (Yanow 1995). We prefer to grapple with the difficulties of analyzing these multiple ideas about the reality of education, because doing so brings to light important elements of our puzzle.

Our purpose is not to determine which claims about education politics and policy are better or worse, true or false. Our aim is, instead, to investigate the process through which various claims and claimants compete in the education arena, and to determine which claims do and which do not become the basis for educational reform, and why. The analysis in this chapter highlights how members of different racial and ethnic groups define education problems and assess the solutions being promoted or implemented in their cities. It reveals a complex arena of problem definitions and assessments of reform ideas, one so infused with issues of race and ethnicity that groups agreeing on some elements of "the education problem" may be kept apart by their differing interpretations of its racial dimensions. These findings suggest that divergent ideas about education problems and solutions pose barriers to collective action and meaningful education reform in multiethnic cities.

The Role of Ideas in Education Politics

Attention to the multiple discourses of education reform in multiethnic cities contributes to our larger analysis. Analyzing the ideas that members of different racial groups hold about the education systems in their cities and the politics surrounding them is useful because it does the following:

- shows us the *meaning* of "interest" in the education arena
- reveals dimensions of power and marginalization in education politics that interest-based analysis overlooks
- identifies sources of conflict and points of consensus across groups
- points toward the role of institutions in promoting or inhibiting cooperation across groups, and in locking particular ideas and interests into place

The first three contributions of ideational analysis improve our understanding of interests, while the fourth looks ahead to our analysis of institutions. Below we discuss each of these points briefly, then turn to an empirical analysis of education discourse in four multiethnic cities.

Defining Interests

A common critique of interest-based analysis is that it tends to assume what actors' interests are, usually based on a relatively simple conception of self-interested actors seeking material gains. Thus, it posits a narrow range of motivations, assuming both that all actors easily understand and perceive their interests in a situation, and also that similarly situated actors will share interests (Hall 1997).

Because of the complexities of human capital as a social "good" and the diversity of racial groups in our cities—and their different situations—we cannot safely presume actors' interests in education, but must investigate them by examining groups' discourse about education. As we outlined in Chapter 1, education has both tangible and intangible dimensions: While it is true that everyone wants it, people have different interpretations of what constitutes a good education and how this definition should be collectively determined and delivered. Education, thus, does not lend itself to a simple politics of compromise and bargaining that may guide traditional distributive politics or even some types of redistributive policy. Thus, we need to empirically examine how groups perceive and define their interests in education—what they want from their school systems and how they define a good education.

Our analysis finds common concern about racial minorities' low achievement levels, school bureaucracies, and the increasing numbers of poor children in urban school systems. But when it comes to identifying the critical dimensions of these problems, we find differences across racial groups, differences in the implications they draw from the changes in urban education that they all agree have occurred, and differences in their views on current reform ideas. Discourse analysis, then, uncovers the complexity of the concept "interest," and empirically shows us what it means in the education arena (Heclo 1994).

Dimensions of Power

Attention to ideas reveals dimensions of power and of marginalization obscured by purely interest-based analyses (Croucher 1997). Problem definitions imply solutions, and create interests—that is, by identifying which aspects of a problem are pertinent, they shape the coalitional activity that will emerge within an issue arena (Rochefort and Cobb 1994; Stone 1989). Thus, a group exercises power when its discourse guides policy solutions, and shapes how other actors understand and act upon issues. A group is marginalized when its ideas do not guide action or shape other actors' understanding of the issues. Power therefore includes the power to control the education agenda, to set the boundaries of what kinds of actions are considered feasible or desirable, and to shape the coalitions and cleavages that will emerge.

This sort of power—control of ideas—can bolster or undermine other sources of power. In education politics, for example, the power of holding a position of authority, such as school board president or superintendent, grows when the person in that position can shape the problem definition. The power of numbers, held primarily by Latinos and Asians in our cities, is undermined when these groups cannot translate numbers into agenda control. In the multiethnic cities we study, the power of whites—and to some extent blacks— emanates in part from their ability to control ideas about education. The marginalization of Latinos and Asians stems from their underrepresentation on decision-making bodies, and their lack of influence over which ideas constitute "policy talk" about education. This dimension of marginalization helps explain why, despite the presence of numerous reform efforts in these cities, Latinos' and Asians' sense of the system's inadequacy persists. This analysis shows the disjunction between these groups' ideas about critical problems and the solutions underway in their cities.

Conflict and Consensus

Attention to the politics of ideas in education reform underscores the degree to which the essence of politics is the struggle among actors to define problems, target groups, and alternative solutions (Rochefort and Cobb 1994; Stone 1989; Schneider and Ingram 1997). In documenting who holds which ideas about education problems and solutions, we reveal the strategic context of education politics, and highlight the difficulty of achieving collective action around school reform. African Americans, Latinos, Asians, and whites share some beliefs about education problems—for example, a dissatisfaction with central administration. But their problem definitions diverge on other points—for example, more racial and ethnic minorities than whites see discrimination in the school system. These differences make an already complex issue even more so, and create a difficult strategic environment for those who would seek to mobilize urban residents around particular education reforms.

Ideas and Institutions

Ultimately, a focus on ideas directs attention to institutions because institutional arenas—with their particular decision rules, evidentiary standards, operating procedures, and norms—privilege particular ideas, which grants legitimacy to certain understandings of education problems rather than others, to certain interests rather than others, and to certain lines of division or conflict rather than others (Heclo 1994; Immergut 1998). To fully understand why Latinos and Asians have difficulty influencing the discourse of education reform, we must consider the institutional barriers they face. That is, we must consider how the institutional arrangements governing the education arena are obstacles to these new school constituencies.

Discourse analysis highlights the degree to which differences in ideas undermine collective action, even in the face of what appear to be shared material stakes. But it also identifies points of consensus among groups. Institutional analysis will highlight the reasons why consensus on ideas and shared material stakes may yet be insufficient to entail collective action or influence on education politics and reforms.

Framing Problem Definitions and Solutions in Multiethnic Cities

One critical way that ideas come into play in the political arena is through the problem definition process. As Rochefort and Cobb explain, policymaking is a function of how decision makers perceive the problem being dealt with, and the contours of the problem can always be contested (1994, 4). From Schattschneider onward, political scientists have recognized the link between language and coalition building; political actors frame problems so as to attract more people to the cause, or to restrict their participation (e.g., Cobb and Elder 1972; Schattschneider 1960). The political process, to a large extent, is a battle of competing claims about problems; the stakes are high because the winning claim may influence the arena in which solutions will be crafted and the nature of the solution itself. As we have discussed in previous chapters, the education issue is inherently complex. Influences on a child's education extend from the individual teacher and school to the larger school district, to family and neighborhood, to city or state, or even national support or interventions in education. Thus numerous claims are possible about what "the problem" is with education today.

Here we present an empirical analysis of such claims in four multiethnic cities. The analysis examines variations in the frames that members of different racial groups used to describe education problems in their cities, and to assess reforms. What respondents in the four cities shared, regardless of race, was a deep dissatisfaction with the schools in their cities. The vast majority of respondents (76 percent) rated their city's efforts in education as "falling short" or "not doing well at all." Even more respondents (81 percent) gave these low ratings to their city's efforts for disadvantaged children. Latinos were most likely to choose the lowest category ("not doing well at all") in answer to this question. But despite a common dissatisfaction with schools in their cities, whites, African Americans, Latinos, and Asians defined education problems and assessed reforms differently.

Data and Methods

The discourse analysis presented here used transcripts from the 191 semi-structured interviews conducted in the four cities. These transcripts constitute the heart of the data for our entire study, but here we code and analyze them to gauge the ideas that members of different racial and ethnic groups hold about education problems and solutions.[1]

We undertook a three-stage coding process using NUD•IST qualitative data analysis software to systematically construct and then analyze two data sets. We first collected statements about problems and statements about solutions.[2] The "problem" data set contains 1,296 statements about education problems that arise in 187 interviews. The "solution" data set contains 680 statements about specific education reforms that arise in 103 interviews. In the second stage, data were analyzed inductively by reading all problem statements to see common themes emerging from them; these became the frames presented below. With the "solution" data, statements were sorted by specific reform idea, and then according to the statement's expression of support of or opposition to it. This enabled us to capture respondents' ambivalence about particular reforms, compared to a survey in which a respondent usually must choose one side or another. Finally, in the third stage, statements were sorted by the race or ethnicity of the speaker. It is likely that respondents' understandings and assessments of education problems and solutions also vary by role; that is, community activists perceive the education arena differently than education professionals. Our study's focus on the multiethnic politics of education, and on the puzzle of limited cooperation across groups of color despite the appearance of shared material stakes, led us to conduct our analysis across race rather than role (see Sidney 2002).

Chi-square tests were calculated for the frequency distributions presented in the tables discussed below; those that are statistically significant are marked as such. In general, where we interpret data to show consensus across groups, chi-squares were not statistically significant, and where we interpret substantive differences in perspectives—for example, on issues of racial and ethnic diversity—chi-squares were statistically significant.

Education Problems: Three Issue Frames

Analysis of problem statements identified three ways respondents framed education problems: They spoke about features of the school system itself, about larger social and economic problems that caused trouble for schools, and about the intersection of racial/ethnic diversity with education politics. Table 5.1 presents summary data of problem statements coded according to the three most commonly used frames, "school system," "broad social problems," and "diversity." There is a high degree of common ground in the first two frames, but not in the third. All three frames do correspond to the realities of urban education problems; urban school districts have high concentrations of low-income and minority students, and by most accounts the systems have not served them well (Stone 1998). But as the analysis shows, despite general agreement on the forces impinging on urban education, important differences persisted among racial groups in understandings about exactly how and why these forces mattered, especially when it came to interpreting the intersection of race with education.

TABLE 5.1 FRAMING EDUCATION PROBLEMS

	TOTAL	WHITE	AFRICAN AMERICAN	LATINO	ASIAN
School System					
Respondents	166 (89%)	89 (90%)	35 (92%)	35 (81%)	7 (100%)
Statements	667 (51%)	348 (54%)	152 (53%)	133 (43%)	34 (61%)
Broad Social Problems					
Respondents	145 (78%)	79 (80%)	32 (84%)	28 (65%)	6 (86%)
Statements	315 (24%)	167 (26%)	76 (27%)	58 (19%)	14 (25%)
Diversity					
Respondents	132 (71%)	67 (68%)	27 (71%)	33 (77%)	5 (71%)
Statements	432 (33%)	183 (28%)	88 (31%)	147 (47%)	14 (25%)
Total					
Respondents	187	99	38	43	7
Statements	1296	643	286	311	56

Note: Percentages and numbers do not add up to column totals, because statements may receive multiple codes and respondents may raise more than one theme within the frame. Chi-squares are not statistically significant.

The "School System" Frame

High proportions of respondents across racial groups framed their discussion of education problems in terms of school system features and practices. In doing so, they placed responsibility for education problems with school administrators, board members, and individual teachers. Table 5.1 shows that 89 percent of all respondents raised these sorts of issues; across racial groups, only among Latinos did this type of criticism drop under 90 percent. Analysis of the data identified two dimensions of school-system flaws that respondents raised: central bureaucracy and local school practices, shown in Table 5.2. Across races, most respondents faulted the central administration and school board for being insulated from, and antagonistic toward, the broader community of parents, business, and local government. They agreed that the system was too slow in diffusing successful reform models throughout the district.

In each city, frequent references to the central administration's street address symbolize insulation and obstruction. Looking at a list of school officials, a Los Angeles community advocate said that anyone whose address was 450 North Grand "is a hindrance." A Boston educator said, "Those that deal with Court Street get very, very frustrated." In San Francisco, a community

TABLE 5.2 DIMENSIONS OF THE "SCHOOL SYSTEM" FRAME

	TOTAL	WHITE	AFRICAN AMERICAN	LATINO	ASIAN
Central Bureaucracy					
Administration & Board (Central)					
Respondents	137 (83%)	76 (85%)	27 (77%)	29 (83%)	5 (71%)
Statements	349 (52%)	211 (61%)	59 (39%)	62 (47%)	17 (50%)
Diffusion of Change					
Respondents	65 (39%)	34 (38%)	14 (40%)	12 (34%)	5 (71%)
Statements	109 (16%)	53 (15%)	23 (15%)	23 (17%)	10 (29%)
Central-Local Links					
Respondents	40 (24%)	24 (27%)	4 (11%)	9 (26%)	3 (43%)
Statements	62 (9%)	36 (10%)	7 (5%)	14 (11%)	5 (15%)
Local School Practices					
Teachers & Teaching Methods					
Respondents	100 (60%)	46 (52%)	25 (71%)	24 (69%)	5 (71%)
Statements	200 (30%)	75 (22%)	69 (45%)	48 (36%)	8 (24%)
School (Local)					
Respondents	33 (20%)	14 (16%)	9 (26%)	10 (29%)	0
Statements	47 (7%)	18 (5%)	16 (11%)	13 (10%)	0
Total					
Respondents	166	89	35	35	7
Statements	667	348	152	133	34

Note: Percentages and numbers do not add up to column totals, because statements may receive multiple codes and respondents may raise more than one theme within the frame. Chi-squares are not statistically significant.

advocate said, "In terms of dealing with the public, I don't think a lot of people at 135 Van Ness are very good at that." And in Denver, several respondents called the central administration office on Grant Street, "Fort Grant."

Respondents described what they perceived to be the inefficiency and irrationality that arises when local school administrators cannot act on issues from building maintenance to teaching methods without going through "red tape" to get approval from the central office. Here, their sympathies were with local school personnel who were hampered by rules from the top and thus "can't go and buy paper on sale at Target," are "inhibited and squelched by the central administration," or worse, "are treated like furniture—moved around without any sense." Yet in other cases, school-level administrators (principals) came under the same attacks lodged against the central office, for their alleged hostility toward community participation in school affairs, sitting in "castles on a hill" without communicating to the outside world. Parents, in particular, "have been excluded from the school unless you pushed your way in," said one Los Angeles community advocate.

Despite this agreement, racial and ethnic minorities were more likely than whites to perceive problems with the local school bureaucracies, and with teachers and teaching methods, revealing a deeper and wider dissatisfaction with schools. About 70 percent of Latinos, African Americans, and Asians cited teachers and teaching methods as problematic, in contrast to 52 percent of whites. These critics wanted teachers to adapt their curricula and teaching styles to contemporary school populations who are more racially diverse and media savvy than previous generations. For example, a black city staffer in Denver said, "Kids are exposed to a lot more these days, and we need to change with the times. If that takes learning their history through a rap song, that's fine." These respondents also complained that teachers resistant to change were able to remain in the system, because of union-imposed procedures making termination difficult. Blacks and Latinos also complained at higher rates than whites or Asians about school-level bureaucracies (26 and 29 percent vs. 16 and 0 percent, respectively), charging school principals with hostility toward community participation in school affairs.

The "Broad Social Problems" Frame

Most respondents, regardless of race (78 percent in Table 5.1), framed education problems in terms of broad socioeconomic changes. In doing so, they placed responsibility for education problems not with the school system itself, but with larger social problems—either increased deviant behavior or poverty. While the data show a high level of general consensus in framing education problems in these terms, some variation is evident in the rate of use, and in the importance groups placed on each of the two dimensions, as shown in Table 5.3. Latinos used this frame less often than other groups, at a rate of 65 percent compared to more than 80 percent of whites, African Americans, and

TABLE 5.3 DIMENSIONS OF THE "BROAD SOCIAL PROBLEMS" FRAME

	TOTAL	WHITE	AFRICAN AMERICAN	LATINO	ASIAN
Deviant Behavior					
Respondents	115 (79%)	64 (81%)	25 (78%)	21 (75%)	5 (83%)
Statements	216 (69%)	115 (69%)	50 (66%)	40 (69%)	11 (79%)
Poverty					
Respondents	103 (71%)	56 (71%)	22 (69%)	21 (75%)	4 (67%)
Statements	155 (49%)	82 (49%)	38 (50%)	31 (53%)	4 (29%)
Total					
Respondents	145	79	32	28	6
Statements	315	167	76	58	14

Note: Percentages and numbers do not add up to column totals, because statements may receive multiple codes and respondents may raise more than one theme within the frame. Chi-squares are not statistically significant.

Asians. Latinos also stood out because they were equally likely to raise the poverty theme as they were to discuss social deviance. By contrast, whites, blacks, and Asians, were somewhat more likely to discuss deviance than to discuss poverty.

In using the deviance dimension of this frame, respondents linked education problems to the social disorder of inner-city neighborhoods, and to pathologies such as crime, the dissolution of families, teenage parents, and drug use. Respondents criticized parents for not providing a home environment conducive to educational achievement. A San Francisco journalist noted, "When I talk to kids, they feel they are getting no structure at home. . . . They just crave some kind of discipline." The problem for educators, then, is that "when [kids] leave school, they go back to an environment that we have no control over." A common refrain was that teachers now are expected not only to teach, but also to be social workers, police officers, babysitters, and substitute parents.

In the poverty dimension, which Latinos were slightly more likely than other groups to invoke, respondents noted that regional disparities resulted in their schools having higher proportions of poor children than suburban schools. Kids who are "not getting enough to eat," "living in garages," and "not getting their inoculations" will have a difficult time achieving in school, explained one respondent. Others talked of challenges relating to homeless children, and the transience of poor families. A Boston nonprofit staffer explained: "Many low-income people with kids in the public schools work, and they work really hard. They may have two or three jobs . . . and they tend to be jobs that don't have a lot of flexibility built into them. . . . We need to stop blaming the parents for not being involved and figuring out how to facilitate their involvement at a structural level." A Denver elected official stated, "I think it's difficult to develop middle-class values if you have less than a middle-class income."

The "Diversity" Frame

For the most part, the analysis thus far has suggested shared interpretations of education problems, suggesting grounds for cooperation across racial groups. When respondents talked about education in terms of district matters, or in terms of broad social problems, they agreed more often than they disagreed. But when they talked about education in terms of racial and ethnic diversity, the picture changed. Analysis of patterns in usage of the diversity frame indicates that racial interpretations of school politics and problems complicate prospects for cooperation. Indeed, the variety of themes within this frame, and the different cleavages across races that emerge within each theme, suggests an overarching complexity to the strategic context for education reform.

On the one hand, a substantial portion of respondents (71 percent, in Table 5.1) linked racial and ethnic diversity to education problems. Table 5.1 shows that racial and ethnic minorities used this frame at a slightly higher rate than whites; whereas 68 percent of white speakers interpreted education problems in racial terms, 77 percent of Latinos, 71 percent of blacks, and 71 percent of Asians did so. The emphasis given differed; nearly half of Latinos' problem statements fell into this frame, whereas less than a third of whites' problem statements did.

But respondents linked race to education differently, depending on their own race/ethnicity. Four themes emerged: divisiveness, disparate outcomes and influence, discrimination, and challenges. As Table 5.4 shows, distinct patterns of usage marked each one, showing agreement across some groups in one area, but disagreement between the same groups in others. For example, whites and Latinos complained more often than blacks and Asians that diversity produced harmful divisiveness in the education arena. Whites, Latinos, and Asians shared a sense of the challenges that diversity poses, particularly relative to language needs, much more so than blacks. But all three minority groups diverged from whites in their propensity to discuss disparate outcomes and influence in education across races, and in their perception of discrimination within the education arena.

DIVISIVENESS As Table 5.4 shows, whites and Latinos were more likely than blacks or Asians to complain that diversity produced conflict and divisiveness in the educational arena. Yet these groups interpreted the conflict differently. Whites called it problematic because it inhibited "rational" decision making; Latinos described how it impeded them in their attempt to have a strong voice in decision making. That is, they "fought battles"—engaged in conflictual political processes—without securing victories. Participation in education politics did not bring representation in the system.

TABLE 5.4 DIMENSIONS OF THE "DIVERSITY" FRAME

	TOTAL	WHITE	AFRICAN AMERICAN	LATINO	ASIAN
Divisive					
Respondents	67 (51%)	34 (51%)	12 (44%)	19 (58%)	2 (40%)
Statements	130 (30%)	69 (38%)	19 (22%)	40 (27%)	2 (14%)
Disparate Outcomes & Influence°					
Respondents	77 (58%)	32 (48%)	21 (78%)	21 (64%)	3 (60%)
Statements	215 (50%)	69 (38%)	55 (63%)	81 (55%)	10 (71%)
Challenge°°					
Respondents	54 (41%)	31 (46%)	2 (7%)	17 (52%)	4 (80%)
Statements	70 (16%)	42 (23%)	3 (3%)	20 (14%)	5 (36%)
Racism°°					
Respondents	47 (36%)	13 (19%)	12 (44%)	22 (67%)	0
Statements	84 (19%)	23 (13%)	28 (32%)	33 (22%)	0
Total					
Respondents	132	67	27	33	5
Statements	432	183	88	147	14

° chi-square p = 0.10; °° chi-square p < 0.001

Note: Percentages and numbers do not add up to column totals, because statements may receive multiple codes and respondents may raise more than one theme within the frame.

Respondents described the racialization of policy decisions, as advocates from different groups see that decisions on many issues have differential consequences for them. For example, according to a white school board member in Los Angeles, a debate about year-round class schedules became a debate about "who's going to win."

On the multi-track year-round schedule [issue], that too is seen as who's going to win. The white suburban campuses that are less overcrowded—why are they given the luxury of a traditional school calendar, while it's just inner-city, mostly Latino schools that are overcrowded and on a multi-track calendar? We should all suffer together. But people in the white community are saying: Wait a minute—why should I have to suffer because way the hell over there they have an overcrowding problem? Why do I have to change my calendar? We have since worked through that, but that has been an ongoing problem with a lot of racial overtones.

Respondents also saw groups competing for district jobs. "The power struggle is constantly going on," said a Latina who had served on the school board in Denver. She continues:

Right now the Blacks feel they dominate the school system because they have a Black superintendent and they have two Black board members.... They want to keep it as long as they can.... There's a certain amount of prestige of knowing 'We have the power, we have a superintendent, we can ask for things. We can get things done. We're not on the outside looking in.' The Hispanics want one of their own in the superintendency. And the Anglos are afraid of both of them.

Conflict emerged at the school level as Latinos moved into black neighborhoods; blacks dominated the administrative and teacher ranks at schools with increasingly Latino student bodies. "It's one hell of a mess," a Latino school official in Los Angeles said. "I can hear the parents screaming, 'Hey, we want someone in the office who will translate for us.'" He added, "I can't even begin to tell you what goes on in some of these schools, and how some of these ... Latino immigrant non-English-speaking parents are treated. You wouldn't believe it."

Respondents thought conflict prevented groups from recognizing shared stakes and working together for change. Differing views on integration and bilingual education were cited as issues that keep Latinos and blacks apart, making them suspicious of one another. Conflict, according to a black school board member in Denver, "revolves around the fear of one group getting too far ahead, and not the belief that, as President Kennedy used to talk about, a rising tide can lift all boats. I don't think we believe that."

Intragroup conflict also came up in the interviews, with respondents particularly critical of conflicts within the Latino community, and descriptions of how these muted broader influence on education decision making. A white school board member in Denver cited a recent school board race in which she felt that Latinos missed a chance for strong representation because they could not agree to rally around one candidate, instead dividing over two "weak" ones. This sort of outcome, she said, leads "Anglo people who are in power to write them off. They'll say: 'These people don't know what they want.'"

THE CHALLENGE OF DIVERSITY   Whites, Latinos, and Asians were much more likely than blacks to describe the challenges posed by a diverse student body, particularly relative to language needs (cf. Schmidt 2000). Only 7 percent of blacks raised this theme, providing empirical evidence of what respondents described as blacks' lack of attention to bilingual education. Sometimes respondents spoke abstractly about the challenge of diversity; for example, a black city official in San Francisco said, "Probably the major challenge is the diversity, which is one of the richest things the city has to offer. At the same time, it is killing us. How do we mainstream all this diversity?"

When they talked in specifics, respondents often focused (albeit inconsistently) on the numbers of non-English speakers in the districts, and the number of languages spoken by them. Clearly, they perceive the districts to be overwhelmed. In Los Angeles, estimates ranged from 35 to 90 languages. An Asian nonprofit director said, "We've got 35 or 40 different languages at Hollywood High." A white activist responded, "I talked to a teacher ... who said that the kids in his school spoke 72 different languages at home. How do you cope...?" Another white activist stated that "A little over 50 percent of our incoming kindergarten kids speak no English. Los Angeles Unified has 84 languages ... other than English spoken in the home." A white school official reported, "There's something like 90 different languages spoken by kids in this school district. It's almost overwhelming."

In Denver, estimates ranged from 27 dialects to 87 languages. A Latino elected official said, "There are 27 dialects spoken in this district, and four major languages." A Latino community advocate responded, "They have over 70 different languages that they have to teach in the Denver public schools in order to communicate with the kids." An white education lobbyist said, "There are 87 languages in the Denver public school district. It's huge, it's astounding. How do you take that and plug it into a school finance formula?"

DISPARATE EDUCATIONAL OUTCOMES AND INFLUENCE ON THE SYSTEM A third dimension emerging in the diversity frame emphasized the disparate educational outcomes between whites and minorities, and minorities' limited influence on the school system. Whereas most blacks, Latinos, and Asians mentioned disparate outcomes and influence, slightly less than half of white respondents did. Respondents cited blacks' and Latinos' lower test scores, their segregation into remedial or special education classes ("little jail classes" according to a white community advocate in Boston, "a caste system" according to a Latino activist lawyer in San Francisco), compared with whites' presence in advanced courses; they noted disparate rates of suspension and expulsion for blacks and Latinos. The same Boston activist complained, "There's a huge dropout rate here. I mean, you ain't going very far if you are black and a boy in this town."

Others described the low numbers of minority teachers, the inability of white teachers to connect with minority students, and the differential treatment they feel minority students receive. According to a Latino elected official in Denver, "I think all too often teachers think because kids are poor or they come from low-income minority neighborhoods, they're not smart, they're dumb. So the expectations are less, and I think our kids are being shortchanged as a result." A black community activist in Denver described her visit to a classroom where most of the students were black and the teacher was white. "They have a little teacher who's scared to death to see so many black kids, wondering are they going to kill me, or do this, that and the other. In reality, [the kids] are nice people, thrown together like that and treated like they're nobody's anything."

Speakers lamented minorities' underrepresentation in the decision-making structure. Some interpreted the void as lack of interest or initiative. A white attorney active on education issues in Boston noted Latinos' absence on site-based management teams, saying, "They are stakeholders who aren't paying attention to their stake." But many others described the school system's failure to respond to these groups when they do demand change. "I think a lot of issues have been brought forward by those groups, but the district and board have failed to act upon them," a white community advocate in Denver said. Some respondents criticized the superficiality of inclusive gestures. For example, a prominent Latino public figure in Denver described being invited to a committee of citizens to review the Denver school district budget:

> At the very first meeting that we went to, Councilman Sandos and I sat down and, I hate to sound so race conscious, but it is reality, 45 percent of the students in [Denver schools] are Hispanic. We sat in this group of probably 100 people that first came out, and there were six Hispanics who were invited to participate. We need people who relate to the issues, and the problems, and the concerns to be able to voice their opinions. When they are not there, then they can't.

Another Denver Latino activist told of school officials' tendency to discount minority parents. She described a school-community meeting held in a Latino neighborhood to discuss proposed changes to middle schools in the district.

> One of the board members said that the problem with education was that parents don't care about their kids' education. I got up and said, 'I take great offense to this. Do you think we came out in 19-degrees-below-zero weather because we don't care about our kids' education?' Oh, I wasn't talking about you, I was talking about the people who aren't here.

DISCRIMINATION AND RACISM A final dimension of respondents' discussion of diversity emerged when speakers attributed disparate outcomes and influence to intentional discrimination or racism. Especially Latinos, but blacks as well, cited racism as a problem; whites were much less likely to see problems in these intentional terms—that is, they might recognize disparate outcomes, but did not characterize the system as discriminatory.

Respondents spoke of white teachers' and administrators' treatment of minority students and parents. "In some schools, it's evident that the Whites do not want these kids there," said a Latino community advocate in Denver. "They do everything in their power to make them unwelcome, to make the parents feel unwelcome. It's done a lot of harm to the kids' psyches, going someplace where they're not wanted." A white PTA leader in Denver spoke of her local school's indifference to parents' language needs:

> If you are in a school—and I'm using a personal example—in which 85 percent of the children are minority, and of that about 60 percent are Spanish-speaking children, and all of your meetings are held in English, that is an intimidation factor. That is a way to—not blatantly, but under the table—prevent those parents from participating. Whether it's done on purpose or not, I can't say. However, 20 years of knowing the population of your school, and not addressing that problem, kind of turns it into blatant: You're not important enough to be involved here; we're not going to hold the meeting in a language you can understand.

Respondents interpreted the general public's lack of support for public education as linked to the system's "majority minority" student body. For example, a Latino education lobbyist in California said, "I think there's been a general bias against the district as the district began to change its complexion.... As the district became more minority, the influential leaders pulled back." Another respondent suggested that as minorities joined the ranks of the school board and administration, the general (white) public began to advocate school vouchers. A Latino nonprofit director in Denver said, "I think that there's been this change where lots of people feel like it's okay that we lose half of the Hispanic kids who enter Denver Public Schools, drop out, and never graduate."

Other respondents said the public's differential concern about education comes to the surface when white students are affected by problems. A Latino principal in Los Angeles described her anger when violence at a primarily white school provoked media attention and public statements of concern. "What angers me personally about that is that as a principal at a predominantly minority school, I've been dealing with gang violence and losing kids, ... but because they were minority students, and 'minority' schools, none of the attention was given. But you have an incident perceived by the public as a White mainstream high school, and they go up in arms."

Assessments of Reform Options

Analyzing how members of different racial and ethnic groups define education problems shows the complex terrain of education reform, and suggests in particular that differing interpretations of diversity's intersection with education infused the arena, potentially complicating coalition building even where consensus existed across groups. The political arena consists not only of competing claims about problems, but also of competing reform alternatives. Sometimes reform ideas emerge directly from problem definitions, but as Kingdon and others have found, sometimes reform alternatives emerge first, and policy entrepreneurs find the problem definition to match it (Cohen, March and, Olsen 1972; Kingdon 1995). The following analysis presents respondents' assessments of the reforms that were in place, or were being proposed, in their cities. As Chapters 1 and 3 emphasized, new school constituencies reacted to many of these ideas, rather than being involved in the processes that led to their adoption.

Analysis of problem statement data shows that when it comes to framing problems, shared understandings exist in some respects but not others—especially interpretations of how racial diversity shapes education politics. When we consider patterns in respondents' views on reforms, we must keep in mind this underlying fault line. Statements about the market-basket of reform ideas in play today show shared preferences coexisting with divergent views. Table 5.5 presents the summary data of this analysis, showing the percentage of comments that were positive and negative about each reform across racial groups. Perceptions of reforms converged on opposition to vouchers, on support for cross-sector strategies, on support for magnet schools, and on ambivalence about measures to decentralize the school system. Perceptions across races diverged on assessments of desegregation, bilingual education, and charter schools.

Points of Consensus

No to Vouchers
Respondents rejected school vouchers as a solution to education problems, as Table 5.5 shows. This reform idea drew the highest proportion of negative comments across racial groups. Respondents feared vouchers would produce unequal schools, reminiscent of the days before desegregation. Others saw it as too individualistic—a dangerous rejection of the concept of public schools—or elitist, a way for rich kids to exit public schools with public money. They saw vouchers as an idea that skirted the complexities of education problems, promoted by people seeking a "quick fix."

Yes to Partnerships
In contrast to vouchers, respondents were unified in their support for broad-based partnerships. Partnerships with business were discussed, but most statements described links with social service agencies, nonprofits, and city government that would make school district boundaries more permeable and would bring community services into the schools. Respondents thought that partnerships would end the "disconnected maze" of services, and would include efforts such as bringing health and counseling services into schools,

TABLE 5.5 ASSESSMENTS OF EDUCATION REFORMS

	WHITE	AFRICAN AMERICAN	LATINO	ASIAN
Vouchers (n=24)				
# Respondents	17	4	3	0
Positive	4 (24%)	0	0	0
Negative	13 (76%)	4 (100%)	3 (100%)	0
Partnerships (n=83)				
# Respondents	45	16	20	2
Positive	43 (96%)	16 (100%)	20 (100%)	2 (100%)
Negative	3 (7%)	1 (6%)	0	0
Magnet Schools (n=48)				
# Respondents	25	7	15	1
Positive	16 (64%)	5 (71%)	13 (87%)	1 (100%)
Negative	10 (40%)	3 (43%)	3 (20%)	0
Decentralization (n=102)				
# Respondents	51	21	27	3
Positive	40 (78%)	15 (71%)	19 (70%)	2 (67%)
Negative	33 (65%)	13 (62%)	20 (74%)	3 (100%)
Charter Schools (n=52)				
# Respondents	23	13	16	0
Positive	16 (70%)	4 (31%)	7 (44%)	0
Negative	11 (48%)	12 (92%)	12 (75%)	0
Desegregation° (n=61)				
# Respondents	32	9	19	1
Positive	5 (16%)	5 (56%)	2 (11%)	1 (100%)
Negative	29 (91%)	6 (67%)	19 (100%)	0
Bilingual Education (n=41)				
# Respondents	15	3	21	2
Positive	7 (47%)	1 (33%)	15 (71%)	1 (50%)
Negative	9 (60%)	2 (67%)	13 (62%)	2 (100%)
Total				
# Respondents	103	38	43	7

° Chi-square p = 0.02.

Note: Columns do not total because not every respondent talked about every reform, and some respondents made both positive and negative comments about the reforms.

bringing schools to public housing, and making schools "one-stop shops," community centers where parents and children could access city and county services. Given students' increasing needs and diversity, respondents felt partnerships were critical because they could bring into the schools the expertise that educators may not have. But generating the will among critical agencies was seen as problematic. Institutional barriers, such as the fragmentation of functions, were hard to overcome given the limited authority of each entity.

Getting two bureaucracies to work together, said one respondent, "is like moving mountains."

Yes to Magnet Schools

Especially among racial and ethnic minorities, this reform received hearty support. Magnet schools had been in place for many years in most cities, so were a familiar idea. Respondents portrayed them as offering parents a way to tailor education to their children's individual needs, and thus as a way to deal with the diversity of the student body. They were praised for contributing to racial integration, and for offering choices within a district. Often magnet schools were perceived to be the best in the district, with superior curricula and achievement levels.

Some respondents criticized magnets for their limited nature. Because every student could not attend these schools, magnets perpetuated inequality. "There aren't that many things to magnetize," as a white community advocate from Denver put it. A white business leader in San Francisco asked about the students who didn't "fit" any of the magnets. "These are the kids not being educated at all," she said. Some described magnets as a desegregation strategy that appealed to white families, and expressed uncertainty about whether magnets could meet the needs of multiethnic school populations.

Ambivalence on Decentralization

Decentralization received high levels of both positive and negative comments, revealing an ambivalence across groups about redistributing power within the school system. Many supported the idea, but were concerned about how it was being implemented in the school system, and worried that decentralization would limit minority representation unless provisions existed to assure access. Respondents recognized that the success and the character of decentralization efforts, such as site-based management, would vary from school to school, introducing the potential for inequality across schools. Some schools would become accountable to parents and run collaboratively, others might become fiefdoms of the principal. The most negative comments called decentralization models, like parent-educator committees, examples of professionals shirking their responsibility. According to a black community advocate in Denver, "It seems as though when all has failed, you dump the problem on the people." Some respondents doubted that school-based management would translate into higher achievement levels. They thought decentralization might overcome the inertia of the central bureaucracy, but were skeptical about whether its benefits would flow to the most needy children.

Points of Conflict

While statements about the above reform options indicated grounds for consensus, other reactions showed a more complex terrain. The reforms most directly linked to racial and ethnic equality—desegregation and bilingual education—split minorities from one another. By contrast, all three minority groups were skeptical about charter schools, whereas higher numbers of whites praised these.

Desegregation

White and Latino respondents clearly were displeased with desegregation efforts in their cities, whereas African Americans were ambivalent, expressing nearly equal levels of positive and negative views. Respondents complained that desegregation broke the link between school and neighborhood. "It's hard for kids to go to each other's birthday parties when they live across the city," stated a black nonprofit leader in Denver. They thought that desegregation made parental involvement more difficult. According to a Latino nonprofit leader in Boston, "You would almost have to have parent busing to get parental involvement and ownership of the school." Respondents thought desegregation burdened minority children without delivering enough benefits, sometimes resulting in more harm than good, and drove whites away from the school district and the city. They spoke of court orders tying the hands of the school district, or being used by administrators as an excuse for not implementing other reforms. And they complained that in "majority-minority" districts, desegregation wasted scarce resources.

African Americans supported desegregation efforts, but recognized their limits. They complained that school districts had resisted desegregation and had never implemented it in good faith. They recalled that equality was the original goal, but that desegregation had come to be understood simply as busing—moving kids around rather than ensuring equal opportunity. These respondents feared that ending mandated desegregation would stop school districts' already halting efforts to achieve racial equality, and would eliminate the leverage that the African American community had gained in school politics. One of the original African American supporters of desegregation in Denver said, "When they get out of the court order, nothing is going to happen that's going to help the youngsters who need it. White people, people with money, will always have what they want. So we will return to what was, and what we were trying to change for the benefit of all."

Bilingual Education

Bilingual education was criticized by all respondents, especially African Americans. Still, high rates of whites, Latinos, and Asians also expressed support. These latter respondents praised the idea of bilingual education, but faulted its implementation. For example, they noted the cultural support that bilingual education offered to Latino and Asian students, but complained about unqualified teachers, low standards, and lack of resources devoted to bilingual education. They linked these conditions to Latino students' low achievement levels.

Charter Schools

Charter schools elicited support from whites, with Latinos moderately supportive, but African Americans generally opposed them. Supporters emphasized charter schools' ability to tailor education to differing needs of students, and their sense that such schools would be more accountable and responsive to parents. Opponents saw them as elitist, "an escape clause for middle-class families" without guarantees that disadvantaged kids would have access to them. Some pointed out that charters' lack of uniformity increased the risk of inequality. Others noted that charters drain money from the public system to benefit only one school's worth of children.

Problem Definitions and Reform Assessments in Four Multiethnic Cities

The discussion thus far of racial and ethnic groups' variations and similarities in defining education problems and in assessing solutions has relied upon data aggregated from the four cities. But each city presents a distinctive context, so we would expect some divergence from the general trends. Here we look briefly at the configuration of problem definitions and opinions about reform ideas in each city. While many of the patterns described thus far hold true across cities, there are some differences. In some cities, respondents reveal higher levels of consensus and emphasize a particular frame more than others. Statements about reforms tend to cluster around those that are most salient in each city. Tables 5.6 and 5.7 rank the use of problem frames and the opinions about reform ideas in each city by racial and ethnic group.

San Francisco

In San Francisco, blacks and Latinos used the broad-social-problems frame most often, whereas whites most often spoke of problems in terms of internal, school-system issues. Across groups, fewer San Francisco respondents used the diversity frame to describe education problems; this is interesting because San Francisco's consent decree was the most specific in its desegregation mandate regarding the relative proportions of each racial and ethnic group to be assigned to specific schools. Whites were most likely to discuss education problems in

TABLE 5.6 RANK-ORDER OF FRAMES BY RACIAL/ETHNIC GROUP IN FOUR CITIES

	1 (Top)	2	3
Aggregate			
White	School System (90%)°	Social Problems (80%)	Diversity (68%)
African American	School System (92)	Social Problems (84)	Diversity (71)
Latino	School System (81)	Diversity (77)	Social Problems (65)
Asian	School System (100)	Social Problems (86)	Diversity (71)
San Francisco			
White	School System (90)	Social Problems (80)	Diversity (65)
African American	Social Problems (100)	School System (83)	Diversity (50)
Latino	Social Problems (90)	School System (60)	Diversity (50)
Asian	School System (100)	Social Problems (80)	Diversity (60)
Denver			
White	School System (88)	Social Problems (79)	Diversity (68)
African American	Diversity (100)	School System (93)	Social Problems (71)
Latino	School System (95)	Diversity (89)	Social Problems (74)
Boston			
White	School System (93)	Social Problems (73)	Diversity (53)
African American	School System, Social Problems (100)	Diversity (60)	
Latino	School System (100)	Diversity (67)	(did not use a third)
Los Angeles			
White	School System (90)	Social Problems (83)	Diversity (77)
African American	School System (100)	Social Problems (88)	Diversity (50)
Latino	Diversity (82)	School System (73)	Social Problems (45)
Asian	All three equally used (100)		

° Percent of respondents from a racial/ethnic group using this frame

terms of diversity, and they especially emphasized the challenges posed by diversity. In the other cities, racial minorities used this frame more frequently.

Latinos stood apart from other groups on a few issues. They focused on the political aspects of diversity more than its challenges—that is, the discrimination and divisiveness they saw in school practices and decision making. Their disinclination to discuss challenges of diversity, such as language issues, distinguished them from Latino respondents in other cities. Latinos also used the broad-social-problems frame differently from members of other groups. Whereas whites, blacks, and Asians emphasized social pathologies and individual behaviors, Latinos were much more likely to emphasize poverty. They diverged most starkly in this way from African American respondents, who all invoked individual behaviors, compared with 56 percent of Latinos. By contrast, nearly 90 percent of Latinos using this frame discussed poverty, while 67 percent of blacks did. Blacks differed from other groups in their perceptions of problems internal to the school system. Only 40 percent spoke of central administration, versus more than 80 percent of respondents of other races;

TABLE 5.7 RANK-ORDER OF REFORMS BY RACIAL/ETHNIC GROUP IN FOUR CITIES

	MOST POSITIVE		MOST NEGATIVE	
	1 (Top)	2	1	2
Aggregate				
White	Partnerships	Decentralization	Desegregation	Vouchers
African American	Partnerships	Decentralization/ Magnet	Vouchers	Charters
Latino	Partnerships	Magnets	Vouchers/ Desegregation	Charters
Asian	Partnerships/Desegregation/ Magnets	Decentralization	Decentralization/Bilingual	
San Francisco				
White	Charter/Decentralization/Bilingual	Partnerships	Desegregation	Vouchers
African American	Charters/Partnerships/Decentralization	--	Charters/Magnets	--
Latino	Partnerships/Magnets/Bilingual/Reconstitution	Bilingual	Chart/Decent/ Desegregation	
Asian	Partnerships/Decentralization/Desegregation/Reconstitution	Bilingual	Decent/Bilingual	--
Denver				
White	Partnerships	Charters	Decentralization	Desegregation
African American	Partnerships	Magnets	Vouchers/Bilingual	Charters
Latino	Partnerships	Magnets	Vouchers/ Decentralization	Desegregation
Boston				
White	Partnerships	Decentralization	Vouchers/Bilingual/ Desegregation	Decentralization
African American	Partner/ Magnets	Decentralization	Charters/ Desegregation	Decentralization
Latino	Partnerships	Decentralization	Charters/Bilingual/ Desegregation	Decentralization
Los Angeles				
White	Partnerships	Decentralization	Vouchers	Desegregation
African American	Partnerships/Decentralization/Magnets	--	Magnets	Decentralization
Latino	Charters/Partnerships/Magnets/Bilingual	Decentralization	Charters/	Desegregation
Asian	Partnerships	Decentralization	Decentralization	--

instead, blacks emphasized teachers and teaching methods, and the lack of diffusion of change across the district.

San Francisco respondents were among the most vigorous supporters of partnership reform ideas; we can connect this to the high rate at which blacks and Latinos especially spoke about socioeconomic trends impinging on schools. The strategy of reconstituting low-performing schools, which involved a school staff and curriculum overhaul overseen by the superintendent, was distinctive to San Francisco, and respondents offered mixed reviews of this approach. Respondents praised the idea of total overhaul rather than tinkering with these schools, noting that it was a way to eliminate bad teachers entrenched in the system and to remove bureaucratic barriers to reform. Reconstitution also brought increased resources for technology and reducing class size. But, as with other school-level reform ideas, respondents complained that not enough schools got the opportunity. They also questioned the selection process, expressed doubt that Latinos benefited as much as African Americans, and criticized it as a top-down approach that didn't allow the school-level staff to have input in designing changes.

Denver

In Denver, black and Latino respondents particularly emphasized diversity issues, doing so more than they discussed socioeconomic trends. On issues of diversity, in fact, Denver reveals a particularly fluid terrain. Whereas whites and Latinos both described the divisiveness of diversity, blacks did so much less often. Whites and Latinos see blacks as holding power, but blacks emphasized disparate impact and outcomes for racial minorities, suggesting they did not necessarily feel as powerful as the others perceived them to be. In this emphasis on disparate achievement levels and influence, blacks and Latinos saw eye to eye with each other more than with whites. Yet when it came to discussion of the challenges of diversity, blacks said little, whereas whites and Latinos both recognized this issue, particularly concerning language needs; blacks' discussion of language needs fell in the political sphere, as an example of issues on which blacks and Latinos disagreed about the allocation of resources. Finally, 50 percent of blacks using the diversity frame invoked racism, along with 71 percent of Latinos. By contrast, only 17 percent of whites did so.

In their opinions of reform ideas, Denver respondents stood out in their negative remarks about decentralization. Denver schools have had Collaborative Decision Making (CDM) teams in place at the school level since 1990. Respondents' views on this version of decentralization were mixed, but leaned toward negative—for whites, 73 percent of their statements were positive versus 86 percent negative; for blacks, 64 percent of their statements were positive, versus 82 percent negative; for Latinos, 76 percent were positive and 82 percent were negative. All respondents, but especially blacks and Latinos, had more unequivocally positive views of magnet schools than of site-managed schools.

Denver also stood out in the frequency and intensity with which respondents assessed desegregation—all of the Latino interviewees' statements were negative, and 85 percent of whites' statements were negative. Even among blacks, 71 percent of their statements were negative, though they had the highest rate of positive statements—57 percent compared with 9 percent for Latinos and 23 percent for whites.

Boston

In Boston, respondents used the diversity frame at low rates relative to respondents in Denver and Los Angeles. Whites emphasized internal school-system issues, with blacks emphasizing those and broad social problems at equally high levels. Boston was the only city in which blacks were more likely to raise the theme of poverty than that of pathology and bad behaviors. No Latinos spoke of education problems in terms of socioeconomic issues, instead focusing either on school-system factors or race and ethnicity. The terrain on diversity issues showed less consistent alignment. Half of the white and Latino respondents using this frame raised the issue of divisiveness, compared to 33 percent of black respondents. Blacks stood out in the opposite way on the issue of disparate outcomes and influence—83 percent of blacks using this frame raised the issue, whereas only half the white and Latino respondents did. Latinos stood out in their emphasis on racism.

Boston respondents were extremely ambivalent about decentralization—this issue attracted high rates of positive and of negative remarks. Members of all groups spoke negatively about desegregation efforts. African Americans and Latinos expressed negative views of charter schools. As in most other cities, partnerships evoked the most praise from respondents.

Los Angeles

In Los Angeles, Latinos and whites were closer to one another in their use of the diversity frame than either was to blacks. Both highlighted the challenge of diversity, often in terms of language needs, though Latinos were more likely to see racism than whites. Blacks focused on the divisiveness of racial politics on education, and on the disparate outcomes and influence of minorities. This diverged from the pattern in the other cities, where blacks were less likely to focus on divisiveness than were whites and Latinos. Respondents showed a greater degree of consensus within the broad-social-problems frame, with all groups emphasizing pathologies and bad behavior, though like in San Francisco and Denver, blacks' rate of use was slightly higher than whites. On internal school issues, Latinos and whites complained at the highest rates about central administration and school board, whereas, like in other cities, Latinos and blacks were more concerned about teachers than were whites. Respondents spoke most frequently about partnerships and decentralization—two reform ideas captured in the LEARN initiative, which brought together actors across sectors and emphasized site-based management. Whites and blacks were most enthusiastic about decentralization, with Latinos expressing high rates of positive and of negative comments, showing their ambivalence about the degree to which decentralization delivered benefits to their children. In Los Angeles, as in most cities, whites and Latinos held extremely negative views about desegregation.

Conclusion

This analysis focusing on how ideas shape politics suggests limited prospects for cross-racial and cross-ethnic mobilization around education reform. On the one hand, consensus across races in use of the school-system frame indicate prospects for broad support of reforms aimed at the top of the school district, and for reinventing school governance to be more responsive and connected to the community. But variations in how respondents invoked this frame indicate that blacks and Latinos wanted reforms to result in concrete changes in teachers and teaching methods. Whites were less likely to perceive a need for attention to the classroom consequences of institutional redesign.

Respondents' use of the broad-social-problems frame suggests widespread support across racial and ethnic groups for reforms helping "at-risk" or disadvantaged children and their families. But differences emerged regarding the nature of such programs. That is, those who focused on social deviance would be likely to support efforts to change parents' behavior through parent training, links with social services, and/or criminal justice systems, along with efforts to change students' behavior through preventive and disciplinary programs. On the other hand, groups who emphasized poverty would be likely to support efforts aimed to improve families' financial status, such as job training and continuing education for parents, child care programs, and links to social services such as health care and food assistance.

Respondents' use of the diversity frame complicates grounds for collective action, similar to findings in other settings (Berrey 2005). Groups perceived race as permeating education problems and politics in different ways, leading us to predict that any multiethnic coalition would be unstable. For example, whites expressed awareness of language as an education issue, so could ally with Latinos for this purpose. But they were less likely to see the discriminatory side of school policies or school personnel's behavior. On that, Latinos and blacks might ally, except for the competitiveness and suspicion that respondents reported exists between them. Differing interpretations of how racial and ethnic diversity infused education politics and policy may be what pre-vented groups with otherwise common understandings from finding one another and working together.

This analysis also shows a complex context when it comes to views on specific reforms. Partnerships linking public and nonprofit agencies with schools received the most vigorous support from all respondents. But this is the solution that in effect consists of broad-based cooperation. In the cities studied, only small-scale examples existed, with little optimism from respondents about the prospects for more cohesiveness among education actors. Additionally, the legacy of desegregation and bilingual education programs was to split Latinos and blacks from one another. Each reform, important to one of these groups, appeared to the other to be a questionable, if not harmful, use of scarce resources.

Another disconnect is that between the problems emphasized by racial and ethnic minorities (including, in particular, a concern about teachers and teaching methods), and the solutions that constituted the dominant "policy talk" in education reform. School vouchers, charter schools, and decentralization elicited responses ranging from extreme antagonism to deep ambivalence. Even though racial minorities understood the positive implications of some of these changes, they were not confident that their children would be the ones to benefit from them.

In sum, the two parts of this discourse analysis—problems and solutions—show a complex terrain of political interests. Although the analysis identifies points of consensus and shared understandings, it suggests that differences—especially in interpretations of how race and ethnicity related to education politics—undermined collective action. These differences lay beneath what appeared on the surface to be shared material stakes. The analysis also showed that racial minorities' limited power in education politics was in part constituted by the fact that their assessments did not match the dominant reforms either in place or proposed. This mismatch was especially true for Latinos and Asians. The power of particular ideas derives in part from the size and resources of the coalitions pushing for them, as well as from the degree of consensus generated behind them. The absence of any of these factors complicates prospects for influence.

But interests and ideas do not tell the whole story of power during this multiethnic moment in education politics. Institutions fix the winners and losers of a particular round of conflict into place. Institutional change, as much as changes in population composition or ideas, offers a window for policy shift. If new interests and ideas are not consolidated into institutions, they cannot in the end assert power in education politics. Chapter 6 turns to the institutional arrangements in multiethnic cities for the final building block of our analysis.

## CHAPTER SIX

Institutions and Education Reform

in Multiethnic Cities

I T SEEMS COMMONPLACE NOW to say that "institutions matter" in the policymaking process. It is almost akin to arguing that "politics matter." Indeed, at the federal level, scholars of American government have explored how formal and informal institutions such as committee organization, rules, and norms structure the outcomes of the policymaking process. Despite being well studied at the federal levels, institutions and the role that they play often are less understood at other levels of government. This holds particularly true for education policymaking processes as well as the implementation of education reform at the local level. As we argue below, the lack of emphasis on institutions is partly due to the fact that a tremendous variety of institutions exist at the local level and their strength in the policymaking arena often waxes and wanes depending upon the issues at hand. Thus, unlike the formation of national policy, the role of institutions in education policy is not necessarily straightforward or consistent.

In Chapters 4 and 5, we made the case that interests and ideas are important factors in understanding the formation of education policy. Chapter 4 concludes that in our four study cities racial and ethnic group interests continue to be ambiguous, fragmented, and difficult to articulate in the educational arena. Thus, despite a numerical superiority within school populations, minority groups have been unable to translate numbers into proportional policy outcomes or to leverage collaboration across minority groups. The analysis of ideas in Chapter 5 shows how various groups interpret problems and appraise solutions. This analysis also points to a fundamental disconnect between the problems emphasized by racial and ethnic minorities and the solutions that constitute the dominant "policy talk." Understanding the role that institutions play within the education policy arena, particularly the role of the courts, sheds light on these unanswered questions. Our analysis of institutions underscores the ways in which institutions shape interests and influence which ideas gain ground. The persistence of these institutional effects over time is a critical factor in determining the effectiveness of subsequent efforts to bring about policy change.

Analyzing the Institutional Context of Education Politics

In particular, the analysis of the institutional context in our four study cities can lead to the following:

- The understanding of how interests emerge. As explained more fully below, court orders or consent decrees in large part determined the membership of coalitions by defining the "problems" and the "victims" in each city.
- The understanding of which ideas dominate the policy arena. To a great degree, the courts in each city shaped the possible solution sets considered, in addition to how groups defined education problems.
- The understanding of the persistence of the status quo despite changing conditions. To varying degrees in our cities, older ideas about education problems persisted, and older coalitions remained ensconced even though new school constituencies emerged and held different ideas about education problems. Court rulings and processes reflected an earlier consensus among interests over particular ideas. Like other institutions, they had the effect of preserving this consensus and previous understandings.
- Attentiveness to institutional change signals likely sites of conflict among interests and ideas. In each city, some degree of institutional change emerged as desegregation orders were removed.

Thus, recognizing and assessing the impact of the institutional primacy of the courts in earlier rounds of education reform is an important part of our story. In addition, contemporary education reform ideas are rooted in institutional arguments about school districts. Charter schools and voucher programs are the two most notable examples. Each seeks to remove a school from its traditional institutional framework by changing the nature of the governance structure, the process by which students are selected to attend the school, and the standards and processes by which the school will be held accountable. Proponents of such reforms argue that a problematic institutional framework is at the heart of contemporary school failures. John Chubb and Terry Moe in 1990 set the framework for the discussion of voucher plans throughout the nation. The basis of their argument for vouchers was an institutional analysis:

> Although everyone wants good schools, and although these institutions are highly sensitive and responsive to what people want, they naturally and routinely function to generate just the opposite—providing a context in which the organizational foundations of effective academic performance cannot flourish or take root. (2)

According to Chubb and Moe, the key institutional challenge for schools lies in the entrenched and unyielding bureaucracy that was built by those seeking to shape and control the schools. As a new idea or program was developed, those who were trying to implement it also established means of guaranteeing compliance and measuring its success or failure by further bureaucratizing schools. As Chubb and Moe write,

> Whatever the technological and intellectual arguments against bureaucracy may be, and however frustrated people from all walks of life may be with the unworkable constraints under which schools are forced to operate, virtually all are driven to pursue their own goals by adding to the bureaucracy problem. (47)

Chubb and Moe's solution to bureaucracy and to other seemingly intractable problems facing schools is to discard the traditional structure of public education in favor of one that rewards schools that succeed with students who carry with them public dollars for tuition and punishes schools that fail with closure. This system of rewards and punishments relies on a market-based concept of schooling with students as consumers of a good that can be realized by a variety of methods.

It is not our intent to argue for or against voucher systems or the logic of the market analogy applied to schools. What we do want to convey is that Chubb and Moe's call for vouchers, and other reformers' support for the proliferation of charter systems throughout the country, in fact make institutional arguments. By shaking up or tearing down the traditional institutional arrangement of schools, they hypothesize that positive change in educational attainment will occur.

In what follows, we trace the institutional context that shaped the struggles for education reform in the four cities. After a brief summary of institutional theory, we apply institutional analysis to the education policymaking arena in the cities, demonstrating the important roles played by institutions in structuring and channeling education reform interests and ideas over the past decades.

Institutionalism and Education

The proliferation of institutional challenges to the organization of schools led the Politics of Education Association to dedicate their 1995 Yearbook to the issue of institutions, entitled "The Politics of Education and the New Institutionalism: Reinventing the American School." The editors of the yearbook argued the importance of institutions to the study of education:

> The central importance of the new institutionalism for educators is that it re-establishes a special interest in the political and social significance of institutions while it simultaneously warns that the reform movement in education must address some 'deep structure' issues in the organization of schooling and in relationships between the schools and the larger society. (Crowson, Boyd, and Mawhinney 1996, 2)

Indeed, it seems that attempts at reform in the 1990s, such as voucher plans or charter schools, addressed the "deep structure" issues by opting out of the traditional organizational framework of schools altogether and allowing students and their families to exercise an option to leave their neighborhood school. The traditional framework of schools was thus seen as a force that limits improved academic achievement or attempts at reform. Proponents of both charter and voucher schools contend that the increased competition created by the resultant market-like system will drive the schools within the traditional institutional frameworks to improve. However, in attempts to address the problems within the organizational framework of schools, reform efforts almost universally ignored the "political and social significance of institutions" by too often not working to imbed solutions within the institutional framework. Thus, these solutions were vulnerable to minor changes within the political and social context of education policy making.

The Institutional Structure of Schooling

Our analysis focuses on the system level rather than the school level.[1] In particular, we focus on the role of the courts, state governments, and school board as most critical in shaping education policy outcomes. Adding to the complexity of developing an understanding of the impact of institutions and education reform is the fact that dozens of different approaches to the study of institutions exist. According to Walter W. Powell and Paul J. DiMaggio (1991, 3),

> There are, in fact, many new institutionalisms—in economics, organization theory, political science and public choice, history, and sociology—united by little but a common skepticism toward atomistic

accounts of social processes and a common conviction that institutional arrangements and social processes matter.

Each of these strands of institutional theory speaks in some way to understanding the institutional structure of schooling. However, for simplicity, we choose to focus on only one strand of theory—the positive political theory of institutions—noting where possible the links to other theories.

As Powell and DiMaggio (1991, 5) state, "The positive theory of institutions is concerned with political decision making, especially the ways in which political structures [or institutions] shape political outcomes." Institutions within this theoretical framework can be defined as "rules, procedures and arrangements" through which decision making occurs (Shepsle 1986). Some scholars within positive theory prefer to focus only on formal institutions, such as written and enforceable rules (Krehbiel 1992). Others note the role played in decision making by informal institutions, such as norms and standards (Moe 1987). Here we discuss formal and informal institutions and their relationship to outcomes in education policymaking and reform efforts.

At the heart of this analysis is the belief that within the education policymaking process, institutions—both formal and informal—shape the political and social context in which ideas and interests compete for attention and acceptance. At times, institutions are the legacy of previous ideas and debates over education reform and policy. They serve to privilege the ideas and interests that were prominent during their creation, often to the exclusion of current ideas and interests. Institutions are also remarkably resilient: Powell and DiMaggio (1991, 6) state that they are "resistant in the short run to political pressures, and in the long run, systematically constraining the options decision makers are free to pursue." Institutions articulate working agreements on what can and can't be done, how reforms will be implemented, and how costs and benefits are to be distributed (Hudson 1995).

Just as cities and communities differ from one another across the nation, so too does the context of education policymaking. Education policymaking is embedded in both a societal environment and also a specific institutional environment. Both are important factors in shaping the outcomes of the policymaking process and work to shape and reinforce the other. James G. Cibulka (Cibulka 1996, 10) describes the societal environment as providing

the overall context for institutional actors. Frequently, there is little or nothing they can do to alter these societal forces. At best they can hope to anticipate and perceive how changes in this societal environment will impact on the institution, and act accordingly. Some examples of exogenous societal changes which have profoundly reshaped American's public schools are the Cold War, the globalization of the economy, decline of traditional family structures, diversification of the population, suburbanization, and increasing individualism.

By contrast, the institutional environment is the place where stakeholders lay claim to outcomes of the education process. Such stakeholders include "producers, consumers, students, taxpayers, interested citizens, as well as social, economic, and political elites. . . . Perhaps the most important are governmental institutions such as bureaucratic regulators, the courts, governmental funding sources and so on" (Cibulka 1996, 11).

In fact, one of the most striking characteristics of the arena of education policymaking is its accessibility to its stakeholders. There are multitudes of access points for stakeholders to use to influence the policymaking process. At its heart, the process of education policymaking is a true example of policymaking in a federal system. Institutional actors include stakeholders at the federal level, such as the, Congress, the Supreme Court, and the Department of Education; stakeholders at the state level, such as governors, legislatures, courts, state school boards, and state departments of education; and stakeholders at the local level, such as mayors, city councils, local school boards, superintendents, principals, and teachers. Furthermore, many stakeholders exert influence across a number of different levels of government. Examples of these stakeholders include parent organizations such as the PTA; teacher unions; specific interest groups that support particular programs in the schools, such as special education and interests groups who are pursuing a larger agenda, such as the Christian Coalition.

The difficulty of characterizing the role of these stakeholders resides in the fact that the institutions that shape the interactions between the stakeholders vary dramatically from city to city and state to state. In some cities, some of the time, school boards play an active and engaged role in decision making, channeling community involvement. In others, the city government is actively involved. Furthermore, the state context varies dramatically as well. Some states provide active leadership and oversight to local school districts by mandating a set of statewide standards and assessment tools. Other states leave a tremendous amount of discretion to the local districts. The four cities described below varied a great deal along these lines. However, three of our four cities shared the characteristic of having the court as an engaged institutional actor for extended periods of time.

Boston, Denver, Los Angeles, and San Francisco

Boston, Denver, Los Angeles, and San Francisco—like other multiethnic cities across the United States—are embedded in an institutional context in which the courts have played a major role. Desegregation court orders and consent decrees controlled and shaped the educational landscape for decades by defining the options and goals for education reform efforts and the membership among various interest groups. To a large extent, the story of each of these cities is a story of a strong institution—the desegregation court order or consent decree—and ultimately the collapse of that institution, that is, the vacating of the desegregation case. In this way, our cities serve not only as individual case studies of multiethnic cities struggling toward education reform. Given that each of these cities was at one point at the forefront of defining desegregation efforts in the United States, their stories also reflect and illustrate the larger trend toward what Gary Orfield and Susan Eaton (1996) call "dismantling desegregation." We see this process as a core element of the multiethnic moment at which various outcomes are possible in a postdesegregation era.

The attempts at desegregation in these cities share a common beginning: The desegregation cases were a response to the inequitable treatment of African American students within the districts. Initially, the cases explicitly addressed the status of African Americans to the exclusion of other ethnic groups, namely Latinos and Asian Americans. In Denver, Latinos became a formal party to the suit in the mid-1980s when numerous complaints about the status of bilingual students and programs were brought before the judge overseeing the desegregation case. In response to a request from the Denver Public Schools to vacate the desegregation order in 1984, Federal District Judge Richard Matsch ruled that the district was not doing enough to address the needs of limited–English proficiency students and upheld the desegregation case.

Neither Latinos nor Asians have been a formal party to the desegregation order in San Francisco. In 1993, Latinos and Asian Americans petitioned to become formal parties to the consent decree in San Francisco. Their petition was denied, although the judge did grant them amicus status and gave them the right to nominate participants for the Committee of Experts. In three of our four cities—Denver, Los Angeles, and Boston—Latino students outnumber African Americans. In Denver and Los Angeles, Latinos are the largest ethnic group in public schools and in Boston, Latinos are the second largest ethnic group among enrolled students. In San Francisco, Latinos are second to Asian Americans as the largest student group.

Supreme Court rulings of the 1980s and 1990s weakened efforts to desegregate across the nation. In *Riddick v. School Board of the City of Norfolk, Virginia* (1986), the court found that a school district could be released from its responsibility to desegregate once it was declared "unitary." Critics of the decision claim that the definition of unitary and the required duration of being unitary was ambiguous and could lead to school districts being turned back to local government control before desegregation took hold. For example, in *Board of Education of Oklahoma v. Dowell* (1991), the court upheld a decision by the Oklahoma School District Board to implement an attendance plan based on neighborhood schools even though this would result in segregation. Because the district had once been found to be unitary by a federal district court it was no longer obligated to desegregate its schools.

In *Freeman v. Pitts* (1992), the Supreme Court found that under certain circumstances school districts could be released from their desegregation plans even if integration had not been achieved in specific areas. And in *Missouri v. Jenkins* (1995), the Supreme Court ruled that remedies "should be limited in time and extent and that school districts need not show any actual correction of the education harms of segregation" (Orfield et al. 1996, xxiii). Gary Orfield (1996, 4), a noted scholar of desegregation and the court, concludes,

> Under *Dowell, Pitts* and *Jenkins*, school districts need not prove actual racial equality, or a narrowing of academic gaps between the races. Desegregation remedies can even be removed when achievement gaps between the races have widened, or even if a district has never fully implemented an effective desegregation plan. Formalistic compliance for a time with some limited requirements was enough, even if the roots of racial inequality were untouched.

Indeed, in cities such as Norfolk, Oklahoma City, Cleveland, and Kansas City, school districts were released from their desegregation plans and responsibilities. All three of our cities with a history of strong court involvement—Boston, Denver, and San Francisco—also had their desegregation court orders vacated in the 1990s.

Some analysts find that the involvement of the court meant that school boards did not play an active and engaged role in Boston, Denver, Los Angeles, and San Francisco. Although it would seem logical that the elected institution of a school board would play a primary role in the formulation of educational policy, our research and the research of others suggests that this was not the case. Fredrick Wirt and Michael Kirst (2001) concluded that "the unstated implication of many reports is that the school boards are part of the problem and have not exercised leadership and authority to improve education" (143) and that "local school boards have seemed to be either ignored or cast in a passive role as weak reactors or even deterrents, rather than partners, in shaping educational improvement" (144). In each the four cities, the school boards indeed played largely a reactive role in the 1990s. In a sense, the institution of the school board and its governing structure was trumped by the ongoing activity of the institution of the court.

Across the nation, however, state legislatures and governors assumed a larger role in education policymaking. This new activist role occurred partly because an increasing share of the state's own tax dollars were being used to fund education. However, nationwide initiatives like Goals 2000 and systemic education reform instigated statewide standards that were often tied to high-stakes testing. Nearly all states engaged in formulating statewide standards, although there was tremendous variation as to the prescriptiveness of each state's program and its implementation timeline.

We now turn to a discussion of each city's institutional context, emphasizing the role of the court, the school board, and the state-level actors. In three of our four cities, we witness a story primarily of an activist court that delineated the educational policy arena for decades.

Boston

Boston's formal effort to desegregate the public schools began on June 21, 1974, when Federal District Judge W. Arthur Garrity found that the Boston School Committee, a governing body,and the school department had knowingly engaged in a systematic program of segregation. Tallulah Morgan and other plaintiffs brought the initial 1972 case that charged that the city failed to implement a 1965 "racial imbalance" law that required all cities to manage school assignments so that no school enrolled more than 50 percent nonwhite students. Garrity's 1974 remedy ordered the state board of education to draw up a massive busing plan—the Phase I plan—involving thousands of students but limited to certain geographical areas. Garrity's decision sparked weeks of unrest among Boston's residents.

The Phase I plan was only in effect for one school year. In a Phase II plan, Garrity ordered the school committee to create a desegregation plan that would balance each school in the city so that it paralleled the racial composition of the city schools overall. After the school committee failed to reach an agreement, a panel of court-appointed experts devised a plan, which divided the city into eight geographical districts with hundreds of small "geocodes." In 1978, approximately 41 percent of the students were bused. By 1985 that percentage had risen to nearly 56 percent. The increase is attributed in some part to the fact that the judge also ordered the closure of twenty-two neighborhood schools.

In 1982, Garrity began to relinquish some control over the day-to-day monitoring of the district. However, Robert Spillane, Boston's school superintendent, continued to accuse Garrity of running the Boston city schools like "his private plantation." In 1989, Garrity approved a controlled-choice plan to replace court-ordered busing and he issued his final orders on racial guidelines for school district employment in 1990. The controlled choice plan put the 74 elementary schools and 19 middle schools in three geographic attendance zones and allowed parents to prioritize school choices within their zone, but did not guarantee placement. However, in the summer of 1999, Boston School officials overturned the controlled choice plan in the wake of a lawsuit brought by the parents of a white child who had been denied admission to the prestigious Boston Latin School. In a 5-to-2 vote, the school committee adopted a race-blind admissions policy in the fall of 2000, signaling the end of major desegregation efforts and a return to neighborhood schooling.

In Boston, the Boston School Committee oversaw education. Its form and structure has changed many times. In 1984, a thirteen-member committee, consisting of nine members elected by district and four members elected at large, replaced a five-member governing board elected at large. In 1992, the structure was again changed, giving the mayor the power to appoint all seven committee members. The committee has long been criticized for "political infighting, racial discord, and fiscal mismanagement" (Portz 1996, 10). A 1989 decision to approve a controlled-choice busing plan illustrates the racial divisions prominent on the board. The 9-to-4 vote to approve the plan was divided by race, with all four black members voting against the plan. As John Portz (1996) reports, in the following year a 7-to-1 vote to oust black superintendent Laval Wilson occurred only after all four black members of the committee walked out in protest.

The Boston School Committee was also limited in its power by the fiscal relationship that the school district had with the city government. While the committee and the district control the allocation of resources within the school budget, the mayor and the city council set the total appropriation. Not surprisingly, this division often resulted in great tension between the district and the city. For example, at the end of the 1980s the district ended every year with a budget deficit, requiring a last minute appropriation from the mayor and the city council (Portz 1994, 11).

The state context of Massachusetts is also important. As in Denver and the California cities, a state initiative limiting local government's ability to raise property taxes went into effect during this same period. In Massachusetts, Proposition 2 1/2 lead to significant cuts in public services, including education, in the early 1980s. In 1993, the state legislature passed an education reform act that provided new roles for superintendents and principals, publicly supported charter schools outside the control of local school boards, expanded school choice across districts, statewide testing, a common core of learning, and a new state education aid formula to improve equalization of resources across districts (Portz 1994).

In sum, as John Portz (1996, 15) reports, " Judge Garrity issued over four hundred orders involving school closings, student assignments, personnel hiring, textbook adoption, community partnerships, and a host of other school matters." Portz writes:

> The court fundamentally reorganized the system, closed schools, and designed a new assignment plan; furthermore, the court pushed businesses, higher education institutions, community organizations, and parents to become more involved in the Boston Public Schools. (Portz, 1996, 15)

In assuming such a major role in Boston, the court as an institution actively structured the context in which parties interested in education reform functioned. Portz reports, "The agenda for educational change was set in the federal courthouse rather than the school department or a community setting" (6). Instead of working to build coalitions and negotiate differences, parties pursued their interests through the court. Thus, the court became the institution through which ideas about education reform or change were funneled, as well as the mechanism that structured coalitions.

Denver

The Supreme Court ruling in *Keyes v. Denver School District* (1973) set what many people in Denver believed to be the institutional context of educational politics for over thirty years. *Keyes* was a monumental decision because it was the first desegregation ruling on school segregation in the North and West and, more importantly, it found that "school districts were responsible for policies that resulted in racial segregation in the school system, including constructing schools in racially isolated neighborhoods and gerrymandering attendance zones" (xxii).

Eight black families in the integrated Park Hill neighborhood who feared that school boundary changes would resegregate local schools originally brought the *Keyes* case. At the time of the suit, the student body was 64 percent white, 21 percent Latino, and 14 percent African American. Despite the fact that Latinos made up a larger portion of the student body, the initial *Keyes* case focused primarily on the needs of black students. The Court found in 1973 that Denver's practices of drawing school boundaries had effectively labeled schools by race and thus was "affecting the racial makeup of neighborhoods throughout the city's housing market" (Orfield and Eaton 1996, 295).

In 1974, busing began for nearly a quarter of the district's eighty-five thousand students. Denver was the only district with court-ordered desegregation in Colorado. While 54 percent of the district enrollment was white in 1974, by the late 1990s it was less than one-third white. The tensions surrounding the school desegregation case in the early 1970s, and the consequent busing order, prompted the passage of a state constitutional amendment in 1974 that requires voter approval of any annexations to the city of Denver. This contributed to the inelasticity of Denver's economic base and protected the suburban white populations from involvement in busing. Furthermore, in 1974, voters approved a constitutional amendment prohibiting busing or assigning students for "the purpose of racial balance." After that time, Denver instituted numerous reforms, such as magnet schools and bilingual programs, along with mandatory busing, to comply with this order.

As noted in Chapter 3, the Denver Public Schools District (DPS) appealed to Federal District Judge Richard Matsch on several occasions for release from the desegregation order on the grounds that it had met its desegregation responsibilities. In 1984, Matsch refused the request, ruling that the district had not met the needs of bilingual students. An agreement between the district and the Congress of Hispanic Educators led to the formation of guidelines for the creation of a bilingual program. In 1985, after Matsch ordered the district to improve integration at three elementary schools, the district developed a plan for magnet schools. In 1993, DPS again petitioned for release from the court order. On September 12, 1995, the request was granted. Matsch wrote in his decision that although differences in test scores, discipline, and program participation continued to exist, the differences "are long-standing and intractable. The mere existence of such differences does not identify them as vestiges from the dual system existing 25 years ago. There are too many variables, including societal and socioeconomic factors."

Beginning with the 1997/98 school year, students within the DPS no longer were bused across the city. Manual High School, once thought of as an example of integration in DPS, pulled almost all its students from the surrounding poor neighborhoods. As a 1997 article in the Denver *Westword* reported, Gordon Greiner, the attorney who represented black families in *Keyes*, claimed that Manual will "clearly become a segregated school, with all the trappings that seems to bring." Greiner went on to claim that "the political tenor of integration changed. Neighborhood schools are what are politically popular" (Witcher 1997).

One year after the end of busing and the subsequent move to neighborhood schools, one third of the district's eighty-four elementary schools had minority populations of at least 90 percent (Illescas 1997b). Manual High's population changed from 54 percent black and Hispanic students in 1996 to 92 percent in 1997, with over three-quarters of the students qualifying for subsidized lunch programs (Illescas 1997a, 16A). But many parents argued that this shift was not so significant, because the busing era's integration program only masked the classroom-level segregation of white students in advanced courses and students of color in special education and remedial courses (Hendrie 1998).

The Denver School Board, long plagued by divisions over the desegregation decision, historically had been a largely dormant player in education policymaking. The six-member board exists independently of city and county government and was until 1992 elected entirely at large. At that time, the state legislature voted to organize the election of the Denver School Board along district lines so that minority representation might be enhanced. In past years, the desegregation case seemed to pervade all decisions about education reform. In fact, due in large part to the disagreement about the case at the school board level, respondents in our study reported that it was as if the school board's hands were tied with regard to education reform.

A 1997 decision of the board—authorizing the superintendent to identify schools that consistently failed to produce students who tested at minimum standards for their own grade level and to replace the principals and teaching staffs—was by far one of the most forward thinking of the board's decisions made during the period under study. This decision to institute a reconstitution process similar to San Francisco was deemed to be quite small in scope and had yet to have a major impact on education policy in Denver as we analyzed it. The mayor at the time, Wellington Webb, established the Mayor's Office for Education and Children, pulling several agencies related to education and youth—including the liaison to DPS—under one roof. Both moves underscored the weak role of the Denver School Board as an institutional player in both the integration and postintegration eras.

In the late-1990s, Colorado instituted a system of statewide standards that each district was required to adopt. Additionally, statewide assessments were also under development. While each district determines how to implement the standards, many in this "frontier" state were uncomfortable with the imposition of standards in the first place. As described in Chapter 3, in 1991, Governor Roy Romer established Collaborative Decision Making Committees (CDMs) at each school site and granted them authority for day-to-day school management. In decentralizing decision making, CDMs removed key responsibilities from the school board and the central administration and placed them in the hands of the school-based committees. But some critics reported that school site officials such as principals or other strong personalities often dominate this new institutional arena. Inexperience in running collaborative processes or declining interest on the part of various participants meant many CDMs became more of a rubber-stamping process than an actual way to generate school-specific ideas for improvement.

Los Angeles

The Los Angeles Unified School District (LAUSD) encompasses nearly all of the City of Los Angeles as well as parts of twenty-seven other cities. In addition to crossing multiple city and municipal jurisdictions, the LAUSD is also unique from our other districts in that it is over ten times larger and it operates 722 K–12 schools. The LAUSD has been the site of notable education reforms, including the 1968 *Serrano v. Priest* lawsuit by LAUSD parents to end inequalities in state-based per-pupil spending.

In 1970, the LAUSD also came under the jurisdiction of a court desegregation order. In February 1970, Superior Court Judge Alfred Gitelson ruled that the LAUSD deliberately perpetuated segregation. He ordered districtwide integration and stipulated that each school have the same ethnic enrollment as the district at large. The Los Angeles Board of Education appealed the ruling in 1972, arguing that it would divert education funds to busing and that desegregation stemmed from housing patterns rather than board policy. The NAACP attempted to circumvent this appeal in 1974 by filing a desegregation suit in federal court. In 1976, the California Supreme Court upheld Gitelson's

1970 decision but relaxed the school enrollment criteria. The Los Angeles Superior Court was given authority to approve an integration plan in compliance with the ruling.

The Los Angeles School Board was embroiled in integration conflicts throughout the 1970s. As in Denver, the School Board resisted large-scale busing and catapulted members into recall elections, eventually prompting a move to district-based board elections. Locked in conflict with the courts and its constituents over how to deal with integration, the board eventually supported three years of mandatory busing until, in 1980, state voters passed Proposition 1, a state constitutional amendment to limit mandatory integration. In response, the LAUSD adopted a voluntary integration plan that included magnet schools. Although its actions were always in response to court pressures, the board eventually developed an all-voluntary desegregation plan that focused on Asians and Latinos as well as blacks, and, in 1986, a bilingual education program.

While issues of segregation and integration continued to make their way to the top of the District's agenda from time to time, the courts in Los Angeles played a significant but limited role early in the integration struggle. Thus, the courts in Los Angeles have been a less strong institutional player than in our other cities, one shaping some ideas for education reform and structuring some interests into working coalitions. This is in marked contrast to the consistent and ongoing role of the court in Boston, Denver, and San Francisco.

San Francisco

The San Francisco Unified School District (SFUSD) has the same geographic and political boundaries as the city-county. The school system is incorporated independently; with the limits of its charter from the state, it can collect its own revenues. Struggles over school segregation go back to 1947 when Governor Earl Warren repealed California laws that segregated Asian and Mexican American children. They continued through the 1960s with pressures from African American organizations and other civic organizations to address *de facto* segregation within the school district. A lawsuit challenging public school segregation was brought in 1970 and again in 1978 by black plaintiffs and the local chapter of the NAACP. Filed in federal district court, the 1978 suit charged both the local district and the state with concentrating students and faculty of certain racial groups in specific schools, the underrepresentation of African Americans among teachers and administrators, and African Americans' unequal treatment in and access to both academic and after-school programs.

In 1981, the court made certain findings of fact and appointed a "Settlement Team" comprised of the parties to the suit and educational experts appointed by the court. In 1983, the SFUSD entered into a consent decree that brought the end to a desegregation challenge by the NAACP. The San Francisco Consent Decree had two major goals. The first was to eliminate racial/ethnic segregation or identifiability in the district's schools or programs by stipulating that all schools must include four of nine recognized ethnic groups, and that no single group should exceed 45 percent of a school's enrollment. The nine groups identified were "Spanish-surname, Other White, African-American, Chinese, Japanese, Korean, Filipino, American Indian, and Other Non-White." The guidelines were even stricter for alternative and magnet schools, including the prestigious college preparatory high school, Lowell. Enrollment of any one group at these schools could not exceed 40 percent. These provisions led to a complex process by which students and parents were able to choose which schools to attend within these broad outlines.

The second goal of the consent decree was to achieve academic excellence throughout the district. These broad goals laid the framework through which the strategy of school improvement called reconstitution was born. Reconstitution gave the district the ability to remove a school's administrators and teachers and replace them with other personnel committed to the philosophical tenets established in the consent decree. Reconstitution also included setting specific student outcome goals at each grade level, improving the technology available at the school site, allowing for more small group instruction, enriching the staff through development programs, and selecting a unique instructional focus for each reconstituted school.

The initial consent decree limited implementation to six schools, called Phase One schools, in the Bayview–Hunters Point area, which was populated primarily by African Americans. Subsequent phases included other schools, but the implementation of reconstitution was not as thorough in these schools as it was in Phase One schools. In 1992, a Committee of Experts appointed by the court (chaired by Professor Gary Orfield) found that the goal of school-building desegregation had largely been achieved. They found that gains in achievement had occurred primarily in Phase One schools and to a lesser degree in the other schools involved in subsequent phases.

Asian Americans challenged the consent decree in the early 1990s. At issue was the decree's ruling that the student body of an alternative school could not be comprised of more than 40 percent of any single ethnicity grouping. Reminiscent of the struggle over a white student's denial of admission to the Boston Latin School, critics claimed that Chinese students were denied admission to Lowell High School although they scored higher on the admission criteria than students from other racial/ethnic groups who were admitted. Thus, attorneys representing Chinese parents and students claimed that the admissions policies discriminated against Chinese students on the basis of their ethnicity by turning away high-performing Chinese students in favor of lower-performing students from other racial or ethnic groups.

Attorney Daniel Girard brought a suit on behalf of the Chinese students in June of 1994. In filing the suit, *Ho v. SFUSD*, he argued that the district, by agreeing to the consent decree, was never actually found in violation of *Brown*. Girard went on to argue that even if the district was once in violation, that the

Committee of Expert's report of 1992 showed that it no longer was. Thus, Girard believed that the district should be released from the decree. Judge William Orrick, who had presided over the decree since its inception, rejected Girard's claim. In his ruling, Judge Orrick wrote that it was true that desegregation orders must be terminated when their goals have been met, but that he was not persuaded that the goals had been met in San Francisco. Amy Chang of the Asian American Legal Foundation was quoted as saying in reaction to the Judge's decision, "We consider the decision today to be anti-progressive. The SFUSD, the state, and the NAACP have put themselves in the same position as George Wallace in the early 1960s—they are saying quotas then, quotas now, and quotas forever" (Schwartz 1997). Nearly two years later, in February of 1999, the judge and San Francisco school officials agreed to stop using race and ethnicity as determining factors in assigning students to schools as a way of bringing the *Ho* case to a final conclusion. The 1999 settlement in effect drew the district's desegregation plan to closure by 2005.

In San Francisco, the school board—elected at large—played a largely supportive role. The court consent decree named the district as a primary actor within the consent-decree process. For nearly ten years after its initial implementation, the school board exercised its superintendent appointment power in such a way as to limit the scope of the district's involvement. In 1992, with the selection of Superintendent Rojas, the board demonstrated greater support for the decree and its reconstitution process. However, beyond the appointment of Rojas and its general appointment power, the school board had assumed the role of a passive monitoring council voting at times on resolutions that were small in scope.

In California, the governor and the state legislature have been quite active in establishing statewide curricular frameworks and assessment tools. However, San Francisco applied—or sued for and won—exemption from many of the state requirements. In doing so, the SFUSD pointed to the consent decree or other court cases that they claimed prevented them from adhering to the governor's initiative on statewide testing. However, San Francisco did take advantage of Governor Pete Wilson's initiative to decrease class sizes in the early years of elementary school.

San Francisco has been somewhat of a renegade district in the state. Each time the state voters pass a proposition out of line with the district's philosophy of educating all of San Francisco's children, the district went to court to block its implementation in the district. In large part, they were successful in blocking the implementation of testing all students in English, the ending of bilingual education programs, and not educating the children of undocumented families. In each instance, the district pointed to the legal requirements established by the consent decree and other relevant court cases as justification for exemption.

The Evolving Role of Institutions in Education

Substantial changes occurred in each of our cities throughout the 1980s and 1990s. In each school system, the percentage of African American and white students continued to decline at the same time that the percentage of Latino students was growing. In the case of San Francisco, the percentage of both Latino and Asian students grew at a very fast pace. At the same time that these districts were experiencing increased levels of ethnic and racial diversity, the role of the federal courts in Boston, Denver, and San Francisco diminished. In contrast, it is possible that the state courts will still be significant in the future development of education issues in Los Angeles, although it must be noted that the court had not been a major player in educational politics during much of the 1990s. How might these changes—that is, the increased diversity coincident with a decline in the role of the courts as a primary institutional actor—affect the configuration of ideas, interests, and institutions? We suggest that the removal of the courts as an active agent affecting educational politics and policymaking could result in any of three distinct scenarios.

Three Scenarios

First, it is possible that education policymaking will largely reflect the same configuration that occurred during the period of active court involvement. As we argued earlier, the interests of certain stakeholders and the ideas that drive their understandings of education policy can achieve near permanent status when organized programmatically within specific institutional configurations. A privileging of interests and ideas can be a desired outcome by those whose visions of educational policy seem to characterize the operation of schools and the education of students. Specific solution sets may be privileged in their continued presence in school politics and policymaking. It is also possible that the institutionalization that characterizes these solution sets leads to long-term patterns of political socialization among newer stakeholders. In this case, although demographics of student enrollment and the role of specific institutions may change, the old patterns of influence in decision making are largely accepted by new stakeholders.

A second possibility is that major changes in the configuration of ideas, interests, and institutions, such as the withdrawal of court involvement, will result in the resurgence of powerful traditional sources of influence in education politics and policymaking. If, for example, the role of the courts compensated for the limited access that certain segments of the population had to education policymaking, court withdrawal might lead to a precourt pattern where the interests of these segments of the population return to marginal status. Among the traditional sources of influence would be the superintendent of the district, the school board, and teachers' unions. These stakeholders in education policy have every incentive to reassert their influence when opportunity arises. Their individual successes, and their constituencies' successes, may become more likely when court intervention is no longer present. Each stakeholder certainly has much to gain by dominating any new configuration of ideas, interests, and institutions. Why not work to reestablish a configuration that seemed to work well for them in the past?

Lastly, it also seems possible that the future of education politics and policymaking in this scenario of reduced court involvement might lead to an undetermined future, at least in the short term. No clear winners and losers would immediately emerge from this major change in the presence of institutions. In this case, a clear contestation among distinct interests—largely unrelated to previous policy cleavages—may emerge, with each interest also contesting for domination of the ideas that will guide educational policymaking. Previously successful strategies of influencing educational outcomes may not work in the new environment. New policy options that were not previously considered seriously may have enhanced potential for success. A call for a district-wide system of vouchers or advocacy of the elimination of bilingual education may now be more seriously considered than before. The likely success of adopting these proposals, however, may be unclear. State-level actors such as the governor or the state legislature may be more active than before in directing educational policy. It is also possible that groups marginalized within previous institutional configurations now find themselves developing innovative policy options that may have a greater probability of adoption than before. This assumes, of course, that these groups either possess or can develop the necessary resources to better influence the course of educational policy.

Which of these scenarios best captures recent educational politics and policymaking in our cities? What configuration of ideas, interests, and institutions seems to be emerging as a result of the removal of a very significant institutional actor?

Three Scenarios in Four Multiethnic Cities

Boston

Latinos continue to be the fastest growing segment of students enrolled in the Boston Public Schools. In the 1999/2000 school year, African Americans comprised 49 percent of all students enrolled, Latinos 11 percent, whites 15 percent, Asians 9 percent, and Native Americans under 1 percent (Boston Public Schools 2000). Stated differently, 85 percent of the students then enrolled in the Boston Public Schools were racial and ethnic minorities. When Judge Garrity originally issued his call for the desegregation of schools in 1974, minority enrollment was 48 percent.

The elimination of the use of race to assign students to Boston's most prestigious public school, Boston Latin, resulted from the case of *Wessman v.*

Gittens (1999). In this decision, the district court ruled unconstitutional the policy of trying to attain levels of racial integration at this school that more closely approximated overall district enrollment than would occur through the use of standardized and other test scores alone. A white student whose scores were higher than those of some admitted African American students brought the suit. Significantly, this decision represented a withdrawal of the court from what had been one of the most active instances of federal intervention in the oversight and implementation of a court order mandating desegregation. And, notably, the response of African American leaders was not substantial; perhaps this reflects acquiescence to the changing nature of federal law in this area.

Throughout this period, city and school leadership was remarkably stable: Superintendent Payzant and Mayor Menino came into office in the mid-1990s and remain there a decade later. As the court retreated, conflict reflecting race and class divisions over student assignment policies shifted to the school board. City councilors and the mayor also weighed in with their views on neighborhood schools vs. "choice." The district developed a "controlled choice" plan begun in the 2000/2001 school year that divided the city into three attendance zones. Half of the seats in every school were reserved for students who lived within walking distance, and half were for students living within the larger zone. Parents submitted their top choices and a lottery was held to assign students. But the School Committee revisited this policy in 2004 as it came under pressure from various constituencies.

Some complained that students were squeezed out of desirable schools in their neighborhoods while other schools had vacancies, some wanted to reduce transportation costs as the district's budget became more constrained (Vaishnav and Talcott 2003). When a new K–8 school opened in the predominantly minority Roxbury section, 75 percent of the seats could be reserved for walkers in recognition of the decades in which Roxbury had no elementary school within walking distance. Parents in the affluent West Roxbury neighborhood responded by asking why schools in their neighborhoods could not also reserve most seats for local students (Tench 2003). And residents of Back Bay and Beacon Hill, the city's wealthiest neighborhoods, raised millions of dollars to buy and renovate a building so that they could have a public school in their neighborhood (Bombardieri 2002).

The school committee appointed a task force of parents and educators to solicit community opinions, to study the issue, and to recommend changes. A predominantly white parents group, Walk 2 School, emerged to support a return to neighborhood schools, while a racially diverse group led by parents of color, Work 4 Quality, argued for improvements in quality across the district's schools before they would support further shifts to neighborhood schools (Naimark 2004; Tench 2004). The court was not entirely ignored; Work 4 Quality leaders threatened to challenge in court any new policy that resulted in increased segregation. Several city councilors offered plans that emphasized neighborhood schools, and the mayor made clear his preference for a change in the current practice (Reilly 2004). In September 2004, the task force presented a six-zone option for elementary school and a three-zone option for middle schools, but the recommendations did not reflect a consensus of the group. The school committee ultimately decided to retain the existing plan and to create a quality work group to study how to create indicators of school quality that would help parents decide where to send their kids (Schwab 2005). The group presented their indicators in February 2005. According to one reporter, "It remains to be seen how the data will be used to improve the quality of schools, a key demand of parents during the student assignment forums" (Schwab 2005, 1A).

Latino leaders have been trying to better influence educational policy to serve their communities. Miren Uriarte and Lisa Chavez (2000), in a report entitled "Latino Students and the Massachusetts Public Schools" noted that Latinos have the highest dropout rates in the state and that they have the lowest rates of passing the Massachusetts Comprehensive Assessment System (MCAS) examination. Interestingly, the report does not recommend any specific changes in educational practice beyond the traditional approaches of having a diversity-sensitive curriculum, targeted initiatives, and an acknowledgement by educational practitioners that past efforts have not been successful in educating many of the state's Latinos. The situation in Boston is similar to that in the state as a whole. The Boston Public Schools contain the largest concentration of Latino students of any public school system in Massachussetts—17 percent of all Latino students in the state. The continued use of standardized testing to determine graduation and other elements of accomplishment in the public schools of Massachusetts could have a profound effect on Latinos.

Denver

As reported by the Denver Public Schools (DPS) in 1999, Latinos comprised 51 percent of all students enrolled, African Americans were 21 percent, Asians 3 percent, and whites 23 percent. As in previous years, Latinos remained the fastest growing group in the DPS (DPS 1999). The end of busing in Denver in 1997 foreshadowed the continued withdrawal of the federal courts from active engagement in educational policy. Three years after the end of the busing era, one of four Denver students chose to attend a school outside their neighborhood (Obmascik 1998). The schools attracting these students are characterized by high test scores and low poverty rates, suggesting the emergence of class-based segregation patterns.

As in Boston, Latinos in Denver have continued to search for new ways to influence educational policy and practice. Some of these leaders saw the arrival of Superintendent Chip Zullinger in 1999 as providing a new opportunity to have their interests served. Zullinger, for example, stated in November 1999,

"I think we have a [Latino] community that we have not done a good job with in making sure they have good access into our system. We need to come up with entirely new strategies to look at changing that" (Illescas 1999b). Zullinger also supported efforts to target developing better relations between schools and their surrounding communities, consistent with work supported by the Piton Foundation (Piton Foundation 2000). These efforts were consistent with the longer tradition in Denver of trying to use state-mandated CDMs.

Zullinger also pushed two changes in the DPS that led to considerable controversy. Early in his tenure he advocated that the district publish individual school "report cards." In these report cards, schools would be assessed in ways that provided the public with useful information. Parents would have the opportunity to use the information to assess the quality of education that their children received (Gottlieb 1999). Superintendent Zullinger also supported the application by the DPS for a federal grant worth "$3.3 million that allow[ed] Spanish-language instruction for five years before mainstreaming students, rather than three" (Hubler 2000a, B1). This was in direct opposition to the preferences of a number of board members who accused him of trying to revive a previously failed bilingual education program.

Within nine months of his hiring, the Denver School Board asked Zullinger to resign. Of the seven members on the board, the only two who wanted him to remain were Latino. Just prior to his resignation one commentator noted, "Several board members are beginning to say publicly what other administrators have been whispering for weeks and months—that Zullinger is a loose cannon who has given a sympathetic ear to several self-appointed activist groups, making promises that the governing board, top administrators and principals know nothing about" (Green 2000, B1). Similarly, *The Denver Post*, in an editorial dated May 14, 2000, criticized Zullinger, writing, "Community support is crucial. But it doesn't supercede the paramount obligation to actually supervise the district. And without a full understanding of the district, a commitment to clear communication, a team-building approach and clear direction, good management cannot exist" (2000, K4). Interestingly, Governor Owens, a Republican, counted among his major accomplishments of the legislative session the passage of a bill that would require all Colorado public schools to receive a letter grade indicative of measures of school performance (Brown 2000, A1).

As in Boston, recent experiences suggest that Latino leaders have yet to find the most effective means to access educational policymaking in Denver. They perhaps had an opportunity with Superintendent Zullinger, but his ouster made it very clear that the power of the school board was substantial. To the extent that some members of the board considered his apparent responsiveness to Latinos misguided, it is evident that the ideas that this community might offer for improving schools in Denver will have a hard time being given a full hearing. Zullinger's successor, Jerry Wartgow, initiated numerous changes, including raising twenty million dollars in a voter-approved school bond, using a decentralized community-based planning process to plan how the money would be spent to revitalize schools, implementing uniform curriculum and new literacy programming across the district, restructuring inside schools to create schools-within-schools at the high school level and K–8 programs elsewhere, and mandating that faculty at several poorly performing schools reapply for their jobs. But test scores have remained flat and community organizations complain of continuing inequity across schools, with poor and minority students experiencing overcrowding and unequal facilities and resources. One school was mandated by state law to be reconstituted as a charter school after three years of unsatisfactory performance, despite a slew of initiatives and a new reform-minded principal who was bilingual in Spanish and English. In 2005, a few others were at risk of similar fates.

Padres Unidos, a Latino organization, and its youth initiative, Jovenes Unidos, issued a report in March 2005 condemning the district for its disproportionate suspension, expulsion, and arrest of minority students. The report criticized school staff for removing students involved in "non-violent subjective offenses, such as verbal fights, obscenities, inappropriate clothing or bullying" (Poppen 2005a). A school board–commissioned task force on high schools issued a report in March 2005 criticizing central administration for being closed and uncommunicative, and calling for considerable decentralization of decision making to the principals. The task force was created as a school board response to data showing half of students who begin high school do not graduate. Their recommendations for school-based plans that introduce distinctive approaches at the school level contrasted with Wartgow's efforts to standardize curriculum over the past four years. Claiming a variety of family and personal reasons, Wartgow announced his resignation effective July 2005. Latino leaders quickly stated their desire to see DPS led by a Latino, pointing out that the district has a majority-Latino student population, and noting that low achievement levels and high dropout rates among Latino students are critical problems facing the district (Poppen 2005a). These demands were thwarted with the naming of Denver Mayor John Hickenlooper's Chief of Staff, a white male, as the new Superintendent of Schools.

San Francisco

On February 15, 1999, the parties in the case of *Brian Ho v. San Francisco Unified School District* (1999) concluded a settlement agreement that would permanently alter the role of the federal court as the primary catalyst of educational reform.[2] Two components of the agreement capture the magnitude of the changes in educational policy that were to occur. First, race and ethnicity could no longer be used to assign students to schools. Second, the consent decree was to be terminated by December 31, 2005.

Especially significant is that this suit was filed by plaintiffs of Chinese descent who successfully argued that the use of race to assign students to schools, in combination with the maximums of 40 to 45 percent enrollment that were mandated under the 1983 decree, violated their equal protection rights under the fourteenth Amendment. In other words, the Chinese plaintiffs prevailed in claiming that the basic provisions of the decree that worked to desegregate San Francisco's elementary, middle, and high schools were unconstitutional. Recent changes in federal law, as noted earlier, gave this argument great weight. Evidently, the plaintiffs felt that their interests, as Chinese, were not met by the desegregation consent decree.

When the 1983 decree was entered, African Americans were the largest group of students in the SFUSD. They constituted 23 percent of all students, with Chinese constituting 20 percent, Latinos and whites each at 17 percent. Since 1985, however, Chinese students have comprised the largest group in the SFUSD. They have grown steadily in their percent of the total student population. In 1999/2000, for example, Chinese students accounted for 30 percent of all students, with Latinos comprising 22 percent, African Americans 16 percent, and whites 12 percent. The district court's refusal in 1993 to allow attorneys for both Chinese and Latino students to be formal parties to the consent decree can be directly linked to the perceived need by the *Ho* plaintiffs to have their interests met only by challenging the constitutionality of the entire consent decree. Interestingly, the district court's unwillingness to pursue a sufficiently inclusive vision of racial and ethnic interests in its continuing oversight of the decree ultimately led to the court determining later that the decree itself was discriminatory against the Chinese plaintiffs (Fraga, Erlichson, and Lee 1998).

Not surprisingly, those advocating on behalf of African Americans, Latinos, and immigrant, working class Chinese students are unsure as to how they should best try to pursue their groups' interests. Problems of resegregation and continued underachievement remain. Consistent with the *Ho* settlement, race and ethnicity have not been used to assign students to schools in San Francisco since the 1999/2000 school year.[3] Instead, an index composed of six socioeconomic factors is used to assign students to oversubscribed schools. As a result, 16 elementary schools, three middle schools, and one high school have at least 60 percent enrollment of students from one particular race or ethnicity (Biegel 2000, 7). Although 32 percent of all students in San Francisco are English-language learners, there is still no systematic method used by the district to assess the annual academic performance of these students (Biegel 2000, 15). The SFUSD has made gradual improvements in district-wide median scores on standardized achievement tests, and similar improvements for all major racial and ethnic groups. However, as Biegel states, "at no time during the entire period [of the Consent Decree] has the achievement *gap* [between whites, Chinese, African Americans, and Latinos] . . . been meaningfully narrowed."

For example, "African Americans had the lowest mean GPA *in all twelve dis-*
trict high schools, and Latinos had the second lowest GPA in ten of twelve
schools" (Biegel 2000, 51, emphasis added). These trends persisted in 2004,
such that the monitoring committee requested an extension of the consent
decree past 2005 (Biegel 2005).

Of continuing concern is the very real possibility that the district will no
longer be eligible for thirty-four million dollars in consent-decree funds currently provided by the State of California after 2002. No contingency plans
existed as to how the district can maintain operations without these monies,
and few have plans to try to convince state leaders that the SFUSD should be
the recipient of special legislative funding (Biegel 2000, 58).

The impending termination of the consent decree coincided with the hiring of a new superintendent. Arlene Ackerman, previously the superintendent
of schools in Washington, DC, was hired in August 2000. The hiring of
Ackerman, who is African American, was seen by some observers as an indica-
tion of the resurgence of the power of the teachers' union, United Educators
of San Francisco (UESF). Ackerman was known as a strong supporter of teachers' unions and she received some of her strongest support on the board from
members who have traditionally been extremely sympathetic to the UESF.
Ackerman continued and expanded the reconstitution process for low-performing schools in her Dream Schools initiative, saw some rise in test scores—
although not in the achievement gap—and cleaned up and reorganized the fiscal management of the district in the wake of financial scandals linked to her
predecessor. She has had difficult relationships with three of seven board
members—including the president—and some parents and teachers who
charge her with an autocratic style (Knight 2005a). She tendered her resignation in Fall 2005.

An increasingly vocal group of Chinese American parents continue to be
dissatisfied with the current student assignment process, staging protests at the
superintendent's office when assignments are released (Knight 2005a).
Although many live relatively close to some of the highest-performing schools,
some students are assigned to schools in other parts of town. A task force,
which was instructed to solicit community input and recommend three options
for student assignment post–consent decree, developed models for plans with
different portions of seats reserved for neighborhood residents. The school
board will adopt a plan in time for the 2006/07 school year.

Although African Americans, Latinos, and Chinese do have representation
on the school board, it is very unclear as to what the Board's plans are to maintain the commitment to both desegregation and enhanced academic achievement after the end of the consent decree. It is also very unclear as to what
the most appropriate strategy is for leaders of these communities to pursue to
make sure that their communities' interests are met. The federal court has
long been the mechanism through which policies for education reform were

pursued in San Francisco. Some of the original parties would like to see court supervision continue. Indeed, no other mechanism has yet emerged to replace it.

Los Angeles

Los Angeles is by far the largest of our school districts and also has the smallest percentage of white students. In school year 1999/2000, 70 percent of students in the LAUSD were Latino, 13 percent were African American, 10 percent white, 4 percent Asian, 2 percent Filipino, and both Pacific Islanders and Native Americans were under 1 percent. The LAUSD has recently dealt with a number of major controversies. It spent millions of dollars to build a state-of-the-art high school in a section of the city that has since been determined to be too hazardous for students and teachers to inhabit. In part as a result of this controversy, Superintendent Ruben Zacharias—the first Latino to hold the post—was released by the LAUSD. Zacharias had great support within the Latino community and the manner in which he was asked to resign was perceived by many to be a clear slap in the face to Latinos. Although Ramon Cortines was chosen as interim superintendent, Cortines did not have the history of work with or the support of many Latino leaders. More recently, the LAUSD hired former Colorado Governor Roy Romer to head its schools. Romer had never been a school superintendent, although he did pursue a number of education initiatives as governor of Colorado, as noted previously. Under Romer, the LAUSD has engaged in an ambitious school-construction program aimed at ending school overcrowding and concomitantly boosting achievement (DiMassa 2004). Romer built a broad coalition of business, labor, and civil rights groups to support bond measures that passed in 2002 and 2004. Seventeen new schools were slated to open in 2004; a total of one hundred and sixty new schools are planned. He shepherded a small-schools initiative through the school board in 2004 that will divide middle and highschools into small clusters of three hundred and fifty to five hundred students over five years (Hayasaki 2004).

Among the most significant issues that Los Angeles periodically faces is the possibility that the district of over seven hundred thousand students might be subdivided into several separate districts. This devolution plan is supported most by leaders in the San Fernando Valley, an area of the city with a very high concentration of both whites and Asians. Some view the call for devolution as a way for these groups to try to maximize their interests at the expense of more working-class Los Angelenos, especially Latinos and African Americans. In 2001, a breakup attempt failed to make it to the ballot because supporters could not meet a host of regulations (Blume 2005).

Any breakup of the LAUSD would also have to be made within the parameters set by previous court orders and related case law within the California courts. Los Angeles was required to desegregate in 1976. In *Crawford v. Board of Education for the City of Los Angeles* (1976) the California Supreme Court ordered the LAUSD to pursue a desegregation plan requiring mandatory reassignment (Biegel and Slayton 1997, 5). The California courts maintained jurisdiction over desegregation through 1981. Despite the passage of Proposition I in 1979—which changed the state constitution such that the state courts could no longer mandate student reassignment based on race, except in the case of a violation of the equal protection clause of the fourteenth Amendment—the LAUSD continued to pursue desegregation through an extensive magnet school program that it has maintained since 1979 (Biegel and Slayton 1997, 5–6). It has also pursued desegregation through an extensive Permits with Transportation (PWT) program. This program allowed students to attend schools other than those close to their homes to promote racial and ethnic desegregation (Biegel and Slayton 1997, 8). Any plan to break apart the LAUSD would have to directly address the possible consequences for racial and ethnic resegregation in subsequently organized schools. Although *Crawford* no longer governs schools in the LAUSD, it is still very likely that the *Crawford* mandates can be revived if devolution results in increased levels of racial segregation.

The powerful United Teachers Los Angeles (UTLA) has, interestingly, taken the position that it opposes devolution on the basis of the possible resegregation of schools. They note as well that the reorganization of the LAUSD would have to comply with relevant federal case law (Biegel and Slayton 1997, 7). Additionally, issues related to the distribution of certified teachers, school funding, charter schools, programs for English language learners, and schools that were part of the Los Angeles Educational Alliance for Restructuring Now (LEARN) program would have to be addressed before reorganization could occur (Biegel and Slayton 1997, 15–22). For each of these issues, the racial and ethnic consequences of devolution are significant and could place major constraints on any reorganization plan.

Important elements of recent educational politics and policymaking in Los Angeles suggest a pattern of decision making where past concerns with desegregation are likely to reassert themselves. It is also clear that whatever the decision regarding the organization of LAUSD it is likely to be pursued by one interest or another in either federal or state court.

Race, Education, and Institutions

Recent politics of educational policymaking in each of our cities suggest that the patterns of interaction among stakeholders that appeared during eras of substantial court supervision are not likely to be maintained in Boston, Denver, or San Francisco. In each of these cities there is some resurgence of traditional centers of power, especially from the superintendent, school board, and teachers' union. In Los Angeles, the court has not been an active player for some time. However, the major issue confronting the LAUSD, its own possible breakup, is likely to be ultimately settled within the domain of the courts.

Two lawsuits have been filed recently in California courts to try to address issues of the unequal distribution of educational resources across school districts within the state. *Williams v. State of California, Delaine Eastin, State Superintendent of Public Instruction, State Dept. of Education, and State Board of Education* (2000) claims that unequal educational facilities, books, certified teachers, and other aspects of education are unconstitutional under California law. The American Civil Liberties Union filed this case in the Superior Court in the County of San Francisco. *Daniel et al. v. State of California, State Board of Education, Delaine Eastin, State Superintendent of Public Instruction, and the Inglewood Unified School District* (1999) claims that the unequal availability of advanced-placement classes detrimentally affects the capacities of students in heavily minority, lower-income school districts to have a chance of entering the University of California system. The plaintiffs in this suit are represented by the ACLU and, until his death, renowned defense attorney Johnnie Cochran. The case was filed in California Superior Court in the County of Los Angeles. Again, the state courts may be major players in structuring elements of educational policymaking in the most ethnically and racially diverse state in the nation.

No dominant set of ideas directly addressing the increasing racial and ethnic diversity in these cities and/or emanating from minority groups themselves has emerged. Instead, the "new populism" ideas that constitute the most prominent reform proposals are something of a mismatch in their policy goals and in their social and ideational origins. Neither, in the short run, has any institution appeared to take the place of the courts in being a means—however limited, effective, and efficient over the long run—for the newer racial minority groups, situated particularly in the second tier, to have their concerns addressed in public education. This unstable configuration of ideas, interests, and institutions directly addressing the needs of the fastest growing segments of students enrolled in public schools may predict much greater education-related conflict in multiethnic cities than has been seen in the past.

## CHAPTER SEVEN

A Developmental Perspective on Education in Multiethnic Cities

F OCUSING ON THE INTERSECTION of interests, ideas, and institutions provides a useful analytical framework for exploring school reforms in multiethnic cities. It is also instructive for broadly comparing the dilemmas of the 1980s and 1990s with the past—that is, the coalitions of interests, ideas, and institutions predominant during different historical periods. In shorthand, we refer to those coalition patterns and orientations as "regimes." From a historical and developmental viewpoint, the multiethnic moments in the 1980s and 1990s brought the prospects of potential regime change: New interests gained ground, mobilized around distinctive ideas and policy paradigms, and contended with institutions geared toward a previous configuration. Yet as we have shown, the outcomes varied substantially in each city. Much of the contingency and variation in the unfolding of these multiethnic moments can be traced to the ways in which lagging institutions shaped possibilities in each of our cities. Concluding our analysis by placing this period in historical perspective further illustrates our central arguments.

Recall that our empirical analysis began by examining ethnic and racial interests in school reform. It became clear, however, that the situations and problematic political impacts of these diverse groups are not easily or fully explicable by an interest-based paradigm alone. As new school constituencies, Latinos and Asians in particular were systematically underrepresented in the formal educational policymaking structures in all four cities. Latino underrepresentation was matched by low levels of educational achievement while Asian students fared somewhat better on educational achievement measures.

Despite being a large and growing share of new school constituencies, Latino and Asian parents and children had yet to find an effective voice in public education. Indeed, our research also showed there is considerable ambiguity about the meaning and implications of this diversity in multiethnic cities, even among and within ethnic and racial minority groups. "Interests" are not as obvious as often assumed, nor are the grounds for cooperation on reform ideas. Even if and when common ground for school reform is carved out, ideational patterns and the institutional venues for educational policymaking can continue to lag behind current realities.

As we try to pull together different pieces of the puzzle, we find that looking at the dynamics of interactions over time more clearly demonstrates how they collectively structure the politics of educational policy. In viewing dilemmas of the 1980s and 1990s from a historical and developmental perspective, we see broadly similar evolutionary patterns in past experiences with school reform. Tracing these historical patterns of reform underscores the decoupling of educational equity from school reform following the civil rights era when equity had been identified with desegregation initiatives. With the easing and lifting of the desegregation orders, equity goals in school-reform debates became more diffuse and, as we argue, displaced by values of competition and choice in the new market-oriented reforms gaining momentum during this period.

This displacement proved particularly significant in multiethnic cities as new school constituencies struggled to articulate their concerns and gain a voice in educational institutions. Just as these groups became more visible—if not more powerful—in schools, they contended with a climate of instability about what is best in public education. Many of the rules, norms, decision procedures, and institutions guiding educational policies over the past decades, which these new constituencies had little impact upon in the first place, gave way to an emphasis on choice, competition, and arguably narrow measures of performance and accountability. The policy paradigm emerging at the time— what can be called "new educational populism"—became a major part of the policy talk (Tyack and Cuban 1995); it privileged some ideas and some interests at the expense of others (Gardner 2000) in part by emphasizing new institutional venues. Just at the point when it seemed that Latinos and Asians might begin to effectively mobilize and to have the ability for pursuing goals of descriptive and substantive representation, this orientation seemed to mitigate that potential.

In public education, institutions matter a great deal in shaping policy change over time; institutions are often the end result of a complex process of competing interests and of ideas. Those who win—those whose values and/or interests prevail—attempt to make their vision of the proper function and focus of public education permanent through the establishment of organizational and related decision-making infrastructures. As a result, those who establish such institutions have considerable advantage in directing the future course of public policy.

As in the past, a good deal of conflict over educational reforms stems from lagging institutional adjustments to new school constituencies and needs. But in the 1990s, multiethnic constituencies had to contend with this institutional inertia as well as with reform strategies advocated by new education populists that seemed to promise few mechanisms for dealing directly with their concerns. New school constituencies were largely relegated to supporting or opposing ideas and proposals emanating elsewhere; they had difficulty defining and putting forth alternatives that were deemed viable. Robin Jones, John Portz, and Lana Stein (1997) suggest that minority group development was actually slowed by court orders because they displaced and/or made it less necessary for minorities to mobilize and develop politically. Although the court orders were not all-encompassing, this demobilizing effect might help account for the inability of new school constituencies to gain ground when the multiethnic moment arrived.

The Historical and Developmental Context of School Reform

Calls for the reform of public schools in the 1980s and 1990s fit within a historical tradition in the United States (Cuban 1990; Peterson 1985). Horace Mann's call for the spiritual enlightenment of students through the common school was promoted as a type of school reform to be made permanent, that is, institutionalized, through a transformation of school curricula. John Dewey couched his claims in terms of school reform when he advocated the comprehensive development of public schooling to assist the nation in its integration of European immigrants. Mass public schools were to be funded by the state and to be available to all youth. The professionalization of public education that occurred during the Progressive Era—a specific vision of public education that continues to affect schooling in fundamental ways—was achieved under the banner of school reform (Tyack and Cuban 1995).

Professionalization, itself grounded in a challenge to existing machine politics, led to the establishment of state certification agencies and the expansion of university-based schools of education. In many cities, including our four multiethnic cities, it also led to the removal of public school systems from the direct control of city mayors and council members. Now efforts to promote school choice, charter schools, site-based management, mandatory standardized testing, competency testing of teachers, and enhanced school accountability are advanced as major school reforms that require changes, sometimes changes in institutional design (Berliner and Biddle 1995). Education historians remind us that there have been few eras in the development of public education in the United States when calls have not been made for school reform (Tyack and Cuban 1995).

One Hundred and Fifty Years of School Reform Proposals

Several dimensions characterize much of the effort to promote school reform over the last one hundred and fifty years. They include the struggle over teacher-centered instruction, the utility of an academic versus a practical curriculum, and the degree of centralization of authority in school administration (Cuban 1990, 8).[1] In the latter decades of the twentieth century, issues of race/ethnicity have been directly and indirectly implicated in these considerations. The debate over teacher-centered instruction appeared in the 1840s and 1850s. This was largely a criticism of teachers whose primary method of instruction was drilling students in their memorization of chapters of a text or even the U.S. Constitution. Reformers called for instruction to be more innovative, interactive, and student centered. The concerns over curriculum were based in disagreements over whether all students should study subjects for their intellectual content and assumed liberal values or whether students should be trained in technical subjects that would enhance their qualifications for jobs that might be available in the current market. In the 1920s, progressive reformers "redefined an equal education, from all students being forced to take the same practical academic curriculum to all students taking different courses to cultivate their varied interests, capacities, and vocational futures" (Cuban 1990, 4). The issue of administrative centralization first appeared over a century ago when reformers wanted to reduce the number of school districts across the country as well as reduce the size of school boards. This reduction was tied to providing more power to trained professionals to run schools (Cuban 1990, 5).

Note how recent calls for systemic school reform fit within this historical context. The focus of the debates regarding site-based management, school councils, charter schools, and school choice is accurately captured as a manifestation of concerns over the centralization of authority (Cuban 1990, 4–5). Enhancing student learning through interactive computer programs and cooperative learning sound very much like many of the concerns about teacher-centered learning described above. The continued focus on standards and competency testing for students is very similar to the debate over liberal versus practical curricula.

Cuban argues that education reform debates have remained similar over the past one hundred and fifty years because they are in fact conflicts over values rather than over rational considerations of policy options (Cuban 1990, 8). As a result, when major societal changes occur, such as demographic shifts, economic booms and busts, or challenges to traditional understandings of equity, schools are likely to be an arena of value conflicts, sometimes pursued by competing interests through changes in formal institutions. In a sense, schools embody past decisions regarding opportunity, upward mobility, empowerment, and public authority. It would be surprising if they were not the focus of calls for reform in periods of noticeable societal transformation. According to Cuban, "Value conflicts, then, are not problems to be solved by the miracles of a science of schooling; they are dilemmas that require political negotiation and compromises among policymakers and interest groups—much like that which occurs in the larger society" (Cuban 1990, 8).

Cuban also notes that political tradeoffs are necessary. It is our sense that, much like in the larger society, certain groups are more likely to be privileged in these tradeoffs and to have their preferences institutionalized by virtue of their resource situations and abilities to develop and present ideas convincingly.

The reasons that schools are often such a focus of value conflicts include the expectations of "elite classes or dominant groups" who "charge the public schools with the responsibility for solving national ills" and "the enduring faith that Americans have placed in schools as an engine of social and individual improvement" (Cuban 1990, 8). But, as two-tiered pluralism would suggest, the minority groups are not likely to be among the "elite classes" and the American faith in education admits to different definitions with some more likely to prevail than others, often because of institutional legacies and interest factors.

The recurrence of reform efforts should not lead us to think that reform does not occur. Rote memorization is less common today than it was in the 1800s. Schools have extremely varied curricula in response to the variety of student interests and perceived abilities. The professionalization of educational practice and certainly educational governance is well entrenched. Unlike the characterizations offered during the 1990s by a number of critics of public schooling, educational reform did occur. It is important to remember, however, that it may not have been as dramatic as some might have preferred, and it occurred within a context where previous decisions created institutional structures that privileged certain ideas and interests. In the end, change—particularly change for historically disadvantaged groups—may be more incremental than some reformers might have hoped.

But what does it mean that one of the most important public institutions in our society continually dissatisfies large segments of the citizenry who, in turn, call for major transformations in institutions of governance, teaching, and evaluation? Clearly, stakeholders have constantly evaluated the public education system in terms of the ideals and the interests that the system advances. Also, the system of public education has never fully satisfied the preferences of important stakeholders. It seems likely that the frequency and intensity of "policy feedback" (Pierson 1994, 27) in public education is distinct from that in other policy arenas. This is likely due to education's pivotal role in efforts to reconcile the goals of individual economic well-being and social equality, and in grappling with concerns for social stability amidst change.

The Decoupling of Educational Equity from School Reform

Calls for greater equality for members of racial and ethnic minority groups in the post–World War II era have seldom been couched in terms of educational reform. The sustained efforts by leaders within African American communities to overcome public school segregation—what they understood to be the major barrier to their enhanced economic, social, and political well-being—were made more in terms of constitutional violations of civil rights than in terms of educational reform per se (*Brown v. Board of Topeka, KS* 1954). The tendency of the federal courts to narrow this claim by identifying enrollment desegregation as the primary means of achieving racial equity in public schools further extended the separation of integration from educational reform. Claims made in the 1960s for "community control" were often understood more in terms of enhanced political power than in terms of altered educational practices that would lead to higher academic achievement. Although such claims sometimes led to the establishment of what came to be known as Afrocentric curricula, this was often couched more in terms of enhancing racial identity than enhancing academic achievement.

Mexican Americans had been successful previously in convincing the courts that their segregation in separate schools was unconstitutional. Notably, the claims made by attorneys for these students were even less linked to calls for institutional educational reform. They claimed that since Mexican Americans were not black, there was no constitutional basis in law justifying their segregation in separate schools (San Miguel 1987). They solely wanted access to white-dominated schools; assumptions were made that such access would lead to the expansion of educational opportunities for these students. No effort was made to call for changes in educational practice or institutional design.

This tendency to separate educational equity for ethnic and racial minorities from school reform also characterized reform efforts of the 1990s. Calls for institutional reform, whether the focus was on governance, instruction, or curriculum, rarely took the ideas and interests of ethnic and racial minorities fully into account. This decoupling of conceptions of educational equity from school reform was particularly significant in multiethnic cities. Multiethnic cities are characterized by a variety of groups whose interests in, expectations of, and needs from public education may differ, sometimes dramatically so. At times their interests may seem compatible, such as when a bond issue is promoted to improve the physical infrastructure of schools or when there is an agreement that teachers' pay should be increased. However, it is just as likely that conflict among groups will appear regarding curriculum, bilingual instruction, the hiring and promotion of teachers, or the assignment of students to a city's highest performing schools. When resources and opportunities are scarce, as they typically are, the multiethnic political environment presents special challenges to those responsible for school governance. Interest competition and interest incompatibility are likely to increase as the number of relevant political actors increases. The decoupling problem is exacerbated when conflicts exist among, and within, a number of different groups. Multiethnic cities, with their numerous stakeholders' interests, and associated competing ideas, are often characterized by such conditions.

Educational institutions mattered in shaping the voices of these new school constituencies. Institutions represent and reflect established solutions responsive to the ideas and interests of influential educational stakeholders. Racial and ethnic minority groups rarely have made claims for greater educational equity in terms of fundamental institutional redesign, or they have done so by treating change as "reform by addition." Calls for institutional redesign not originating from racial and ethnic communities tended not to take the interests of these communities specifically into account, again reflecting a two-tiered structure of influence. The new educational populism emerging in multiethnic cities was not an agenda promoted by any particular group but, rather, a political struggle defined by institutional legacies and competing ideas about "the problem" with schools. It was also comprised of emerging interests seeking to respond to the struggles, but seldom, if ever, playing a successful role in them. To better understand this evolutionary process, we set out a developmental perspective that traces critical elements of educational policy regimes over time.

A Developmental Perspective on School Reform

In our view, the politics of urban education have evolved through various periods, closely paralleling historical patterns of urban politics that have been suggested by Clarence N. Stone, Robert K. Whelan, and William J. Murin (1986). The time frame and configurations in multiethnic settings of the 1980s and 1990s, however, were somewhat different. Here we place the policies and outcomes described in earlier chapters in a broader temporal context.

Stone, Whelan, and Murin define several periods of urban politics on the basis of two dimensions: an orientation toward common or nondifferentiated interests, versus an orientation toward differentiated or competing interests, and a traditional versus a modern outlook. They write: "The trend from a traditional to a modern outlook represents a broad shift over time ... an adaptation to changes in the scale of life, which in turn are related to changes in technology and the organization of the economic system" (177). In terms of the interest dimension, there has been movement back and forth, with " nondifferentiated" interests ascendant in some periods, then giving way to competing and "differentiated" interests in other periods; one might also refer to these as focused on the "politics of similarity" and "the politics of difference." In the twentieth century, common interests were most clearly ascendant with urban "reform" style politics, and gave ground to "differentiated interests" with the rise of "postreform" politics that emerged in the mid-1960s.

"Village politics" had a traditional, that is, a personal and somewhat informal, style and a nondifferentiated, consensus-based orientation. "Machine politics" also had something of an informal style, but it also had considerable competition and conflict—often associated with "ethnic politics"—in large, industrial cities of the Northeast and Midwest. Despite this emphasis on material rewards and "status" politics, however, the machines tended to be nonideological and were typically not oriented toward substantive, redistributive policies. Nonetheless, the perceived corruption and inefficiency of machines were the target of the Progressives' efforts to "reform" and "professionalize" local politics in ways that fundamentally redefined urban politics and education. Indeed, as we argued earlier, contemporary education politics can scarcely be understood without reference to the ideas, interests, and institutions associated with "reform" and "professionalization."

In the urban government context, "reform" refers to a specific movement beginning in the early 1900s; that movement had further implications regarding education. The reform style of politics includes a "modern" view of political processes and relations in its emphasis on impersonal and formal, or rule-based, systems. The reform model paralleled the "business model" of administrative efficiency, which it sought to imbed through several institutional features. There was a belief in a strong chief executive officer (CEO)—such as the school superintendent (in the education arena) and the city manager (in city government)—as well as the preference for a legislative body that was small in number, paralleling a board of directors. The governmental CEO was not directly elected by voters, but selected by the legislative body so as to buffer this leader from mass popular opinion and to base selection on "expertise," not popularity. In the education arena, specialization and division of labor were promoted, both throughout the curriculum and in the structural separation of the school district from city government.

The legislative bodies themselves—city councils and school boards—were to be selected through a particular kind of electoral mechanism defined by its status of being at-large, nonpartisan, longer (for example, six-year versus one- or two-year year) terms of office, and staggered elections. All this was designed to produce "good government" and an ostensible "common good" leading to efficient, "responsible" government by purportedly insulating government from partisan, parochial influences. The political reform paradigm was, and is, powerful in its claims about the common good and the attainment of the public interest through specific institutional designs. While couched in the language of "good government," the implications of reform were significant and tilted toward certain interests, its claims notwithstanding.

The middle and upper classes tended to benefit from the formal administrative and electoral structures embodying reform ideas, at the expense of working and lower classes. And the historical reform orientation overlooked the fact that these reforms occurred within a larger context of "separate but equal" and much de facto segregation in the aftermath of formal desegregation. The perception that these reform systems were biased prompted the postreform ideas championed by blacks, which emerged most clearly in the 1960s.

The postreform era in city government openly suggested "that we are a society of diverse interests, that these interests expect to be represented, and that politics, the process through which this representation is obtained, is an inescapable part of modern life" (Stone, Whelan, and Murin 1986, 134). Movements of black constituents and others made "the service-providing agencies [administrative agencies] of local government ... the direct target of efforts to make government more responsive and effective" (Stone, Whelan, and Murin 1986, 136). There was growing recognition that problem solving, especially if it involves person-to-person activity, is to some degree culture bound and is, in any event, heavily intertwined with value choices. Once this perception gained currency, the decisions of experts and professionals, no longer protected by the claim of being politically neutral, came to be questioned.

While the postreform ideas challenged reform ideals, they clearly did not displace them. Stone, Whelan, and Murin note, "The process of change can best be described as one of absorption rather than substitution. New elites join but never totally replace old elites" (Stone, Whelan, and Murin 1986, 179). These authors make several other noteworthy points. The competitive interest orientation, most often espoused by minorities and disadvantaged groups, is institutionally unstable because "while conflict can be defended as a source of innovation and as a prompter of adaptation to new conditions, it is hard to cope with" (Stone, Whelan, and Murin 1986, 180). Conflict management often ends up leaving some interests unrepresented. Elites maintain order through arrangements that bring together selected interests in a system of exchange and mutual support. But other interests may be excluded or provided only meager benefits. For those who are part of an ongoing system of exchange and mutual support, governance appears to support the general welfare, if not always fully. But for those who are excluded or underrepresented, the system is one of exploitation and favoritism (Stone, Whelan, and Murin 1986, 180). Our argument has been that underrepresentation and unresponsive systems in multiethnic cities are rooted not only in resource and interest-based factors, but also in the ideas that are most influential and in the institutions that favor certain interests and ideas. These configurations contribute to the two-tiered structure of influence shaping local politics in American cities.

Evolving Educational Policy Regimes

As with broader urban patterns, the reform and postreform eras are also evident in education. Note, for instance, that in the cities examined here the basic structural components of urban education associated with the reform era remain largely intact. At the same time, the desegregation orders call for more minority teachers and curriculum changes to reflect minority experiences reflect postreform concerns. The 1990s also had certain notable characteristics and orientations. As described in earlier chapters, proposals for systemic reform such as charter schools, site-based management, and the like, while in some ways challenging conventional practices, nonetheless seemed to speak more to middle-class and to white concerns than to those of emerging minority groups in multiethnic settings.

Table 7.1 identifies various ideas, interests, and institutions that have coalesced around school politics to form policy regimes or orientations dominant in different eras. That is, these policy regimes denote coalitions of interests mobilized around particular policy paradigms and agendas. Using the regime concept reminds us that mobilization involves norms, principles, decision procedures, and institutions, as well as interests. While the three eras are somewhat distinct, there are "carry-over" impacts on the institutions, ideas, and interests from era to era, although each era reframes them somewhat differently. By creating institutions that address their distinctive concerns, each regime shapes future policies; in doing so they also constrain responsiveness to interests and ideas that emerge later on.

The Reform Policy Regime

The major ethnic cleavages of the reform era concerned white and white-ethnic relations: "Yankee Protestants" contested the Irish, Italians, and other southern and eastern European groups in urban politics. While education sought to "Americanize" new immigrants, local schools also sought to insulate against the new interests. Indeed, historians have come to view reform efforts as aiming to curb the urban ethnic "machines" and various related orientations and practices. A major reason for the rhetorical power of the reform movement was that it suggested positive, "good government" beliefs on behalf of universal, general interests, as opposed to what were portrayed as narrow, particular interests. A major concern of the reform policy regime was to constrain or deny and reshape racial/ethnic, place-based, and "partisan" interests; the major methods for doing so were institutional. Hence, reformers sought to have at-large, nonpartisan elections to deflect interests away from allegedly narrowly focused group and partisan voices to city-wide ones. Once the structures preferred by the reformers were put in place, the expression of their interests could flow readily and implicitly therefrom. But the reformers' suggestion that the policy focus of government should be "city wide" ignored the presence of policies and practices that promoted racial and social class differences, and a great deal of residential segregation.

The reform policy regime norms emphasized "responsible" government, that is, government that would be attentive to the general well-being, perceived to be "big picture," "long term," effective, and noncorrupt. In many

TABLE 7.1 REFORM ERAS AND EDUCATION POLICY REGIMES

	REFORM	POSTREFORM	NEW EDUCATIONAL POPULISM
INTERESTS			
Ethnic Cleavages	White vs. white ethnic	White vs. black	Multi-ethnic
Politics of ...	Good government	Interest group liberalism	Interest group conservatism
Group relations	Constrain or deny group consciousness	Recognition of historical group relations	Inattentive
Expression of voice	Implicit	Explicit	Through individual choice
IDEAS			
Substantive goal	Responsible government	Responsive government	Accountable government
Procedural goal	Administrative efficiency	Procedural	Market efficiency
Policy orientation	Effective distribution; consensus is structurally induced	Redistributive; social regulation; challenge or addition to consensus	New distributive; deregulation; structural creation of choice
Social order	Community	Command	Community and competition
Notion of public	Assumed	Collection of groups	Aggregation of individuals
INSTITUTIONS			
Reform approach	Institutional design	Addition or modification of existing programs and practices	Circumvent existing programs through market mechanisms
Administrative orientation	Strong superintendent	Representative bureaucracy	Extra-bureaucratic
School Board Election	At-large	District	Mixed
Administrative specialization	By function	By clientele	In response to choice
School/city relations	Separation	Nonissue	Informal links and partnerships

ways, the reform regime norms favored a "trustee" approach to governance, implying that there should be deference to appropriate leaders. These leaders included community members both elected to the school board through specified processes and also selected on the basis of expertise, such as the superintendent. In these ways, common or community interests could be affirmed and advanced. These claims belied a middle- or upper-class bias, however.

The reform regime's principles, norms, and procedures also emphasized efficiency—defined in administrative or bureaucratic terms of hierarchy, division of labor, specialization, span of control, and expertise—and favored the allocation of resources in accordance with managerial and professional principles. The administrative apparatus of city government and school districts were to reflect these. A notable quality of the reform era was that it saw itself as oriented toward an inclusive, collective, community based means to social order. The reform ethos advocated that public policy should be "nonpolitical," as suggested by the politics/administration dichotomy. These goals could best be accomplished through designing formal governmental structures and policies that were (thought and claimed to be by reformers) for the benefit of all.

What makes the legacies of each era more or less broad and/or deep in their impacts and more or less stable is the imbedding of these ideas and interests into ongoing formal arrangements, that is, institutions. Despite significant challenges, reform institutions remain pretty much in place today. This is because the reform era's ideas, interests, and institutions benefit from being perceived as normal, natural, and neutral: "normal" in being viewed as in accord with [dominant] norms, rules, principles; natural in that they are thought to be "based on an inherent sense of right and wrong," or "occurring in conformity with the ordinary course of nature"; and neutral, meaning "not biased nor engaged on either side, not aligned with a political or ideological grouping."

At a broad level, the reform era was grounded in a belief in the efficacy of institutional design to produce desired outcomes. That much of our education system still reflects structures from the reform era is strong testimony to their impact. While there has been considerable consolidation of school districts over the years, for example, the reform idea of separating school districts from city government remains common. The reform regime's administrative emphasis was on professionalization, merit, and the strong executive in the person of the superintendent. The superintendent was the CEO and was to be selected on the basis of expertise; and the superintendent was also to be "buffered" from direct link to the voters by school board selection. In short, the reform model's biases were toward the superintendent, with the school board and bureaucracy essentially functioning as "trustees." There was to be accountability to the voters, but indirectly. Critics would later argue that accountability primarily was to middle-class voters.

These reform influences were successful to the point that numerous scholars (for example, Meier and Stewart 1991) have argued that during much of the 1900s education was seen as apolitical, that is, as above or beyond politics. As a result, various issues—including those concerning racial equality—were largely submerged by the prevalent ideas and practices.

The Postreform Policy Regime

During the postreform era, especially as manifest in the desegregation and related court cases of the 1960s and 1970s, the dominant actors were organized largely in terms of white and white ethnics versus blacks. The civil rights movements of the postreform era argued for the equality of blacks as a group, to be achieved through school desegregation, "descriptive representation" among teachers and administrators, and other mechanisms. Descriptive representation was to be encouraged by reestablishing the district (or ward) elections that had been criticized during the reform era. Notably, city governments tended to readopt district elections more readily than did school districts. For example, the city of Denver reestablished district elections in the late 1960s, while the school district did not do so until the 1990s. However, the postreform challenges did not, by and large, raise larger questions about many of the other structures, procedures, and practices associated with the reform orientation.

The postreform policy arrangements preferred by blacks called for desegregation of schools and for the appropriate recognition—through curriculum change and the like—of the condition of blacks in American society. Latinos and Asians later succeeded in having bilingual programs added to the formal structures. However, major institutional changes were not advocated; most often "reform by addition" occurred, but did not fundamentally alter existing institutional patterns or policy outcomes.

The postreform policy regimes strongly challenged the tenet that politics and administration were separable, arguing that merit systems unfairly limited employment opportunities for blacks and other minorities in city government and education, and were otherwise unresponsive or insensitive to minority concerns. Postreform policy regimes were ambivalent about the notion of efficiency as that was conventionally understood. The postreform arguments suggest there had been real, detrimental policy implications associated with earlier reform ideas and practices, challenging the reform era's claims of simple distributive effects. Instead, the postreform perspective questioned such practices as at-large elections and argued for formal school desegregation.

Perceiving that the reform vision was much narrower than claimed, the postreform regimes sought the intervention of formal institutions of government to require, that is, command, more inclusive behavior. Civil rights legislation, busing, and other mechanisms are examples. The postreform policy regime was oriented toward descriptive representation, and sought to achieve this through district elections and a (descriptively) representative bureaucracy. But that came to be criticized as a perverse form of interest group liberalism, even as "clientelism" by conservative analysts. Some liberal observers have argued that group entrenchment in school bureaucracies has led to "cartels" (Rich 1996), further suggesting narrow group self-interest. Indeed, certain of the criticisms sound somewhat similar to those made about the urban machines of the early twentieth century.

The Emergence of Multiethnic Politics and a New Educational Populism in the 1990s

Multiethnic political divisions and relations, especially regarding education, were central features for a growing number of cities in the 1990s. As we have argued previously, this multiethnic condition often is analyzed, incompletely or inappropriately, through the black/white paradigm of the previous era. That paradigm is hardly irrelevant; it is, however, insufficient in that it does not adequately consider the importance of "new" and rapidly growing minority groups, and the resulting uncertainties about problem definitions and policy solutions. In important respects, the politics of education during this era—a "new educational populism"—appears most influenced by groups seeking goals that are not necessarily hostile to minority groups, but that do not directly address minority groups' central concerns. In fact, group competition seems to create outcomes that are particularly problematic for emerging minority groups. At the same time, we noted that minority intergroup relations, while often competitive or conflictual, are not only or always so; they are at times cooperative. There are possible patterns other than groups, as well, such as minorities making small gains individually.

During the time of our study, a renewed emphasis on "responsible" government—somewhat differently defined in broad notions of accountability—appeared to take place. It was more outcome or bottom-line oriented and less structurally or procedurally oriented than the reform era; proponents argued that its favored solutions were equally beneficial to all individuals and groups of students. Examples are standards-based assessment such as through testing, school accountability committees, and the like. Advocacy of mechanisms to deregulate or partly degovernmentalize certain aspects of public education were evident—as with charter schools and voucher systems—or to allow for new mechanisms to distribute education resources, such as site-based management.

This educational populism stresses notions of community (for example, citizen/parental involvement through site-based management) and of competition (through market-like mechanisms). These are two prominent ideas in American political thought, representing the "republican" and "liberal" traditions, respectively. With both the community and competition approaches, there is reliance on noncoercive approaches. These seemed more consistent with historical American ideals; they also privileged the reform and contemporary models, in contrast to the postreform reliance on court orders. This orientation differed from postreform regimes in that it disaggregated policies from government responsibility to a series of individual, market-like choices. In this fashion, policy questions were thought, and claimed, to be depoliticized because the "invisible hand" of the market is not viewed as political.

Federal court desegregation orders, and their specific provisions, were central to shaping education politics in multiethnic settings. Similarly, state governments became more involved in the 1970s around school finance questions and in the 1990s with legislative and initiative activities affecting charter schools, school finance, and so on. Yet, these federal and state activities did little to change the formal structures of urban school governance. Despite the visibility of the federal No Child Left Behind Act, its primary impact has been on school practices—standardized testing—rather than school governance. Indeed, in some ways a major impact of federal and state actions was to open the way for other, new players in school politics, namely nonprofits and private-sector groups. The ultimate impact of these groups is still not entirely clear, but in general they tended not to be closely associated with minority group issues.

The educational populist orientation of the nineties, like the reform perspective, also stressed efficiency, but defined this in *market*, not administrative or bureaucratic, terms on the assumption that market mechanisms assure lean, cost-effective practices. Frustrated with the bureaucratic norms and centralized procedures integral to the reform era goals, this orientation stressed such extrabureaucratic, institutional mechanisms as charter schools, vouchers, and a form of decentralization, through site-based management. The new educational populist policy coalitions shared more in common with the reform than with postreform regime goals, although the institutional approach is rather different. That is, quality, effectiveness, professionalization, and other things are to be achieved from "the outside in" as much as or more than from "the inside out." To a considerable degree, the goals echoed the "good government" sentiments of an earlier era, but new ways of achieving the goals are now suggested.

In the 1990s, a variety of aspects were so taken for granted that they were seldom questioned. For example, the formal separation of cities from school districts was hardly challenged during the postreform era. We saw few direct challenges to this by new educational populist policy regimes, although there were highly publicized instances of city takeovers of schools, such as in Chicago, and other efforts to develop informal links (Chambers 2002). Where more formal links and oversight occurred, it often was through state government directives and mayoral initiatives (Henig and Rich 2003). The strong tradition of localism, including the very existence of school district boundaries as historically drawn, was rarely discussed. Such major changes would not necessarily be "better" but the point is that they have not been serious agenda items, even though minority concerns have fared somewhat better on city government agendas than in school districts' politics. The market-oriented ideas and proposals of the new educational populism seem to drown out such considerations.

Also, one consequence of the 1990s policies to increase choice through market institutions might allow for a "new separatism," or even a "new segregationism" (Goldberg 1996), partly because of the distributional consequences embedded in these new reforms.

Interests, Ideas, Institutions, and Civic Capacity: The Prospects for Transformation in Local Educational Politics

Hugh Heclo's (1994) framework emphasizing the intersection and reciprocal influences of ideas, interests, and institutions organized and guided our analysis. It underscores ways in which political institutions privilege some options and weaken others. While political institutions set parameters that constrain options for both individuals and groups, they also are dynamic settings that "carry forward continuities of conflict rather than immutable answers" (Heclo 1994, 378). In this regard, they not only affect preferences, options, and previous understandings, but they "can also provide the means for changing ideas about our interests and preferences." As Heclo sees it, this suggests "a more open-ended, transformational capacity in the politics of democratic institutions" (1994, 379).

This transformational capacity centers on the presence of "evolutionary bids" (1994, 386) and evolutionary learning. In this view, institutional constraints can generate new ways of thinking about issues. When "some expectation has not been met or an opportunity is perceived that wasn't there before" (1994, 387), bids for alternative solutions may rise and serve to "coordinate the expectations necessary for cooperation, the interaction of ideas and institutions [that] can make results possible that could not be achieved otherwise" (1994, 381). When these new ideas are adopted, "evolutionary learning" has occurred.

Evolutionary bids to overcome institutional constraints were apparent in each of the cities. Factors such as intervention of the courts, the substantial overhauling of entire school administrations, the consistent and insistent presence of outside experts evaluating the process, voter support for school bond issues, and the leadership available in the superintendent's office are powerful bids but not easily sustained. Students of color, their parents, and advocates presented new policy ideas, but these ideas led, at most, to marginal institutional transformation. Additionally, the self-identified interests of African Americans, Latinos, and in the case of San Francisco, Chinese, were often understood as competitive, if not incompatible. This made it even more difficult for educational institutions to be transformed in fundamental ways that would lead to systematic improvements in educational opportunity for these students. In Heclo's terms, the multiethnic context within which educational policy exists in these cities presented formative challenges to the "transformational capacity" of educational institutions.

Our study of educational policy in four multiethnic cities leads us to question the transformational capacities of local education institutions. Racial desegregation and the increased availability of instruction for English-language learners signified historical transformations in traditional educational practice in each of our cities. But it is apparent that these enhancements of opportunity did not lead to the anticipated magnitude of improvement in educational outcomes for students of color. Change that focused on desegregation was insufficient to contribute directly to enhanced academic achievement. Change in instruction modes for English-language learners, similarly, did not lead to major improvements for many Latino and Asian students. Although our analysis indicates that new policy images, reframing of education issues, and redesign of educational institutions are critical to systemic reforms, the evidence from these four cases should give us pause about the difficulties in accomplishing these efforts.

The Prospects for Change in Urban Schools

Absent the desegregation orders, a political free-for-all occurred as multiethnic moments unfolded in our four cities. Given the values articulated by new educational populist regimes coupled with the logic of two-tiered pluralism, incremental changes responding to new school constituencies were possible, but negative distributional outcomes seemed at least equally likely. Although the moment for school reforms responsive to multiethnic constituencies arrived, the outcomes were less than anticipated. That Latinos and Asians did not gain greater influence during this time suggests, again, the broad difficulties in overcoming interest configurations, policy legacies or ideas, and institutional inertia, as well as the structural disadvantages described by two-tiered pluralism.

Our analysis of the interests, ideas, and institutions involved leads us to believe that without significant modifications in each of these arenas, transformational change that addresses the concerns of new school constituencies is likely to be quite limited. That is, substantial changes would be needed in the following areas: the minority groups' resources, cohesion, articulation, coalition formation, and other things; the creation of policy images, problem definitions, and policy solutions responsive to multiethnic concerns, but also resonating with broad values and wider audiences; and the creation of institutional arrangements that consolidate and reinforce new interests and ideas. These are, clearly, daunting challenges, but nothing less will overcome the barriers identified by our analyses and the constraints imposed by two-tiered pluralism.

METHODS APPENDIX

In order to address the complex question of school reform in multiethnic cities, we necessarily drew on multiple data collection and analysis methods. No one method is privileged in the analysis; the different methods described here are all seen as important but partial approaches to the questions we are interested in. Bringing together the information with diverse methodologies provides a more nuanced understanding of the different dimensions and meanings of school reform issues.

PROJECT GOALS

It is useful to keep in mind the broader purposes of the National Science Foundation (NSF) study.[1] The focus was on the context of public education, rather than on an analysis of the classroom dynamics or an evaluation of particular programs. The conceptual focus was on the political coalitions and dynamics in which education policymaking is embedded and the different types of civic arrangements associated with various reform efforts. School systems are seen as one part of an interrelated network of political institutions situated at the local level, but not necessarily controlled entirely by local officials. Schools' capacity to make innovative choices is contingent on these contextual features and collaborative political arrangements. The overall project goals, therefore, included mapping the patterns of alliances and civic dynamics providing the context in which school policies are formed; assessing the range and variation in education and other human capital investment initiatives in each city; and identifying the coalitions, decision processes, and ideas associated with different school reform initiatives.

Research Design

Eleven cities were included in the NSF project: Atlanta, Baltimore, Boston, Denver, Detroit, Houston, Los Angeles, Pittsburgh, St. Louis, San Francisco, and Washington, DC. All have substantial minority populations and large numbers of students from poverty households. The field research began in May 1993 and extended through December 1994. The initial hypothesis postulated that more systemic school reforms were more likely in cities with more civic capacity. The dependent variable in the larger study measured human capital investments in terms of the aggregate effort (tapping wealth and school expenditure measures), the scope of the effort (the number and types of programs serving disadvantaged students), and the extent to which these efforts constituted systemic reform (rather than incremental tinkering). For each dimension, there were attempts to determine whether the initiatives were sustained, whether the efforts were real or symbolic, and whether they were targeted to the disadvantaged in the schools. Data for these measures came from aggregate statistical sources as well as from interviews in each city.

Measures of civic capacity were the key independent variable. Civic capacity is the ability to build and maintain effective alliances between public and private sectors for problem-solving goals. This is akin to the notion of social capital, but concerns the trust and communication among diverse elites developed over time in each city. Mobilization around human capital issues is likely to depend on how these civic actors define community issues and the issue definitions associated with education particularly. Understanding civic capacity on a city-by-city basis meant relying on interviews in each city. Eventually, each research team assessed the overall civic capacity in their city based on these interviews; these individual assessments were matched with the assessments of each city by researchers from other cities.

Although the findings vary by city, overall, it appears that the findings support the central proposition. However, the cities had only varying degrees of civic capacity, and they also fell short of systemic reform to varying degrees. Though the most conspicuous barrier to greater civic capacity is racial and other intergroup tensions, the problem of concentrated poverty itself stands as the major obstacle. In addition, elite perceptions of the nature of the urban education problem were fundamentally ambiguous and diffuse, and proposals for reform were primarily incremental even though aspiration levels were high. In the face of a large and resistant problem, but lacking a "well-structured" understanding of the challenge, players in urban education tend to be deflected into piecemeal efforts, some even treating education as an employment regime.

Data Collection

Trends

We collected aggregate data on socioeconomic, demographic, fiscal, political, and educational trends for each city over time as well as school district statistics, according to the guidelines set out by the NSF project Principal Investigators (Clarence Stone, Jeff Henig, and Bryan Jones). These guidelines, and the resulting comparative data for the eleven project cities, were detailed in the *Field Research Guide for the Civic Capacity and Urban Education Project* (September 1993). The NSF project primarily focused on data collection for a five year period: 1989/90 through 1993/94; historical data going back to the 1960s was included for some topics.

In addition to these data, each city team compiled data on the institutional and administrative changes in education policy subsystems over time. This included the ethnicity, race, gender, tenure, and backgrounds of key administrative and elected officials, as well as changing conditions in the educational policy environment, for example, shifts to district elected school board elections.

Interview Data

Each city in the NSF project used similar data collection instruments and sampling procedures for the structured interviews. The aim was to gain an understanding of the policy world as each respondent saw it—who is important, what the views of others might be, and what were the grounds for cooperation and conflict over education issues. Three key sets of respondents were targeted, defined by their role positions—the kind and range of information they were able to provide: General Influentials in the community, Community Activists, and Program Specialists. Since the project focused on the capacity for systemic reform in local education, these three groups appeared the most likely to be directly involved in such efforts.

In each city, the research teams followed general guidelines on whom to interview within each set of respondents, though they had the discretion to adjust the quota to better match the city context. General Influentials were people likely to be active across a range of policy issues, including education. This group included the mayor, two city council members, the city manager or chief administrative officer, two school board members, the director or president of the Chamber of Commerce, and others involved in education issues from business organizations, the CEO of at least one major private employer, minority business executive, Private Industry Council chair, directors of United Way and other prominent charitable organizations and foundations, local newspaper editors and reporters, state legislators from the city, a judge or attorneys on desegregation cases. Community based representatives included two heads of children's advocacy groups, the system wide PTA officer, influential religious leaders and members of religious alliances or coalitions, minority organization representatives, education specialists from good government groups such as League of Women's Voters. Program Specialists included the school superintendent and several assistants, the Head Start administrator, principals involved in innovative programs, an administrator of school-business partnerships, a Private Investment Council (PIC) staff member involved in education issues, and a lobbyist for the school district in city hall or the state capitol.

The majority of the interviews in each city were conducted between June and December 1993. For each set of respondents, a distinctive interview form was used; this protocol was the same in each city, so that it is possible to compare the responses of each set of respondents across all eleven cities. In general, questions asked respondents about the broad political context of their city, how education issues were understood and what key problems existed, lines of conflict and cooperation, key program initiatives, and reform efforts. Core elements of the interview were the same for each set of respondents; additional items were tailored to tap the expertise and experiences of each group of respondents, with these items common to all cities. In addition, city teams added questions they found useful and specific to their city. Project personnel also collected and assembled program and finance data from each city. These semistructured interviews were conducted primarily in person, at the work setting or other location chosen by the respondent. With the consent of the respondent, interviews were taped and later transcribed. The transcribed tapes were coded and analyzed at Texas A&M University by a team headed by Bryan D. Jones and Whitney Grace.

The Interview Data
As a result of this collaborative effort, there is a unique data set for eleven cities of the attitudes, beliefs, and observations about school reform of three key groups in local politics. These data have been used in various ways by the different research groups, resulting in numerous conference papers, scholarly articles, and analyses, including *The Color of Reform, City Schools and City Politics, and Building Civic Capacity*.

The project data consists of the coded interviews with the three groups of community education elites, along with a codebook for each of the datasets. For the convenience of future analysts, a codebook and associated dataset containing the questions asked of all three groups is also available. See project data, in Excel format, at http://depts.washington.edu/ampol/research/individual _research_projects/civic_capacity_and_urban_education.html.

Elite Interviews and Codebooks

Interview Group	Codebook Size	Download Codebook	Data Set Size	Download Data Set
Community Advocates	57k	cacode.doc	312k	caspread.xls
General Influentials	59k	gicode.doc	257k	gispread.xls
Program Specialists	60k	pscode.doc	319k	psspread.xls
Overlapping Questions	93k	olcode.doc	808k	olspread.xls

Respondents in Four Multiracial Cities

	All Cities	Boston	Denver	Los Angeles	San Francisco
Race/Ethnicity					
Anglo	103	16	35	30	22
Black	38	10	14	8	6
Asian	7	0	0	2	5
Latino	43	3	19	11	10
Role					
City officials, business leaders	78	8	33	20	17
Community activists, nonprofit directors	50	8	20	11	11
School system officials, teachers, principals	63	13	15	20	15
Total	191	29	68	51	43

THE GENERAL INFLUENTIAL QUESTIONNAIRE

Codebook: General Influentials: First Release 10/18/94 (revised 2/24/95) (revised 4/4/95) (revised 6/26/96)

City Codes:
1. Atlanta
2. Baltimore
3. Boston
4. Denver
5. Detroit
6. Houston

7. Los Angeles
8. Pittsburgh
9. St. Louis
10. San Francisco
11. Washington, DC

City Type:
1. Black-led Cities
2. Sunbelt Cities
3. Machine Cities

Interviewee Coded as:
General Influential
10. Mayor (Mayor office)
11. City Council Members
12. City Manager/deputy mayor
13. City Government, generally (includes court)
14. State Legislator
15. School Board
16. State/Federal Government or Courts
17. Education Community (universities, educational foundations)
18. Teachers Union
19. Chamber of Commerce
20. Minority Chamber of Commerce
21. Education Committee of Chamber of Commerce
22. Business
23. PIC
24. Community Development Planning Body
25. Minority Foundations
26. Other Foundations
27. United Way
28. Media
29. Urban League
30. Employment Services/Agencies
31. Labor
32. Political Parties

Community Advocates
40. Community/Advocacy Organizations with concern for children
41. Religious Organizations/Leaders
42. PTA
43. Non-PTA Parent Advocacy Groups
44. Good Government-Education Committee
45. Minority Organizations

Program Specialists
50. School Superintendent
51. Assistant Superintendent
52. Police Officer
53. Head Start Administrator
54. Chapter I Administrator
55. Social Services Liaison with Schools
56. Principal
57. Principal of Innovative School
58. Economic Development Administration with Education Portfolio
59. Business - Education Partnerships
60. PIC with Education Responsibilities
61. United Way with Education Responsibilities
62. Lobbyist
63. School System Administrator/Department

Q1: What do you see as the major problems facing City X? (Allow up to five problems)
1. Inadequate governmental bureaucracy
2. Inadequate city economic resources (poverty, unemployment, city resources)

3. Loss of tax base
4. Ineffective leadership (to include too much conflict)
5. Social problems of individuals (housing, health, family breakdown)
6. Crime
7. Drugs
8. Inadequate education
9. Race relations/white flight
10. Inadequate workforce
11. No problems
98. Question was not asked or answered in another question
99. Question was asked but not answered

A2. *For each problem mentioned, was it mentioned spontaneously or in response to a question?*
1. Mentioned spontaneously (in response to the major problems question)
2. In response to a question (in response to a probe following the major problems question)
98. Question was not asked or answered in another question
99. Question was asked but not answered

A3. *How specific was the respondent when mentioning the problems?*
1. Specifically (with elaboration)
2. Not very specifically (merely named the problems without much elaboration)
98. Question was not asked or answered in another question
99. Question was asked but not answered

Q2: *Are there important new policy ideas to come on the scene in the county during the past few years?*
1. No new ideas
2. New ideas
98. Question was not asked or answered in another question
99. Question was asked but not answered

B1. *If response is 2:*

What are the ideas? (Allow up to 3)
1. Concerning problem of crime
2. Concerning problem of unemployment
3. For improving governmental structures
4. Tto confront health issues/social issues
5. To remove racial inequalities
6. Concerning economic problems/development
7. Concerning education (including school-to-work)
8. Concerning community self-esteem/awareness/involvement
9. No new ideas
98. Question was not asked or answered in another question
99. Question was asked but not answered

B2. *For each named, was it clear that this is a project which the respondent was/is involved with?*
1. Yes
0. No
98. Question was not asked or answered in another question
99. Question was asked but not answered

B3. *How specific was the individual when discussing the policy idea?*
1. Mentioned policy idea specifically (with elaboration)
2. Mention was not very specific (naming the problem with little elaboration)
98. Question was not asked or answered in another question
99. Question was asked but not answered

B4. *Who is supporting the idea? (Allow up to 5)*
1. Mayor/county executive

2. City government in general
3. State government
4. Federal government
5. City council
6. School board
7. School superintendent
8. Educators
9. Chamber of commerce
10. Business community (specific business, corporations, or general mention of business community)
11. University community
12. Community groups (to be used only when the term community groups is given with no elaboration and no mentions of specific groups or types of groups)
13. Nonprofit community
14. Ethnic groups
15. Neighborhood citizen groups
16. Parent organizations
17. Unions (dealing with schools)
18. Media
19. Church groups/leaders
20. State courts
21. Labor
22. Political parties
23. Response of everyone in general, but no particular groups/individuals mentioned
24. None
98. Question was not asked or answered in another question
99. Question was asked but not answered

Q6: *Looking at the area of children and youth, especially education, what do you see as the major challenges facing the county? (Allow up to 3)*
1. Lack of workforce preparedness of students
2. Low self-esteem of students/lack of community involvement
3. Health and social issues
4. Crime and drug issues
5. School board problems
6. City government problems
7. Social service problems
8. Before/after school care
9. Finances
10. Minority relations
11. Union conflict
12. Inadequate school resources (poor buildings, teachers' salaries, lack of books and equipment)
13. No problems
14. Poor quality of teaching (curriculum and school organization)
98. Question was not asked or answered in another question
99. Question was asked but not answered

Q7: *Still focusing on education, has there been much change lately in the thinking about approaches and program ideas in City X? If so, what innovative approaches and ideas have been considered?*
1. Yes
0. No
98. Question was not asked or answered in another question
99. Question was asked but not answered

D1. *Ideas and approaches concerning social and educational issues facing schools and youth (Allow up to 3):*
1. Crime prevention programs/strategies
2. Crime enforcement programs/strategies
3. Job training and placement programs/strategies

4. Programs/strategies to educate youth concerning sexually transmitted disease and pregnancy prevention
5. Programs/strategies to deal with youth drug and alcohol abuse
6. Programs/strategies to deal with other health issues not included in 4 or 5
7. Programs/strategies to deal with poverty, lack of parental guidance, and one parent families
8. Programs/strategies to deal with dysfunctional families (child abuse, drug and alcohol abuse of parent/s)
9. Programs/strategies to increase civic involvement in education (including parents groups, church groups, community groups)
10. Choice, including private schools
11. Public school choice, within district
12. Public school choice, cross-district
13. Charter schools
14. Contracting out school management
15. Expanded preschool programs
16. Expanded after-school programs (also summers)
17. Promotion of parental involvement (not including parent groups)
18. School-private partnerships (adopt-a-school programs)
19. Increased business involvement (other than adopt-a-school programs)
20. Interagency collaboration
21. Increased funding to schools
22. Change in curriculum
23. Site-based management of schools
24. More city/county centralized management of schools
25. Quality control (increase quality of teaching, methods of evaluating progress)
26. None or nothing
98. Question was not asked or answered in another question
99. Question was asked but not answered

D2. *For each named, was the respondent involved with this project?*
1. Yes
0. No
98. Unable to code (could not tell if involved or not)

D3. *For each named, how specific was the individual when discussing the policy idea?*
1. Mentioned the policy idea specifically (with elaboration)
2. Mention was not very specific (with little elaboration)
98. Question was not asked or answered in another question
99. Question was asked but not answered

D4. *Who are the players backing the policy/ideas: (Allow up to 5)*
1. Mayor/country executor
2. City government in general
3. State government
4. Federal government
5. City council
6. School board
7. School superintendent
8. Educators
9. Chamber of commerce
10. Business community (specific businesses or corporations, or general mention of business community)
11. University community
12. Community groups (to be used only when the term community groups is given with no elaboration and no mentions of specific groups or types of groups.)
13. Nonprofit foundations
14. Ethnic groups
15. Neighborhood citizen groups
16. Parent organizations
17. Unions(dealing with schools)
18. Media

19. Church groups/leaders
20. State courts
21. Labor
22. Political parties
23. Response of everyone in general, but no particular groups/individuals mentioned
24. None
98. Question was not asked or answered in another question
99. Question was asked but not answered

Q8: *What are the major groups in the county, the active stakeholders ... by that I mean those that play a major part in decision making? (Allow up to 5)*
1. Mayor/county executive
2. City government in general
3. State government
4. Federal government
5. City council
6. School board
7. School superintendent
8. Educators
9. Chamber of commerce
10. Business community (specific businesses or corporations, or general mention of business community)
11. University community
12. Community groups (to be used only when the term community groups is given with no elaboration and no mentions of specific groups or types of groups.)
13. Nonprofit foundations
14. Ethnic groups
15. Neighborhood citizen groups
16. Parent organizations
17. Unions (dealing with schools)
18. Media
19. Church groups/leaders
20. State courts
21. Labor
22. Political parties
23. Response of everyone in general, but no particular groups/individuals mentioned
24. None
98. Question was not asked or answered in another question
99. Question was asked but not answered

Q10: *How do things get done in City X? (what is the informal process)*
1. Formal process
2. Informal process
3. Combination of 1 and 2
4. Things just don't get done (management by crises)
98. Question was not asked or answered in another question
99. Question was asked but not answered

F1. *If there is an informal process or a combo of formal and informal, which players are mentioned as important? (Allow up to 5)*
1. Mayor/county executive
2. City government in general
3. State government
4. Federal government
5. City council
6. School board
7. School superintendent
8. Educators
9. Chamber of commerce
10. Business community (specific businesses or corporation, or general mention of business community)

11. University community
12. Community groups (to be used only when the term community groups is given with no elaboration and no mentions of specific groups or types of groups)
13. Nonprofit community
14. Ethnic groups
15. Neighborhood citizen groups
16. Parent organizations
17. Unions (dealing with schools)
18. Media
19. Church groups/leaders
20. State courts
21. Labor
22. Political parties
23. Response of everyone in general, but no particular groups/individuals mentioned
24. None
98. Question was not asked or answered in another question
99. Question was asked but not answered

Q11: Do the major players work well together?
1. Very well
2. Fairly well
3. Not so well
4. Poorly
5. Admits to the existence of general lines of conflict, but does not elaborate the severity of the problem.
98. Question was not asked or answered in another question
99. Question was asked but not answered

G1. If any answer is not classified as very well (2, 3, 4, or 5 in Q1), then what are the major recurring lines of conflict? (Allow up to 3)
1. Government v. business
2. State or federal government v. local government/school board
3. Citizens v. local government/school board
4. Intra-city/school board conflict
5. Citizen v. business (includes regimes)
6. City v. suburbs
7. Ethnic conflicts
8. Inability of government to get much of anything done
9. Inability of government to deal with social problems
10. Lack of leadership/agenda-setting process
11. Union problems
12. Interest group v. interest group (can include any two (or more) business or community groups)
13. Conflict, but no specific recurring lines
98. Question was not asked or answered in another question
99. Question was asked but not answered

G2. For each choice, is the conflict over
1. Differences in definition of problems
2. Differences in solutions
3. Different interests
4. One groups' inability to be heard
98. Question was not asked or answered in another question
99. Question was asked but not answered

Q13: Is community education a specialized arena or do general leaders play an important role in education?
1. Specialized
2. Several players are involved
98. Question was not asked or answered in another question
99. Question was asked but not answered

H1. If Several players are involved, who are they? (Allow up to 5)
1. Mayor/county executive
2. City government in general
3. State government
4. Federal government
5. City council
6. School board
7. School superintendent
8. Educators
9. Chamber of commerce
10. Business community (specific businesses or corporations, or general mention of business community)
11. University community
12. Community groups (to be used only when the term community groups is given with no elaboration and no mention of specific groups or types of groups.)
13. Nonprofit community
14. Ethnic groups
15. Neighborhood citizen groups
16. Parent organizations
17. Unions (dealing with schools)
18. Media
19. Church groups/leaders
20. State courts
21. Labor
22. Political parties
23. Response everyone in general, but no specific mention of particular groups/individuals
24. None
98. Question was not asked or answered in another question
99. Question was asked but not answered

Q14: When building support for an important educational reform, would you start with one particular player?
1. Yes, there is one particular player to begin with
2. No, there are several players to begin with
98. Question was not asked or answered in another question
99. Question was asked but not answered

I1. If yes, then who is the major player?
1. Mayor/county executive
2. City government in general
3. State government
4. Federal government
5. City council
6. School board
7. School superintendent
8. Educators
9. Chamber of commerce
10. Business community (specific businesses, corporations, or general mention of business community)
11. University community
12. Community groups (to be used only when the term community groups is given with no elaboration and no mentions of specific groups or types of groups)
13. Nonprofit community
14. Ethnic groups
15. Neighborhood citizen groups
16. Parent organizations
17. Unions (dealing with schools)
18. Media
19. Church groups/leaders
20. State courts

21. Labor
22. Political parties
23. Response of everyone in general, but no specific groups/individuals mentioned
24. None
98. Question was not asked or answered in another question
99. Question was asked but not answered

I2. If no, then which players are in the group to begin with? (Allow up to 5)
1. Mayor/county executive
2. City government in general
3. State government
4. Federal government
5. City council
6. School board
7. School superintendent
8. Educators
9. Chamber of commerce
10. Business community (specific businesses, corporations, or general mention of business community)
11. University community
12. Community groups (to be used only when the term community groups is given with no elaboration and no mentions of specific groups or types of groups)
13. Nonprofit community
14. Ethnic government
15. Neighborhood citizen groups
16. Parent organizations
17. Unions (dealing with schools)
18. Media
19. Church groups/leaders
20. State courts
21. Labor
22. Political parties
23. Response of everyone in general, but no specific individuals/groups mentioned
24. None
98. Question was not asked or answered in another question
99. Question was asked but not answered

Q15: Are education decisions in city X highly visible and generate a lot of attention or are they handled pretty routinely and out of the public eye?
1. Highly visible
2. Out of the public eye
3. Becoming more visible
4. Becoming less visible
5. A combination of 1 and 2
98. Question was not asked or answered in another question
99. Question was asked but not answered

Q16: When there is conflict, what is its source? (Allow up to 3)
1. Local government v. business
2. State or federal government v. local government/school board
3. Citizens v. local government/school board
4. Intracity government/school board conflict
5. Citizens v. business (includes regimes)
6. City v. suburbs
7. Ethnic conflicts
8. Inability of government to deal with educational problems (i.e., the processes which would facilitate this are not in place)
9. Inability of government to deal with social problems
10. Lack of leadership/agenda-setting process
11. Unions
12. Interest group v. interest group (can include any two (or more) business or community groups)

13. Conflict, but no specific recurring lines
98. Question was not asked or answered in another question
99. Question was asked but not answered

Q17: In the area of education and youth, which groups are especially effective? (Allow up to 5)
1. Mayor/county executive
2. City government in general
3. State government
4. Federal government
5. City council
6. School board
7. School superintendent
8. Educators
9. Chamber of commerce
10. Business community (specific businesses or corporations, or general mention of business community)
11. University community
12. Community groups (to be used only when the term community groups is given with no elaboration and no mentions of specific groups or types of groups)
13. Nonprofit community
14. Ethnic groups
15. Neighborhood citizen groups
16. Parent organizations
17. Unions (dealing with schools)
18. Media
19. Church groups/leaders
20. State courts
21. Labor
22. Political parties
23. Response of everyone in general, but no specific groups/individuals mentioned
24. None
98. Question was not asked or answered in another question
99. Question was asked but not answered

L1. Why are these players/groups effective?
1. They have financial backing
2. They have large numbers of individuals involved
3. They have connections to other groups with power and funding
4. They are persistent
5. They know the rules
6. Other
98. Question was not asked or answered in another question
99. Question was asked but not answered

Q18: Over the past several years, what do you see as the major change in public education in this community? (Allow up to 3)
1. Decline in quality
2. Increase in quality
3. Change in ethnicity of children serviced
4. Change in important actors
5. Major education reforms
6. Financial stress has increased
7. Financial stress has decreased
8. Social problems have increased
9. Social problems have decreased
10. Crime has increased (included violence and drugs)
11. Crime has decreased (including violence and drugs)
12. Health problems have become more serious
13. Health problems have become less serious
14. School government has become more effective

15. School government has become less effective
98. Question was not asked or answered in another question

99. Question was asked but not answered

Q19: Recognizing that no city can do everything that it would like to do in education, how would you generally characterize the effort in City X?
1. Doing everything that can be done
2. Doing fairly well
3. Falling short of what we could be doing
4. Not doing well at all

Q20: What about for children and youth, especially those from economically disadvantaged backgrounds? What kinds of efforts are being made? (Allow up to 3)
1. To remove educational disadvantages
2. To deal with health problems
3. To lift self-esteem
4. To provide better employment opportunities
5. No effort
6. General realization of problems but no specific effort
98. Question was not asked or answered in another question

99. Question was asked but not answered

O1. If 1 through 4, are these programs targeted at:
1. Individual schools
2. The entire city
3. The region
4. A combination of 1 and 2
5. A combination of 2 and 3
98. Question was not asked or answered in another question

99. Question was asked but not answered

O2. Who is making these efforts? (Allow up to 5)
1. Mayor/county executive
2. City government in general
3. State government
4. Federal government
5. City council
6. School board
7. School superintendent
8. Educators
9. Chamber of commerce
10. Business community (specific businesses, corporations, or general mention of business community)
11. University community
12. Community groups (to be used only when the term community groups is given with no elaboration and no mentions of specific groups or types of groups)
13. Nonprofit community
14. Ethnic groups
15. Neighborhood citizen groups
16. Parent organizations
17. Unions (dealing with schools)
18. Media
19. Church groups/leaders
20. State courts
21. Labor
22. Political parties
23. Response of everyone in general, but no specific groups/individuals mentioned
24. None
98. Question was not asked or answered in another question

99. Question was asked but not answered

Q21: What is done well? (Allow up to 3)
 1. Crime prevention programs/strategies
 2. Crime enforcement programs/strategies
 3. Job training and placement programs/strategies
 4. Programs/strategies to educate youth concerning sexually transmitted disease and pregnancy prevention
 5. Programs/strategies to deal with youth drug and alcohol abuse
 6. Programs/strategies to deal with other health issues not included in 4 or 5
 7. Programs/strategies to deal with poverty, lack of parental guidance, and one parent families
 8. Programs/strategies to deal with dysfunctional families (child abuse, drug and alcohol abuse of parent/s)
 9. Programs/strategies to increase civic involvement in education (including parent groups, church groups, and community groups)
 10. Choice, including private schools
 11. Public school choice, within district
 12. Public school choice, cross-district
 13. Charter schools
 14. Contracting out school management
 15. Expanded pre-school programs
 16. Expanded after-school programs (also summer)
 17. Promotion of parental involvement (not including parent groups)
 18. School-private partnerships (adopt-a-school programs)
 19. Increased business involvement (other than adopt-a-school programs)
 20. Interagency collaboration
 21. Increased funding to schools
 22. Change in curriculum
 23. Site-based management of schools
 24. More city/county centralized management of schools
 25. Quality control (increase quality of teaching, methods of evaluating progress)
 26. None or nothing
 98. Question was not asked or answered in another question
 99. Question was asked but not answered

P1. What groups or individuals are doing these things? (Allow up to 5)
 1. Mayor/county executive
 2. City government in general
 3. State government
 4. Federal government
 5. City council
 6. School board
 7. School superintendent
 8. Educators
 9. Chamber of commerce
 10. Business community (specific businesses, corporations, or general mention of business community)
 11. University community
 12. Community groups (to be used only when the term community groups is given with no elaboration and no mentions of specific groups or types of groups)
 13. Nonprofit community
 14. Ethnic groups
 15. Neighborhood citizen groups
 16. Parent organizations
 17. Unions (dealing with schools)
 18. Media
 19. Church groups/leaders
 20. State courts
 21. Labor
 22. Political parties
 23. Response of everyone in general, but no specific groups/individuals mentioned
 24. None
 98. Question was not asked or answered in another question

99. Question was asked but not answered

P2. Are these things being done at:
1. Individual schools
2. The entire city
3. The region
4. Combination of 1 and 2
5. Combination of 2 and 3
98. Question was not asked or answered in another question
99. Question was asked but not answered

Q23: What would enable City X to make a greater effort in the area of education?
1. Government bureaucracy better able to deal with financial, social, and educational issues
2. More involvement by mayor/council (to include stronger commitment/ leadership)
3. Stronger superintendent
4. Cut central bureaucracy
5. Redistribute resources
6. More capable school board
7. More control to school board
8. More control to individual schools
9. More motivation/ control to parents
10. More involvement by the unions (dealing with schools)
11. Achievement of agenda status by educational issues (systemic agenda)
12. Creation of an agenda by those involved in education policy (governmental agenda)
98. Question was not asked or answered in another question
99. Question was asked but not answered

R1. What are the obstacles to these efforts:
1. Those capable of making the change do not see the problem
2. Little motivation among groups necessary to make the change
3. Little power among groups necessary to make the change
4. Distraction from integration issues
98. Question was not asked or answered in another question
99. Question was asked but not answered

Q24: What reasons would you give for City X to put extra resources into education or programs for education? (Allow up to 3)
1. Problems in City X are greater than the problems in other cities
2. This city's expenditures are not comparable to the expenditures put forth by other cities
3. More funding would attract higher quality teachers
4. Better school environments would motivate children and raise their self-esteem
5. More funding could provide a safer environment for teachers and students
6. Better schools lead to better workforce/economic development
7. Better schools lead to less crime
8. More resources should not be put into the schools
98. Question was not asked or answered in another question
99. Question was asked but not answered

S1. If 8, then why not:
1. The structure of school government must change before more funding can make a difference
2. Already enough funding and resources now, but they are not being used properly
3. There are no problems with the system we have today
98. Question was not asked or answered in another question
99. Question was asked but not answered

Q26: Other reports?
1. Yes
0. No
98. Question was not asked or answered in another question
99. Question was asked but not answered

Q27: Other issues? (Allow up to 3)
1. Lack of workforce preparedness of students
2. Low self-esteem of students
3. Health and social issues
4. Crime and drug issues
5. School board problems
6. City government problems
7. Social services problems
8. Before/after school care
9. Finances
10. Minority relations
11. Union conflict (unions dealing with schools)
12. Education reform
13. No problems
14. Poor quality of teaching (curriculum and school organization)
98. Question was not asked or answered in another question
99. Question was asked but not answered

Gender?
0. Female
1. Male

Race?
1. White
2. Black
3. Eurasian
4. Hispanic

Years lived in City?

Children in public schools?

ADDITIONAL QUESTIONS ASKED
OF COMMUNITY ACTIVISTS

Q3: What policy initiatives or programs are you especially concerned with currently?
1. No policy initiatives or programs
2. New policy initiatives or programs
98. Question was not asked or answered in another question
99. Question was asked but not answered

B1. if response is 2: What are the policy initiatives or programs concerned with? (Allow up to three)
1. Concerning problems of crime
2. Concerning problems of unemployment
3. For improving governmental bureaucracy
4. To confront health issues/social issues
5. To remove racial inequalities
6. Concerning economic problems/development
7. Concerning education (include school-to-work)
8. Concerning community self-esteem/awareness/involvement
9. No new ideas
98. Question was not asked or answered in another question
99. Question was asked but not answered

B2. How specific was the individual when discussing the policy idea?
1. Mentioned policy specifically (with elaboration)
2. Mention was not very specific (naming the problem with little elaboration)
98. Question was not asked or answered in another question
99. Question was asked but not answered

Q4: Who are the major players in the issue areas you are concerned with? (Allow up to 5)
1. Mayor/county executive
2. City government in general
3. State government

4. Federal government
5. City council
6. School board
7. School superintendent
8. Educators
9. Chamber of commerce
10. Business community (specific business, corporations or general mention of business community)
11. University community
12. Community groups (to be used only when the term community groups is given with no elaboration and no mentions of specific groups or types of groups.)
13. Nonprofit community
14. Ethnic groups
15. Neighborhood citizen groups
16. Parent organizations
17. Unions (dealing with schools)
18. Media
19. Church groups/leaders
20. State courts
21. Labor
22. Political parties
23. Response of everyone in general, but no particular groups/individuals mentioned
24. None
98. Question was not asked or answered in another question
99. Question was asked but not answered

Q9: What do you think are the top policy priorities of the major elected officials in the county? (Allow up to 3)
0. Don't know
1. Education
2. Proactive youth programs
3. Government infrastructure
4. Crime (to include prevention of, police enforcement)
5. Drugs
6. Economic redevelopment
7. Dealing with social problems (poverty, unemployment, city resources)
8. Dealing with problem of poor race relations
9. Health care
10. Redistribution of power and resources
11. Government services (not dealing specifically with social problems, like: transportation)
12. Self-interest
13. Reducing bureaucracy
14. Improving efficiency
98. Question was not asked or answered in another question
99. Question was asked but not answered

Q10: Are those priorities generally shared by others? For example, by business? Various community groups?
1. Yes
2. No
3. Don't know
4. Combination of 1 and 2
98. Question was not asked or answered in another question
99. Question was asked but not answered

E1. If 1, then specifically, who shares these general priorities? (allow up to 5)
1. Business community
2. Nonprofit community
3. Religious groups
4. Community groups in general
5. Parent organizations
6. Everyone

7. State government
8. Federal government
98. Question was not asked or answered in another question
99. Question was asked but not answered

Q12: *Of the various government offices and officials, which ones do you work with most often? (Allow up to 5)*
1. Governor
2. State legislators
3. State agencies/departments
4. County officials
5. Mayor
6. Aldermen/City Council
7. School Board
8. School System
9. District Attorney's office/Judges/Sheriff's office/Police Department
10. Department of Social Services
11. Federal government
12. Federal/state courts
13. Local agencies/departments
14. Local government in general
15. State government in general
16. State Education Dept./Board of Education
17. Other
98. Question was not asked or answered in another question
99. Question was asked but not answered

Q13: *Who are your most dependable allies in the public sector? [Probe: What roles do they play?] (Allow up to 5)*
1. Governor
2. State legislators
3. State agencies/departments
4. County officials
5. Mayor
6. Aldermen/City Council
7. School Board
8. School System
9. District Attorney's office/Judges/Sheriff's office/Police Department
10. Department of Social Services
11. Federal government
12. Federal/state courts
13. Local agencies/departments
14. Local government in general
15. State government in general
16. State education dept./Board of Education
17. Other
98. Question was not asked or answered in another question
99. Question was asked but not answered.

Q14: *What about business groups and organizations—are there some you work with? [Probe: Who are they?] Do you see them as close allies? (Allow up to 5)*
1. Specific businesses or corporations
2. Chamber of Commerce
3. Labor organizations
4. Business-education cooperative organizations
5. Entrepreneur training programs
6. Business alliances (e.g., New Detroit, Detroit Renaissance)
7. Don't know
98. Question was not asked or answered in another question
99. Question was asked but not answered.

Q15: *What about nonprofit groups, volunteer organizations and other community groups— whom do you work with most closely? (Allow up to 5)*
1. Child development groups (e.g., YMCA, YWCA, 4-H)

2. Educators groups
3. University system
4. Ethnic organizations (e.g., NAACP, Urban League, United Negro College Fund)
5. Church organizations
6. Foundations
7. Community Chests (e.g., United Way)
8. Parent groups (e.g., PTA)
9. Political groups (e.g., League of Women Voters)
10. Don't know
98. Question was not asked or answered in another question
99. Question was asked but not answered .

Q16: *Who are your most dependable allies among these groups and organizations?* *(Allow up to 5)*
1. Child development groups
2. Educators groups
3. University system
4. Ethnic organizations/communities
5. Church organizations
6. Foundations
7. Community chests (e.g., United Way)
8. Parents groups (e.g., PTA)
9. Political organizations (e.g., League of Women Voters)
10. Specific businesses or corporations
11. Chamber of Commerce
12. Labor organizations
13. Business -Education cooperative organizations
14. Entrepreneur training programs
15. Business alliances (e.g., New Detroit, Detroit Renaissance)
16. Don't know
98. Question was not asked or answered in another question
99. Question was asked but not answered

TEXT ANALYSIS

In our study we relied on this common data collection and analysis to provide the foundation of our argument about the distinctive nature of multiethnic school politics. The semistructured interviews asked respondents about education problems and about the political relationships between school district actors and others, such as business, nonprofits, and city government. They also inquired about reform efforts and their origins, and how well the schools served disadvantaged children. But the coding and categorization necessary for the larger comparative analysis could not do justice to the subtleties and sensibilities uncovered in our interviews. To explore the multiple meanings of school reform to different ethnic and racial groups in our cities, we turned to textual analysis of the transcribed interviews. Although there are many text analysis software programs available, we used NUD•IST (Non-numerical Unstructured Data with Indexing, Searching, and Theorizing), now supplanted by NVivo. This approach allowed us to retain the context of the interview comments by comparing the respondents within each city in terms of their race/ethnicity and their membership in the three groupings. Since the city samples were constructed in terms of potential policy influence rather than race/ethnicity, using race/ethnicity to group respondents can result in imperfect clusters for some cities.

The analysis in Chapter 5 draws on 191 interview transcripts from fieldwork in four multiracial cities. It relies on two data sets: a problem set and a solution set. Both were built by coding interview transcripts using NUD•IST software. Statements about problems and solutions were sorted by city, and by the race of the speaker. NUD•IST's feature of keeping code and text together enables creation of summary data such as the percentages presented in the tables in the chapter, but also keeps the analyst close enough to the text to pay attention to variations and nuances within code categories. The data set about education problems consists of 1,296 paragraphs, called problem statements, which arise in 187 interviews. The second data set consists of statements from interviews about specific education reforms, and includes 680 paragraphs arising in 173 interviews.

DATA APPENDIX

I. CITY AND METROPOLITAN AREA CHARACTERISTICS, 1970–2000

	1970 Denver	1970 MSA	1980 Denver	1980 MSA	1990 Denver	1990 MSA	2000 Denver	2000 MSA
Population	514,678	1,227,612	492,360	1,428,708	467,610	1,622,980	554,636	2,109,282
Race & Hispanic Origin								
White	459,734 (89.3%)	1,162,860 (94.7%)	326,549 (66.3%)	1,156,443 (80.9%)	287,162 (61.4%)	1,272,389 (78.4%)	287,997 (51.9%)	1,489,610 (69.9%)
Black	47,187 (9.2%)	50,164 (4.1%)	58,408 (11.9%)	74,875 (5.2%)	57,793 (12.4%)	92,296 (5.7%)	64,370 (11.6%)	124,352 (5.9%)
Hispanic	86,345 (16.8%)	138,928 (11.3%)	92,348 (18.8%)	163,388 (11.4%)	107,382 (23.0%)	211,005 (13.0%)	175,709 (31.7%)	397,236 (18.8%)
Asian	6,136 (1.2%)	11,497 (0.9%)	7,025 (1.4%)	18,283 (1.3%)	11,005 (2.4%)	37,134 (2.3%)	18,158 (3.3%)	75,021 (3.6%)
Under 18	156,508	432,500	128,172	506,704	102,879	420,670	121,766	545,034
White	133,132 (85.1%)	405,203 (93.7%)	81,313 (63.4%)	430,906 (85.0%)	43,118 (41.9%)	301,170 (71.6%)	35,988 (29.6%)	333,867 (61.3%)
Black	20,025 (12.8%)	21,210 (4.9%)	22,210 (17.3%)	29,981 (5.8%)	17,019 (16.5%)	28,928 (6.9%)	19,735 (16.2%)	41,451 (7.6%)
Hispanic	39,600 (25.3%)	65,383 (15.1%)	40,105 (31.2%)	77,775 (15.3%)	38,132 (37.1%)	75,506 (17.9%)	60,004 (49.3%)	139,698 (25.6%)
Asian	N/A	N/A	3,140 (2.4%)	8,570 (1.6%)	3,139 (3.1%)	11,717 (2.8%)	3,970 (3.3%)	21,565 (4.0%)
Median Income	$9,654	$10,896	$15,506	$19,989	$25,106	$32,852	$39,500	$51,196
White	N/A	N/A	16,233	20,567	27,636	N/A	44,022	55,550
Black	7,287	7,341	12,344	13,633	19,469	N/A	30,895	35,720
Hispanic	7,323	8,085	12,606	15,643	19,268	N/A	32,636	38,115
Asian	N/A	N/A	16,578	19,272	21,250	N/A	36,194	49,468
Per Capita Income	3,557	3,497	8,555	8,900	15,590	16,539	24,101	26,206
White	N/A	N/A	9,618	9,328	18,191	17,613	33,765	30,735
Black	2,234	2,239	5,833	6,056	10,442	11,125	16,939	18,533
Hispanic	1,979	2,117	4,510	5,143	7,778	9,220	11,990	13,688
Asian	N/A	N/A	6,023	6,570	9,556	11,284	18,705	20,825

CITY AND METROPOLITAN AREA CHARACTERISTICS, 1970–2000 (continued)

	1970 Denver (%)	1970 MSA (%)	1980 Denver (%)	1980 MSA (%)	1990 Denver	1990 MSA	2000 Denver	2000 MSA
Poverty Rate (%)	10.7	7.3	13.7	8.4	17.1	9.7	14.3	8.0
White	N/A	N/A	10.2	6.9	9.9	8.8	7.8	4.7
Black	24.2	24.1	23.3	21.1	27.0	24.6	19.2	16.0
Hispanic	23.0	18.3	23.9	17.5	30.6	22.3	22.4	17.7
Asian	N/A	N/A	24.0	16.1	26.2	14.6	17.0	10.0
Education (%)								
High School Graduate								
White	66.4	70.6	78.0	83.0	83.5	88.2	91.8	92.7
Black	54.1	54.6	70.1	73.5	75.0	79.4	79.7	83.6
Hispanic	33.6	40.9	42.8	52.2	50.4	60.2	46.1	55.9
Asian	N/A	N/A	70.8	78.3	69.8	78.0	77.0	79.8
College Graduate								
White	18.1	18.7	27.9	27.2	33.9	32.2	47.8	39.7
Black	6.9	7.7	12.0	14.2	14.5	17.5	17.8	21.0
Hispanic	3.9	6.2	6.1	8.4	6.9	9.6	7.8	10.6
Asian	N/A	N/A	26.8	30.2	32.1	34.1	40.7	40.6
Segregation								
White/Black	84.6	84.7	72.2	69.1	67.1	64.5	63.0	61.8
White/Hispanic	N/A	N/A	55.9	49.0	54.6	46.7	57.0	50.2
White/Asian	N/A	N/A	26.7	26.5	31.4	29.8	30.8	30.0
Black/Hispanic	N/A	N/A	72.9	71.3	72.2	68.6	62.3	56.0
Black/Asian	N/A	N/A	61.6	59.9	60.6	54.0	58.3	50.8
Hispanic/Asian	N/A	N/A	51.5	46.1	44.5	42.3	46.8	45.3

CITY AND METROPOLITAN AREA CHARACTERISTICS, 1970–2000 (continued)

School Segregation	1970 Denver	1970 MSA	1980 Denver	1980 MSA	1990 Denver	1990 MSA	2000 Denver	2000 MSA
White/Black	N/A	N/A	N/A	N/A	46.3	67.0	63.1	68.4
White/Hispanic	N/A	N/A	N/A	N/A	39.3	55.8	57.5	59.7
White/Asian	N/A	N/A	N/A	N/A	33.2	35.8	34.5	35.5
Black/Hispanic	N/A	N/A	N/A	N/A	71.9	70.3	64.4	58.7
Black/Asian	N/A	N/A	N/A	N/A	50.9	56.6	56.5	56.6
Hispanic/Asian	N/A	N/A	N/A	N/A	46.0	51.6	48.9	51.7

	1970 Boston	1970 MSA	1980 Boston	1980 MSA	1990 Boston	1990 MSA	2000 Boston	2000 MSA
Population	641,056	2,753,804	562,994	3,147,313	574,283	3,226,935	589,141	3,405,985
Race & Hispanic Origin								
White	524,709 (81.8%)	2,602,741 (94.5%)	382,123 (67.9%)	2,856,929 (90.8%)	338,734 (69%)	2,779,570 (86.1%)	291,561 (49.5%)	2,725,194 (80.0%)
Black	104,596 (16.3%)	126,276 (4.5%)	122,203 (21.7%)	160,121 (5.1%)	136,887 (23.8%)	198,224 (6.1%)	151,246 (25.7%)	247,675 (7.3%)
Hispanic	17,984 (2.8%)	36,190 (1.3%)	36,068 (6.4%)	71,918 (2.3%)	61,995 (10.8%)	137458 (4.3%)	85,089 (14.4%)	202,510 (5.9%)
Asian	7,320 (0.3%)	9,265 (1.4%)	15,150 (2.7%)	38,590 (1.2%)	30,388 (5.3%)	97,732 (3.0%)	46,919 (8.0%)	181,984 (5.3%)
Under 18	181,805	878,293	151,155	787,441	109,456	672,022	115,874	765,856
White	132,625 (72.9%)	817,627 (93.1%)	85,245 (56.3%)	664,697 (84.4%)	45,982 (42.0%)	540,801 (80.5%)	29,640 (25.6%)	566,991 (74.0%)
Black	45,510 (25.0%)	53,187 (6.1%)	49,820 (32.9%)	61,961 (7.9%)	44,611 (40.8%)	57,995 (8.6%)	43,233 (37.3%)	76,998 (10.1%)
Hispanic	7,676 (4.2%)	15,299 (1.7%)	16,233 (10.7%)	29,015 (3.7%)	18,846 (17.2%)	43,469 (6.5%)	27,355 (23.7%)	66,176 (8.6%)
Asian	N/A	N/A	4,487 (2.9%)	12,255 (1.5%)	6,602 (6.0%)	25,153 (3.7%)	7,650 (6.6%)	43,213 (5.6%)
Median Income	9,563	11,449	12,530	18,694	29,180	40,491	39,629	55,183
White	N/A	N/A	13,701	19,384	32,261	52,411	47,668	59,323
Black	5,023	5,106	10,277	11,099	23,809	32,220	31,061	35,291
Hispanic	4,970	6,203	8,745	10,673	19,504	30,777	27,141	33,051
Asian	N/A	N/A	12,136	16,998	22,337	N/A	27,732	51,277

CITY AND METROPOLITAN AREA CHARACTERISTICS, 1970–2000 (continued)

	1970 Boston	1970 MSA	1980 Boston	1980 MSA	1990 Boston	1990 MSA	2000 Boston	2000 MSA
Per Capita Income	3,099	3,713	6,555	8,182	15,581	19,288	23,353	29,227
White	N/A	N/A	7,448	8,471	18,939	20,455	32,709	32,215
Black	2,054	2,169	4,620	5,008	10,420	11,323	15,186	16,932
Hispanic	1,939	2,488	3,583	4,261	8,364	9,461	11,931	13,774
Asian	N/A	N/A	4,697	6,487	9,400	13,470	15,537	22,586
Poverty Rate (%)	16.2	8.5	20.2	9.4	18.7	8.3	19.5	17.9
White	N/A	N/A	15.7	8.1	13.3	6.3	13.1	
Black	28.4	26.5	28.6	26.1	24.2	21.2	21.9	
Hispanic	34.4	22.1	41.9	34.4	33.9	28.4	30.5	
Asian	N/A	N/A	22.4	16.4	29.5	N/A	30.0	
Education (%)								
High School Graduate								
White	N/A	N/A	71.9	78.2	81.2	85.4	88.4	90.1
Black	45.1	47.1	61.7	64.7	66.7	70.7	73.0	76.4
Hispanic	40.1	53.6	48.4	53.2	52.8	58.8	57.3	61.0
Asian	N/A	N/A	75.4	71.7	61.9	75.8	64.3	78.3
College Graduate								
White	N/A	N/A	23.6	25.2	36.7	34.1	48.8	41.5
Black	4.1	5.8	8.7	12.1	14.0	17.9	15.6	20.8
Hispanic	10.9	17.9	11.7	16.5	13.9	18.2	15.3	18.7
Asian	N/A	N/A	47.3	41.6	31.5	47.1	37.0	53.4
Segregation								
White/Black	81.2	79.3	78.6	76.5	75.3	69.5	70.4	65.7
White/Hispanic	N/A	N/A	59.0	55.4	54.2	55.3	53.3	58.8
White/Asian	N/A	N/A	57.9	48.2	43.2	44.3	39.9	44.9
Black/Hispanic	N/A	N/A	52.0	52.0	47.3	46.2	43.5	43.4
Black/Asian	N/A	N/A	82.7	72.8	74.5	62.3	69.4	56.6
Hispanic/Asian	N/A	N/A	64.1	53.8	52.1	47.1	55.1	51.4

CITY AND METROPOLITAN AREA CHARACTERISTICS, 1970–2000 (continued)

Boston	1970 MSA	1980 Boston	1980 MSA	1990 Boston	1990 MSA	2000 Boston	2000 Los Angeles	2000 MSA
School Segregation								
White/Black	N/A	N/A	N/A	N/A	32.8	71.1	44.8	70.7
White/Hispanic	N/A	N/A	N/A	N/A	48.8	71.5	46.5	71.5
White/Asian	N/A	N/A	N/A	N/A	55.6	53.7	46.2	54.5
Black/Hispanic	N/A	N/A	N/A	N/A	40.1	45.5	46.2	48.8
Black/Asian	N/A	N/A	N/A	N/A	63.5	60.1	57.0	55.8
Hispanic/Asian	N/A	N/A	N/A	N/A	64.0	61.5	63.2	59.8

	1970 Los Angeles	1970 MSA	1980 Los Angeles	1980 MSA	1990 Los Angeles	1990 MSA	2000 Los Angeles	2000 MSA
Population	2,816,061	7,032,075	2,966,836	7,471,200	3,485,398	8,854,200	3,694,820	9,519,338
Race & Hispanic Origin								
White	2,173,600 (77.2%)	6,006,499 (85.4%)	1,419,402 (47.8%)	3,949,861 (52.9%)	1,299,604 (37.3%)	3,618,030 (40.9%)	1,099,188 (29.7%)	2,959,614 (31.1%)
Black	503,606 (17.9%)	762,844 (10.8%)	495,722 (16.7%)	924,9939 (12.4%)	454,289 (13%)	932,888 (10.5%)	422,819 (11.4%)	950,765 (10.1%)
Hispanic	518,791 (18.4%)	1,289,311 (18.3%)	816,075 (27.5%)	2,065,155 (27.6%)	1,391,411 (39.9%)	3,345,047 (37.8%)	1,719,073 (45.5%)	4,242,213 (44.6%)
Asian	110,787 (3.9%)	202,844 (2.9%)	196,017 (6.6%)	434,655 (5.8%)	341,807 (9.8%)	954,432 (10.8%)	398,888 (10.8%)	1,232,085 (12.9%)
Under 18	849,202	2,260,018	850,292	2,298,265	861,436	2,325,988	978,575	2,667,976
White	614,196 (72.3%)	1,861,301 (82.4%)	451,531 (53.1%)	1,402,492 (61%)	370,404 (42.9%)	638,200 (27.4%)	165,733 (16.9%)	528,353 (19.8%)
Black	194,024 (22.8%)	312,383 (13.8%)	172,418 (20.2%)	352,037 (15.3%)	130,566 (15.1%)	266,133 (11.4%)	106,334 (10.9%)	287,541 (10.8%)
Hispanic	209,060 (24.6%)	552,367 (24.4%)	333,125 (39.1%)	885,306 (38.5%)	468,410 (54.4%)	1,173,685 (50.5%)	609,586 (62.3%)	1,534,979 (57.5%)
Asian	N/A	N/A	56,771 (6.7%)	139,682 (6.1%)	75,452 (8.8%)	247,923 (10.7%)	64,994 (6.6%)	283,351 (10.6%)

CITY AND METROPOLITAN AREA CHARACTERISTICS, 1970–2000 (continued)

	1970		1980		1990		2000	
	Los Angeles	MSA	Los Angeles	MSA	Los Angeles	MSA	Los Angeles	MSA
Median Income	10,535	9,280	15,735	17,551	30,925	34,965	36,687	42,189
White	N/A	N/A	17,931	19,051	40,325	N/A	51,516	53,978
Black	7,200	6,506	10,756	12,423	21,353	N/A	27,236	31,885
Hispanic	8,241	8,291	12,481	14,645	23,398	N/A	28,759	33,820
Asian	N/A	N/A	17,157	20,580	32,018	N/A	37,195	47,656
Per Capita Income	3,977	3,884	8,408	8,303	16,188	16,149	20,671	20,683
White	N/A	N/A	10,316	9,560	22,191	20,531	39,272	35,785
Black	2,435	2,398	5,463	5,714	11,257	12,018	16,894	17,484
Hispanic	2,474	2,489	4,340	4,627	7,111	8,066	10,070	11,100
Asian	N/A	N/A	7,251	7,654	13,875	14,584	19,611	20,652
Poverty Rate (%)	13.3	10.9	16.4	13.4	18.9	15.1	22.1	17.9
White	N/A	N/A	11.5	9.9	8.2	10.6	10.0	8.5
Black	25.5	24.0	26.2	23.1	25.3	21.2	28.0	24.4
Hispanic	17.4	14.7	24.2	20.5	28.2	22.9	29.6	24.2
Asian	N/A	N/A	15.6	12.8	14.8	13.2	16.9	13.7
Education (%)								
High School Graduate								
White	N/A	N/A	74.4	73.3	75.8	76.7	90.1	89.4
Black	50.3	51.7	64.3	68.6	69.9	73.8	76.0	79.3
Hispanic	39.9	40.9	34.9	39.9	35.4	39.2	35.5	42.1
Asian	N/A	N/A	87.7	80.2	77.6	79.7	82.1	82.4
College Grad								
White	N/A	N/A	23.5	20.5	28.8	25.6	42.6	37.7
Black	6.2	5.7	9.7	11.2	13.3	14.8	17.1	17.8
Hispanic	6.4	5.5	5.5	5.6	6.0	6.0	6.1	6.8
Asian	N/A	N/A	40.4	34.9	35.1	37.2	42.4	42.9

CITY AND METROPOLITAN AREA CHARACTERISTICS, 1970–2000 (continued)

	1970 Los Angeles	1970 MSA	1980 Los Angeles	1980 MSA	1990 Los Angeles	1990 MSA	2000 Los Angeles	2000 MSA
Segregation								
White/Black	88.6	88.5	85.0	81.2	78.4	73.2	71.5	67.5
White/Hispanic	N/A	N/A	62.0	57.3	64.5	61.1	65.6	63.2
White/Asian	N/A	N/A	51.7	47.1	47.8	46.4	44.9	48.3
Black/Hispanic	N/A	N/A	73.0	72.5	59.3	59.7	53.2	54.3
Black/Asian	N/A	N/A	78.3	76.2	72.6	69.0	67.2	66.2
Hispanic/Asian	N/A	N/A	44.2	49.5	45.3	50.2	50.2	55.0
School Segregation								
White/Black	N/A	N/A	N/A	N/A	74.2	69.5	72.9	66.8
White/Hispanic	N/A	N/A	N/A	N/A	69.5	65.8	72.4	69.3
White/Asian	N/A	N/A	N/A	N/A	49.0	48.0	46.8	52.2
Black/Hispanic	N/A	N/A	N/A	N/A	61.7	58.5	60.3	55.9
Black/Asian	N/A	N/A	N/A	N/A	72.6	67.4	70.0	66.2
Hispanic/Asian	N/A	N/A	N/A	N/A	57.3	57.3	61.2	61.2

	1970 San Francisco	1970 MSA	1980 San Francisco	1980 MSA	1990 San Francisco	1990 MSA	2000 San Francisco	2000 MSA
Population	715,674	3,109,519	678,972	1,487,530	723,959	1,603,678	776,733	1,731,183
Race & Hispanic Origin								
White	511,186 (71.4%)	2,574,802 (82.8%)	355,159 (52.3%)	969,833 (62.2%)	337,118 (46.6%)	923,914 (57.6%)	338,909 (43.6%)	885,518 (51.2%)
Black	96,078 (13.4%)	330,107 (10.6%)	84,857 (12.5%)	124,810 (8.4%)	76,343 (10.5%)	117,872 (7.4%)	64,070 (8.2%)	99,199 (5.7%)
Hispanic	101,901 (14.2%)	363,893 (11.7%)	83,373 (12.3%)	165,089 (11.1%)	100,717 (13.9%)	233,274 (14.5%)	109,504 (14.1%)	291,563 (16.6%)
Asian	97,995 (13.7%)	176,638 (5.7%)	147,426 (21.7%)	209,087 (14.1%)	210,876 (29.1%)	329,599 (20.6%)	253,047 (32.6%)	430,1469 (24.8%)

CITY AND METROPOLITAN AREA CHARACTERISTICS, 1970–2000 (continued)

	1970		1980		1990		2000	
	San Francisco	MSA	San Francisco	MSA	San Francisco	MSA	San Francisco	MSA
Under 18	159,876	941,393	133,801	868,399	116,883	302,275	116,883	302,275
White	91,234 (57.1%)	746,203 (79.3%)	52,253 (39.0%)	569,693 (65.6%)	29,537 (25.3%)	132,752 (43.9%)	29,537 (25.3%)	132,752 (43.9%)
Black	35,831 (22.4%)	130,064 (13.8%)	26,968 (20.1%)	197,234 (22.7%)	18,704 (16.0%)	29,152 (9.6%)	18,704 (16.0%)	29,152 (9.6%)
Hispanic	34,624 (21.6%)	140,054 (14.9%)	26,187 (19.5%)	133,170 (15.3%)	24,254 (20.8%)	64,596 (21.4%)	24,254 (20.8%)	64,596 (21.4%)
Asian	N/A	N/A	40,709 (30.0%)	100,392 (11.5%)	44,883 (38.4%)	76,468 (25.3%)	44,883 (38.4%)	76,468 (25.3%)
Median Income	11,750	10,064	15,866	20,017	33,414	40,494	55,221	63,297
White	N/A	N/A	16,217	21,085	36,434	N/A	65,431	70,948
Black	7,676	6,813	11,254	12,631	21,733	N/A	29,561	35,490
Hispanic	9,497	9,658	14,509	17,964	29,816	N/A	46,553	50,905
Asian	N/A	N/A	18,440	21,367	32,977	N/A	49,607	60,493
Per Capita Income	4,289	4,122	9,265	9,593	19,695	22,049	34,556	36,651
White	N/A	N/A	11,295	10,751	26,222	26,580	51,986	50,732
Black	2,585	2,476	5,994	6,064	11,829	12,237	19,352	20,924
Hispanic	2,979	3,028	5,944	6,276	11,400	11,583	18,584	17,137
Asian	N/A	N/A	6,761	7,386	12,665	14,286	22,352	25,593
Poverty Rate (%)	10.0	14.0	13.7	9.8	12.7	9.0	11.3	8.4
White	N/A	N/A	11.1	7.1	9.0	6.5	7.7	5.4
Black	24.6	23.4	25.1	22.3	26.2	22.5	25.0	21.0
Hispanic	14.1	11.2	17.1	13.1	16.4	14.2	15.6	13.0
Asian	N/A	N/A	12.7	11.0	12.6	10.3	10.7	8.5

CITY AND METROPOLITAN AREA CHARACTERISTICS, 1970–2000 (continued)

	1970 San Francisco	1970 MSA	1980 San Francisco	1980 MSA	1990 San Francisco	1990 MSA	2000 San Francisco	2000 MSA
Education (%)								
High School Grad								
White	N/A	N/A	80.0	82.1	86.8	87.6	94.7	94.4
Black	48.5	47.1	62.4	67.0	72.4	57.4	76.1	75.9
Hispanic	52.5	51.9	57.6	58.9	60.7	60.7	62.5	59.2
Asian	N/A	N/A	64.3	72.7	64.7	72.0	67.3	75.6
College Grad								
White	N/A	N/A	33.1	28.2	44.6	39.4	63.2	54.8
Black	5.7%	5.6%	11.2	11.7	14.9	15.6	18.1	18.5
Hispanic	9.7%	8.3%	13.4	11.4	15.1	13.8	20.3	16.2
Asian	N/A	N/A	25.1	30.1	25.5	30.6	31.2	38.9
Segregation								
White/Black	67.8	77.3	62.5	67.9	58.2	64.1	57.0	60.9
White/Hispanic	N/A	N/A	47.9	45.6	50.9	50.0	53.1	53.9
White/Asian	N/A	N/A	35.2	51.1	38.0	50.1	40.3	48.7
Black/Hispanic	N/A	N/A	62.6	59.0	59.3	54.4	53.2	49.8
Black/Asian	N/A	N/A	64.4	59.8	58.2	55.0	54.5	52.1
Hispanic/Asian	N/A	N/A	48.9	45.3	47.6	46.9	44.9	48.1
School Segregation								
White/Black	N/A	N/A	N/A	N/A	69.9	46.0	71.6	58.6
White/Hispanic	N/A	N/A	N/A	N/A	59.4	52.8	62.4	59.6
White/Asian	N/A	N/A	N/A	N/A	63.1	33.2	64.2	37.3
Black/Hispanic	N/A	N/A	N/A	N/A	44.3	32.5	49.5	39.8
Black/Asian	N/A	N/A	N/A	N/A	43.3	40.2	49.3	50.3
Hispanic/Asian	N/A	N/A	N/A	N/A	46.8	45.2	51.0	44.0

II. SCHOOL DISTRICT CHARACTERISTICS

A. Size, Enrollment, Poverty, Finance

	BOSTON	DENVER	LOS ANGELES	SAN FRANCISCO
Number of Students[1]				
1995/96	63,293	64,322	647,612	61,374
2000/01	63,024	70,847	721,346	59,979
% Free & Reduced Price Lunch Eligible				
1995/96	N/A	N/A	N/A	49.7
2000/01	72	59.9	73.5	53.5
2002/03	74	62	74	N/A
% English Language Learners				
1995/96	N/A	N/A	N/A	30.5
2000/2001	21	27.7	43.2	31.5
Enrollment				
% African American				
1995/96	47.9	21.3	14.3	17.4
2000/01	48.4	20.3	12.8	15.6
% Hispanic				
1995/96	24.6	46.4	67.3	20.5
2000/01	27.4	53.1	70.8	21.7
% White				
1995/96	17.8	27.1	11.3	13.1
2000/01	14.7	22.0	9.9	11.0
Enrollment Change[2]				
1967–2000	−28,584	−24,148	68,738	N/A
% change				
1967–2000	−31.2	−25.4	10.5	N/A
1986–2000	2,858	10,557	133,984	N/A
% change				
1986–2000	4.8	17.5	22.8	N/A
Percentage Distribution of District Revenues				
1994–1995[3]				
% Federal	6.8	8.4	12.3	8.3
% State	27.7	28.0	59.7	30.3
% Local	65.5	63.7	28.0	61.4
2001–2002[4]				
% Federal	8.4	9.6	10.8	14.0
% State	34.8	32.0	67.7	33.3
% Local	56.8	58.3	21.5	52.7
Current Expenditure Per Pupil[5]				
1992–1993/94	$7,076	5,034	5,706	4,853
1995/96	$9,126	5,596	5,393	5,357
2000/01	$11,040	5,897	6,245	5,787

B. EDUCATIONAL OUTCOMES

Graduation and Retention

	Boston	Denver	Los Angeles	San Francisco
GRADUATION RATE 2002–2003[6]	66	56	45	N/A
PROMOTION POWER/ % COMPLETION[7]				
1993	0 (0)	50 (5)	80 (40)	33 (4)
1996	27 (4)	80 (8)	78 (40)	23 (3)
1999	27 (4)	90 (9)	57 (29)	54 (7)
2002	33 (5)	73 (8)	68 (39)	29 (4)

Test Scores by Race/Ethnicity

BOSTON: MASSACHUSETTS COMPREHENSIVE STATE ASSESSMENT, % PROFICIENT AND ABOVE ON ENGLISH LANGUAGE ARTS, GRADE 4

	1998	1999	2000	2001	2002	2003	2004
Grade 4: English Language Arts[8]							
White	10	13	18	41	48	52	53
African American	2	3	3	17	19	21	25
Hispanic	2	2	2	19	20	20	26
Asian	12	15	16	49	44	44	47

DENVER: COLORADO STATE ASSESSMENT PROGRAM, % PROFICIENT AND ABOVE ON READING, GRADE 3

	1998	1999	2000	2001	2002	2003	2004	2005
Grade 3: Reading[9]								
White	66	69	72	74	79	81	81	77
African American	37	34	39	45	47	53	50	45
Hispanic	37	33	38	40	40	45	43	42
Asian	N/A	N/A	N/A	N/A	N/A	69	62	66

SAN FRANCISCO: CALIFORNIA STANDARDS TEST (CDT), % PROFICIENT AND ABOVE ON READING, GRADE 4

	2002	2003	2004
Grade 4: Reading[10]			
White	58	62	67
African American	17	17	17
Hispanic	18	24	24
Asian	N/A	N/A	N/A

LOS ANGELES: CALIFORNIA STANDARDS TEST (CDT), % PROFICIENT AND ABOVE ON READING, GRADE 4

	2002	2003	2004
Grade 4: Reading[11]			
White	57	60	61
African American	22	23	23
Hispanic	17	22	21
Asian	N/A	N/A	N/A

C. Impacts of Desegregation

Enrollment and Integration

School District Enrollment and Integration Levels at Two Periods[12]

YEAR		TOTAL ENROLLMENT	PERCENT MINORITY[13]	DISSIMILARITY	INDEX[14]
Los Angeles	1968	653,549	46.3		0.73
	1984	583,044	79.9		0.60
San Francisco	1968	94,154	58.8		0.41
	1984	62,696	83.4		0.32
Denver	1967	96,420	33.4		0.62
	1985	59,128	62.4		0.24
Boston	1968	94,174	31.5		0.71
	1985	59,539	72.6		0.36

Impacts of School District Desegregation Initiatives

	BOSTON	DENVER	LOS ANGELES	SAN FRANCISCO
Racial Composition				
% African American				
1995/96	47.9	21.3	14.3	17.4
2000/01	48.4	20.3	12.8	15.6
% Hispanic				
1995/96	24.6	46.4	67.3	20.5
2000/01	27.4	53.1	70.8	21.7
% White				
1995/96	17.8	27.1	11.3	13.1
2000/01	14.7	22.0	9.9	11.0
Change in % Black and White Enrollment[15]				
White				
1967	73	66	55	N/A
1976	44	48	37	N/A
1980	35	41	24	N/A
1986	26	37	18	N/A
2000	15	22	10	N/A
Change 1967–2000	−58	−44	−45	N/A
Change 1980–2000	−20	−19	−14	N/A
Black				
1967	26	14	22	N/A
1976	43	21	24	N/A
1980	46	23	23	N/A
1986	47	22	18	N/A
2000	48	22	13	N/A
Change 1967–2000	22	8	−9	N/A
Change 1980–2000	2	−1	−10	N/A
Change in Dissimilarity Index[16]				
1968	0.71	0.62	0.73	0.41
1985	0.36	0.24	0.60 (1984)	0.32 (1984)
Exposure of Blacks to Whites[17]				
1988	20.4	34.9	11	N/A
2000	11.2	19.4	8	N/A

Impacts of School District Desegregation Initiatives (continued)

	BOSTON	DENVER	LOS ANGELES	SAN FRANCISCO
Exposure of Minorities to Whites[18]				
2000/01				
Black	11.2	19.4	6.6	N/A
Latino	12.8	14.6	9.3	N/A
Changes in White Exposure to Blacks, 1986–2000[19]				
	3.5	–4.0	N/A	–7.5
% Racial Groups In 50–100% Minority Schools[20]				
% White	84	66	80	N/A
% Latino	99	97	99	N/A
% Black	99	92	98	N/A

Plan Components and Integration

Types of Desegregation Plans and Accompanying Changes in Dissimilarity Index[21]

	IMPLEMENTATION YEAR	PLAN COMPONENTS	CHANGE IN DISSIMILARITY INDEX
Los Angeles	1978	Magnets/Pair	–5.2
	1980	Magnets/Pair	–1.1
	1981–1984	Magnets/(Major Voluntary)	2.8
San Francisco	1970	Pair	–1.0
	1971	Pair	–16.7
	1974	Rezoning	–0.2
	1978	Magnets/Rezoning/Pair	6.8
	1983	Magnets/Transfers	–2.7
Denver	1969	Transfers/Rezoning	–6.9
	1974	Rezoning/Pair	–13.1
	1976	Rezoning/Pair	–13.1
	1979	Rezoning/Pair	0.9
	1982	Magnets/Rezoning/Pair	2.4
Boston	1969	Transfers	0.7
	1974	Rezoning/Pair	–19.8
	1975	Magnets/Pair	–19.5
	1981	Rezoning	0.6

1. Council of the Great City Schools, *Beating the Odds: A City-by-City Analysis of Student Performance and Achievement Gaps on State Assessments: Results from the 2001–2002 School Year* (Washington, DC: Author, 2003).

2. Erica Frankenberg, Chungmei Lee, and Gary Orfield. Derived from Table 20. *A Multiracial Society with Segregated Schools: Are We Losing the Dream?* (Cambridge, MA: The Harvard Civil Rights Project, 2003). http://www.civilrightsproject .harvard.edu.

3. National Center for Education Statistics, *Digest of Education Statistics* Table 94 (Washington, DC: U.S. Dept. of Education, 1998). http://nces.ed.gov/programs/digest.

4. National Center for Education Statistics, *Digest of Education Statistics* Table 90, 2005.

5. National Center for Education Statistics, *Digest of Education Statistics* Table 91, 1995; Table 94, 1999; Table 90, 2005.

6.Gary Orfield and Chungmei Lee, *Why Segregation Matters: Poverty and Educational Inequality*. Derived from Table 26. (Cambridge, MA: The Harvard Civil Rights Project, 2005).

7. Robert Balfanz and Nettie Legters, *Locating the Dropout Crisis*. Derived from Table 2. (Baltimore, MD: Johns Hopkins University, Center for Social Organization of Schools, 2004). The "promoting power" measure compares the number of freshmen with the number of seniors in high schools four years later; this ratio measures the ability of schools to move students through to completion and is designed to overcome the absence of a standard measure of dropouts. Schools included in this table for each city are those with 60 percent fewer seniors than original freshmen; the number of these schools in each city follows the promoting power measure, in parentheses. The 60 percent cutoff directs attention to schools with a very low graduation rate and high dropout rate— what Balfanz and Legters refer to as "dropout factories."

8. Source: Massachusetts Comprehensive State Assessment, Results of Spring 2004, Boston Public Schools, Office of Research, Assessment, and Evaluation, 15.

9. Years 2003–2005 from Denver Public Schools, Department of Planning, Assessment and Research. CSAP. "District Level: CSAP Proficient & Advanced Score Summary (2003–2005 sorted by subject and grade level and disaggregated by gender and ethnicity)." August 2, 2005. http://testing.dpsk12.org/rescsap05a.htm.

10. Years 1998–2002 from Council of the Great City Schools, *Beating the Odds IV: A City-by-City Analysis of Student Performance and Achievement Gaps on State Assessments: Results from the 2003–2004 School Year* (Washington, DC: Author, 2005), 342.

11. Ibid., 236.

12. Finis Welch and Audrey Light, *New Evidence of School Desegregation* (U.S. Commission on Civil Rights. Clearinghouse Publication 92, 1987), 74–78.

13. Here "minority" includes all nonwhite groups, i.e., African American and Asian; Hispanics are included as white in this tabulation.

14. The dissimilarity index shows "the extent of racial imbalance among schools (the more that the proportion minority in the individual schools diverges from the district-wide proportion, the greater the degree of segregation)." A decline in the dissimilarity index indicates a decline in segregation (Welch and Light, New Evidence, v).

15. Frankenberg, Lee, and Orfield, Derived from Table 21, p. 57.

16. Welch and Light, *New Evidence*. Derived from Table A2. 75–78. The index of dissimilarity (or segregation) shows the extent of racial imbalance among schools; a decline in the index score indicates a decline in segregation (v).

17. Frankenberg, Lee, and Orfield, *A Multiracial Society with Segregated Schools*, 21. According to the authors, the exposure index describes the "percentage of a particular group present in the school of the average student in another group." A black-white exposure of 11 percent indicates there are 11 percent white students in the school of the average black student. This is not a measure of discrimination per se but reflects group exposure and potential isolation: trends of lower levels of interracial exposure suggest resegregation, (4).

18. Frankenberg, Lee, and Orfield, *A Multiracial Society with Segregated Schools*. Derived from Table 19.

19. Erica Frankenberg and Chungmei Lee, *Race in American Public Schools: Rapidly Resegregating School Districts*. Derived from Table 3. (Cambridge, MA: The Harvard Civil Rights Project, 2002). The trend indicates growing isolation of white students from black students. These districts are among the twenty districts with the largest declines in white exposure to blacks from 1986 to 2000. Los Angeles is not in this top-twenty list, possibly because it is a primarily Latino district.

20. Orfield and Lee, *Why Segregation Matters*. Derived from Table 26.

21. Welch and Light, *New Evidence of School Desegregation*, 83–87.

REFERENCES

Aguilar-San Juan, Karin. 2005. Staying Vietnamese: Community and place in Orange County and Boston. *City and Community* 4: 37–66.

Ancheta, Angelo. 1998. *Race, rights, and the Asian American experience*. New Brunswick, NJ: Rutgers University Press.

Applebome, Peter. 1997. *Dixie rising: How the south is shaping American values, politics, and culture*. New York: Harvest Books.

Baird, Frank, ed. 1977. *Mexican Americans: Political power, influence or resource*. Lubbock, TX: Texas Tech University Press.

Balfanz, Robert, and Nettie Legters. 2004. *Locating the dropout crisis*. Baltimore: Johns Hopkins University, Center for the Social Organization of Schools.

Banfield, Edward C., and James Q. Wilson. 1963. *City politics*. Cambridge, MA: Harvard University Press.

Barker, Lucius J., Mack H. Jones, and Katherine Tate. 1999. *African Americans and the American political system*. 4th ed. Upper Saddle River, New Jersey: Prentice-Hall.

Barker, Lucius J., and Jesse McCrory. 1994. *Blacks and the American political system*. New York: Prentice-Hall.

Barrera, Mario. 1979. *Race and class in the Southwest: A theory of racial inequality*. Notre Dame, IN: University of Notre Dame Press.

Barrow, Clyde W. 1993. *Critical theories of the state: Marxist, neo-Marxist, post-Marxist*. Madison, WI: University of Wisconsin Press.

Baumgartner, Frank R., and Bryan D. Jones. 1993. *Agendas and instability in American politics*. Chicago, IL: University of Chicago Press.

Berger, Peter L. and Thomas L. Luckman. 1967. *The social construction of reality*. New York: Doubleday.

Berk, Gerald, and Todd Swanstrom. 1995. *The power of place: Capital, (im)mobility, pluralism and regime theory*. Proceedings of the Urban Affairs Association Annual Meeting, Portland, OR.

Berliner, David C., and Bruce J. Biddle. 1995. *The manufactured crisis: Myths, fraud and the attack on America's public schools*. Reading, MA: Addison-Wesley.

Berrey, Ellen C. 2005. Divided over diversity: Political discourse in a Chicago neighborhood. *City and Community* 4: 143–70.

Biegel, Stuart. 2000. San Francisco Unified School District desegregation: Paragraph 44 independent review, report 17, 1999–2000. Submitted to the United States District Court for the northern district of California.

————. 2005. Reports of the consent decree monitoring team for the years 1997–2005. http://www
.gseis.ucla.edu/courses/edlaw/sfrepts.html.
Biegel, Stuart, and Julie Slayton. 1997. Access to equal educational opportunity:
Policy issues and prospects of the LAUSD breakup. http://www.gseis.ucla.edu/
gseusdic/study/equal1.html.
————. 1994. Strike puts decision making teams on trial. *Denver Post*, 12 October.
Bingham, Janet. 1997. Keeping score: Just 1/3 of pupils pass test. *Denver Post*, 13 November.
Bluestone, Barry, and Mary Huff Stevenson. 2000. *The Boston renaissance: Race, space, and eco-
nomic change in an American metropolis.* New York: Russell Sage Foundation.
Blume, Howard. 2005. Decrepit district is tough to demolish. *Los Angeles Times*, 2 January.
Blyth, Mark. 2002. *Great transformations: Economic ideas and political change in the twentieth
century.* Cambridge: Cambridge University Press.
Bobo, Lawrence D., Melvin L. Oliver, James H. Johnson Jr., and Abel Valenzuela Jr. 2000.
Prismatic metropolis: Inequality in Los Angeles. New York: Russell Sage Foundation.
Bombardieri, Marcella. 2002. Beacon Hill parents go public: Pledges of money for an elementary
school stir debate. *Boston Globe*, 23 November.
Boston Public Schools Enrollment. 2000. http://boston.k12.ma.us/bsp/enrollment.asp (accessed 1
October 2000).
Brackman, Harold, and Steven Erie. 1995. Beyond "politics by other means?" Empowerment
strategies for Los Angeles' Asian Pacific community. In *The bubbling cauldron: Race, ethnic-
ity, and the urban crisis,* ed. Michael Peter Smith and Joe R. Feagin, 282–303. Minneapolis,
MN: University of Minnesota Press.
Brown, Fred. 2000. Record session comes to close: Owens wins handful of key measures. *Denver
Post*, 4 May.
Browning, Rufus P., Dale Rogers Marshall, and David H. Tabb. 1984. *Protest is not enough: The
struggle of blacks and Hispanics for equality in urban politics.* Berkeley, CA: University of
California Press.
————. 1995. *Racial politics in American cities.* 2nd ed. New York: Longman.
————. 2003a. *Racial politics in American cities.* 3rd ed. New York: Longman..
————. 2003b. Has political incorporation been achieved? Is it enough? In *Racial politics in
American cities,* ed. Rufus P. Browning, Dale Rogers Marshall, and David H. Tabb, 357–387.
New York: Longman.
Brown v. Board of Education of Topeka, Kansas, 347 U.S. 483; 74 St. Ct. 686; 98 L.Ed 873 (1954).
Brown v. Board of Education of Topeka, Kansas, 349 U.S. 294; 75 St. Ct. 753; 99 L.Ed 1083 (1955).
Burnham, Walter Dean. 1974. The United States: The politics of heterogeneity. In *Electoral
behavior: A comparative handbook,* ed. Richard Rose, 653–726. New York: Free Press.
California Department of Education, Education Data Partnership. *District Reports.* http://www
.ed-data.k12.ca.us/welcome.asp.
Camarota, Steven A. 2002. Immigrants in the United States—2002: A snapshot of America's foreign-born population. Washington, DC: Center for Immigration Studies, November.
Carter, Prudence L. 2005. *Keepin' it real.* New York: Oxford University Press.
Center for Education Reform. 1998a. I. Charter Schools: The new neighborhood schools. http://
www.edrefrom.com.
————. 1998b. Charter school highlights and statistics. http://www.edreform.com
————. 2001. What research reveals about charter schools. http://www.edreform.com.
————. 2005. CER quick facts: All about charter schools. http://www.edreform.com.
Chambers, Stefanie. 2002. Urban education reform and minority political empowerment. *Political
Science Quarterly* 117: 643–65.
Chang, Gordon H., ed. 2001. *Asian Americans and politics: Perspectives, experiences, prospects.*
Stanford: Stanford University Press.
Chubb, John E., and Terry M. Moe. 1990. *Politics, markets and America's schools.* Washington,
DC: Brookings Institution Press.
Cibulka, James G. 1996. The reform and survival of American public schools: An institutional per-
spective. In *The politics of education and the new institutionalism: Reinventing the American
school,* ed. Robert L. Crowson and William Lowe Boyd, 7–22. Washington, DC: The Falmer
Press.
Citrin, Jack, Donald P. Green, Beth Reingold, and Evelyn Walters. 1990. The "official English"
movement and the symbolic politics of language in the United States. *Western Political
Quarterly* 43 (3): 535–60.
Clark, William A. V. 1998. *The California cauldron.* New York: Guilford Press.

————.2003. *Immigrants and the American dream: Remaking the middle class.* New York: Guilford Press.

Clarke, Susan E., and Gary L. Gaile. 1998. *The work of cities.* Minneapolis, MN: University of Minnesota Press.

Clarke, Susan E., Lynn Staehli, and Laura Brunell. 1995. Women redefining local politics. In *Theories of urban politics*, ed. David Judge, Gerry Stoker, and Harold Wolman. London: Sage Publications.

Cobb, R., and C. D. Elder. 1972. *Participation in American politics: The dynamics of agenda building.* Baltimore, MD: Johns Hopkins University Press.

Cobb, R., and M. H. Ross. 1996. Agenda building as a comparative political process. *American Political Science Review* 70: 126–38.

Cohen, Michael D., James G. March, and Johan P. Olsen. 1972. A garbage can model of organizational choice. *Administrative Science Quarterly* 17, 1: 1–25.

Cohen, Mara, and Fernando Guerra. 1995. Latinos and educational reform in Los Angeles: The case of the missing giant. Proceedings of the annual meeting of the Western Political Science Association, Portland, OR.

Collet, Christian. 2005. Bloc voting, polarization, and the panethnic hypothesis: The case of little Saigon. *Journal of Politics* 67: 907–14.

Consent Decree. 1983. *NAACP v. SFUSD*, Civ. No. C-78-1445 WHO, 576 Supp. 34.

Cookson, Peter W., ed. 1992. *The choice controversy.* Newbury Park, CA: Corwin Press.

Coons, John E., and Stephen D. Sugarman. 1978. *Education by choice: The case for family control.* Berkeley, CA: University of California Press.

Council of the Great City Schools. 1997. *A Marshall Plan for urban schools: A framework for improving America's urban public schools.* Washington DC: Council of the Great City Schools. http://www.cgcs.org.

————. 2003. *Beating the odds III: A city-by-city analysis of student performance and achievement gaps on state assessments: Results from the 2001–2002 school year.* Washington, DC: Author.

Crawford v. Board of Education for the City of Los Angeles. 17 Cal. 3d at 297, 130 Cal. Rptr. (1976).

Cross-City Campaign for Urban School Reform. 2001. Annual decentralization progress comparison across ten cities. http://www.crosscity.org.

Croucher, Sheila. 1997. *Imagining Miami.* Charlottesville, VA: University Press of Virginia.

Crowson, Robert L., William L. Boyd, and Hanne B. Mawhinney. 1995. The politics of education and the new institutionalism: Reinventing the American school. In *Politics of education association annual yearbook.* London: Falmer Press.

Cuban, Larry. 1990. Reforming again, again and again. *Educational Researcher* 19: 3–13.

————. 1998. How schools change reforms: Redefining success and failure. *Teachers college record* 99 (3): 453–77.

Daniel et al. v. State of California, State Board of Education, Delaine Easton, State Superintendent of Public Instruction, and the Inglewood Unified School District. 27 July 1999.

De la Garza, Rodolfo O. 1985. As American as tamale pie: Mexican-American political mobilization and the loyalty question. In *Mexican-Americans in political perspective*, ed. Walter Connor, 225–42. Washington, DC: Urban Institute Press.

————, ed. 1987. *Ignored voices: Public opinion polls and the Latino community.* Center for Mexican American Studies, 158–69. Austin, TX: University of Texas Press.

De la Garza, Rodolfo O., and Louis DeSipio, eds. 1996. *Ethnic ironies: Latino politics in the 1992 elections.* Boulder, CO: Westview Press.

DeLeon, Richard. 1992. *Left-coast city: Progressive politics in San Francisco, 1975–1991.* Lawrence, KS: University Press of Kansas.

————. 1997. Progressive politics in the left-coast city: San Francisco. In *Racial politics in American cities*, ed. R. P. Browning, D. R. Marshall, and D. H. Tabb, 137–60. New York: Longman.

DeSipio, Louis. 1996. More than the sum of its parts: The building blocks of a pan-ethnic Latino identity. In *The politics of minority coalitions: Race, ethnicity and shared uncertainties*, ed. Wilbur C. Rich, 177–89. Westport, CT: Praeger.

Denver Public Schools. 1999. Total DPS enrollment continues to soar: Hispanic students are now 51.5 percent of membership. http://www.denver.k12.co.us/news/press/99/11/19b.html (accessed 16 Sept 2000).

DiMassa, Cara Mia. 2004. An education in expansion: L.A. school district says a years-long building program will "change the face" of the city. *Los Angeles Times*, 23 November.

Dionne, E. J., Jr. 1998a. In education, money and reform both matter. *Daily Camera*, 14 March.

————. 1998b. Good teachers do make a difference. *Washington Post Weekly Edition*, 17 August.

Donnell-Kay Foundation. 2003. *Amendment 23 and public school finance reform in Colorado.* Denver: Donnell-Kay Foundation. http://www.dkfoundation.org.

DPS board OKs bilingual plan. 2000. *Daily Camera*. 12 May.

DPS leadership lacking. 2000. *Denver Post*. 14 May.

Dunn, W. N. 1994. *Public policy analysis: An introduction.* 2d ed. Englewood Cliffs, NJ: Prentice Hall.

Dyer, Jones, Arnold Vedlitz, and Stephen Worchel. 1989. Social distance among racial and ethnic groups in Texas. *Social Science Quarterly* 70 (3): 607–16.

Eaton, Susan E. 2001. *The other Boston busing story.* New Haven, CT: Yale University Press.

Edelman, M. 1988. *Constructing the political spectacle.* Chicago, IL: University of Chicago Press.

Education Commission of the States. 1999. Governing America's schools: changing the rules. http://ecs.org.

Elections '96; state propositions: A snapshot of voters. 1996. *Los Angeles Times*, 7 November.

Elkin, Stephen L. 1987. *City and regime in the American republic.* Chicago, IL: University of Chicago Press.

Elmore, Richard F. 1991. Public school choice as a policy issue. In *Privatization and its alternatives*, ed. William T. Gormley, 55–78. Madison, WI: University of Wisconsin Press.

Evans, W. N., S. E. Murray, and R. Schwab. 1997. Schoolhouses, courthouses and state houses after Serrano. *Journal of Policy Analysis and Management* 16 (1): 10–31.

Falcon, Angelo. 1988. Black and Latino politics: Race and ethnicity in a changing urban context. In *Latinos and the American political system*, ed. F. Chris Garcia, 171–94. Notre Dame, IN: University of Notre Dame Press.

Finn Jr., Chester E., Bruno V. Manno, and Greg Vanourek. 2000. *Charter schools in action: Renewing public education.* Princeton, NJ: Princeton University Press.

Fraga, Luis Ricardo, and Bari Anhalt Erlichson. 1994. The politics of educational reform in San Francisco. Civic Capacity Project. Unpublished paper.

Fraga, Luis Ricardo, Bari Anhalt Erlichson, and Sandy Lee. 1998. Consensus building and school reform: The role of the courts in San Francisco. In *Changing urban education*, ed. Clarence N. Stone, 79–82. Lawrence, KS: University Press of Kansas.

Frank, Laura. 2005. Refs C&D: Budget breakdown, the ABCs of K–12. *Rocky Mountain News*, 18 October.

Frankenberg, Erica, and Chungmei Lee. 2002. *Race in American public schools: Rapidly resegregating school districts.* Cambridge, MA: The Harvard Civil Rights Project.

Frankenberg, Ericka, Chungmei Lee, and Gary Orfield. 2003. *A multiracial society with segregated schools: Are we losing the dream?* Cambridge, MA: The Harvard Civil Rights Project. http://www.civilrightsproject.harvard.edu.

Garber, Judith. 1990. Law and the possibilities for a just urban political economy. *Journal of Urban Affairs* 12 (1): 1–15.

Garcia, F. Chris, and Rodolfo O. de la Garza. 1977. *The Chicano political experience: Three perspectives.* North Scituate, MA: Duxbury.

Gardner, Howard. 2000. Paroxysms of choice. *The New York Review of Books* XLVII: 44–51.

Giles, Michael, and Melanie Buckner. 1993. David Duke and black threat: An old hypothesis revisited. *Journal of Politics* 55 (3): 702–13.

Glazer, Nathan. 1993. A human capital policy for the cities. *The Public Interest* 112: 27–49.

Goldberg, David Theo. 1997. *Racial subjects: Writing on race in America.* New York: Routledge.

Gottlieb, Alan. 1999. Zullinger brings winds of change to DPS. *Denver Post*, 28 November.

Great Education Colorado. http://www.greateducation.org.

Green, Chuck. 2000. Is DPS leader abusing his power? *Denver Post*, 10 May.

Grofman, Bernard, and Lisa Handley. 1989. Minority population and black and Hispanic Congressional success in the 1970s and 1980s. *American Politics Quarterly* 17 (4): 436–45.

Guerra, Fernando, and Mara A. Cohen. Educational restructuring in Los Angeles. Civic Capacity Project, 1994. Unpublished paper.

Gutherie, Julian. 2002. A good rap: Leadership high hopes to chart the way with smaller classes, devoted teachers. *San Francisco Examiner*, 8 March.

Hajnal, Zoltan, and Jessica Trounstine. 2005. Where turnout matters: The consequences of uneven turnout in city politics. *Journal of Politics* 67: 515–36.

Hall, Peter A. 1997. The role of interests, institutions, and ideas in the comparative political economy of the industrialized nations. In *Comparative politics: Rationality, culture, and structure,* ed. Mark I. Lichbach and Alan S. Zuckerman, 174–207. Cambridge and New York: Cambridge University Press.

Hassel, Bryan C. 1998. Charter schools: An innovation in policy or practice? Paper presented at the annual meeting of the American Political Science Association, Boston, MA.

Hassel, Bryan, and Paul Peterson, eds. 1998. *Learning from school choice.* Washington, DC: Brookings Institution Press.

Hayasaki, Erika. 2004. 5-year plan for smaller schools ok'd. *Los Angeles Times,* 6 October.

Heclo, Hugh. 1994. Ideas, interests, and institutions. In *The dynamics of American politics,* ed. Lawrence C. Dodd and Calvin Jillson, 366–92. Boulder, CO: Westview Press.

Hendrie, Caroline. 1998. A Denver high school reaches out to the neighborhood it lost to busing. *Education Week on the Web* 17 (June): 1, 22–23.

———. 2004. In U.S. schools, race still counts. *Education Week* 1 (21 January): 16–19.,

Henig, Jeffrey. 1995. *Rethinking school choice: The limits of the market metaphor.* Princeton, NJ: Princeton University Press.

Henig, Jeffrey R., Richard C. Hula, Marion Orr, and Desiree S. Pedescleaux. 2001. *The color of school reform: Race, politics, and the challenge of urban education.* Princeton, NJ: Princeton University Press.

Henig, Jeffrey R., and Wilbur C. Rich, eds. 2003. *Mayors in the middle: Politics, race, and mayoral control of urban schools.* Princeton, NJ: Princeton University Press.

Henig, Jeffrey, and Clarence Stone. 1994. Positioning the study of civic capacity and urban education: Some prefatory remarks. Unpublished paper.

Hernandez, Romel. 1994. Power to parents and schools. *Rocky Mountain News,* 6 March.

Hero, Rodney E. 1990. Hispanics in urban government and politics. *Western Political Science Quarterly* 43 (2): 403–14.

———. 1992. *Latinos and the U.S. political system: Two-tiered pluralism.* Philadelphia: Temple University Press.

———. 1998. *Faces of inequality: Social diversity in American politics.* Oxford: Oxford University Press.

Hero, Rodney E., and Anne G. Campbell. 1996. Understanding Latino political participation. *Hispanic Journal of Behavioral Sciences* 18 (2): 129–41.

Hero, Rodney E., and Susan E. Clarke. 1995. The politics of education reform in sunbelt cities: Changing demography, changing institutions, and distributional consequences. Paper presented at American Political Science Association annual meeting, Chicago, IL.

———. 2002. Latinos, blacks, and multi-ethnic politics in Denver: Realigning power and influence in the struggle for equality. In *Racial politics in American cities,* 3rd ed, ed. Rufus Browning, Dale Rogers Marshall, and David Tabb, 310–30. New York: Longman.

Hero, Rodney E., Susan E. Clarke, and Mara S. Sidney. 1994. Civic capacity and urban education: Denver. Civic Capacity Project. Unpublished paper.

Hero, Rodney E., and Caroline J. Tolbert. 1996. A racial/ethnic interpretation of politics and policy in the States of the U.S. *American Journal of Political Science* 40 (3): 851–71.

Hess, Frederick. 1998. *Spinning wheels: The politics of urban school reform.* Washington, DC: Brookings Institution Press.

Hess, Frederick, and David Leal. 2001. Quality, race, and the urban education marketplace. *Urban Affairs Review* 37: 249–66.

Hilgartner, S., and Charles L. Bosk. 1998. The rise and fall of social problems: A public arenas model. *American Journal of Sociology* 94 (1): 53–78.

Hill, Paul, et al. 1995. *Reinventing education.* Santa Monica CA: The RAND Corporation.

Hill, Paul T., and J. Bonan. 1991. *Decentralization and accountability in public education.* Santa Monica, CA: Rand Corporation.

Hill, Paul T., Christine Campbell, and James Harvey. 2000. *It takes a city: Getting serious about school reform.* With the collaboration of Paul Herdman, Janet Looney, Lawrence Pierce, Carol Reed, and Abigail Winger. Washington, DC: Brookings Institution Press.

Hill, Paul T., and M. B. Celio. 1998. *Fixing urban schools.* Washington, DC: Brookings Institution Press.

Hill, Paul T., and James Harvey, eds. 2004. *Making school reform work.* Washington, DC: Brookings Institution.

Hirsch, Eric. 1993. Analysis of the Colorado charter schools policy. University of Colorado at Boulder, Department of Political Science. Unpublished paper.

Ho v. SFUSD et al., 59 F. Supp. 2d. 1021 (N.D. Cal. 1999). ("July 1999 Opinion and Order Approving the Ho Settlement Agreement.")

Hochschild, Jennifer. 1984. *The new American dilemma: Liberal democracy and school desegregation*. New Haven, CT: Yale University Press.

———. 1995. *Facing up to the American dream: Race, class and the soul of the nation*. Princeton, NJ: Princeton University Press.

Hochschild, Jennifer, and Bridget Scott. 1998. Governance and reform of public education in the United States. *Public Opinion Quarterly* 62: 79–120.

Hubler, Eric. 2000a. City schools OK bilingual option: Board votes 4–3 to endorse controversial grant for 5-year offering. *Denver Post*, 11 May.

———. 2002b. School governing boards rethought. *Denver Post*, 28 August.

Hudson, Ray. 1995. Institutional change, cultural transformation, and economic regeneration: Myths and realities from Europe's old industrial areas. In *Globalization, institutions, and regional development in Europe*, ed. Ash Amin and Nigel Thrift, 196–216. Oxford: Oxford University Press.

Huntington, Samuel P. 1981. *American politics: The promise of disharmony*. Cambridge, MA: Belknap Press.

Illescas, Carlos, 1997a. All eyes on Manual as DPS year begins. *Denver Post*, 31 August.

———. 1997b. Slavens a challenge to DPS' diversity goals. *Denver Post*, 11 November.

———. 1998. DPS Gets passing grade in teaching white children. *Denver Post*, 8 April.

———. 1999a. Thousands of students hold secret. *Denver Post*, 7 September.

———. 1999b. Hispanics top 50% of DPS student body. *Denver Post*, 20 November.

Immergut, Ellen M. 1998. The theoretical core of the new institutionalism. *Politics and Society* 26: 5–34.

Inglehardt, Ronald. 1990. *Culture shift in advanced industrial democracies*. Princeton, NJ: Princeton University Press.

Jencks, Christopher. 1970. Giving parents money to pay for schooling: Education vouchers. *New Republic* 4 (July): 19–21.

Jencks, Christopher, and Meredith Phillips. 1998. *The black-white test score gap*. Washington, DC: Brookings Institution Press.

Johnson, Judith, and Alex Medler. 2000. The conceptual and practical development of charter schools. *Stanford Law and Policy Review* 11 (2): 291–94.

Jones, Bryan D. 1994. *Reconceiving decision-making in democratic politics: Attention, choice and public policy*. Chicago, IL: University of Chicago Press.

Jones, Bryan D., Lynn Bachelor, and Carter Wilson. 1993. *The sustaining hand: Community leadership and corporate power*. Lawrence, KS: University Press of Kansas.

Jones-Correa, Michael. 1998. *Between two nations: The political predicament of Latinos in New York City*. Ithaca, NY: Cornell University Press.

Jones, Robin, John Portz, and Lana Stein. 1997. The nature of civic involvement and educational change in Pittsburgh, Boston and St. Louis. *Urban Affairs Review* 32 (6): 871–91.

Judd, Dennis R., and Todd Swanstrom. 1994. *City politics: Private power and public policy*. New York: Harper Collins College Publishers.

Key, V. O. 1949. *Southern politics in state and nation*. New York: Alfred Knopf.

Kim, Claire Jean. 1999. The racial triangulation of Asian Americans. *Politics and Society* 27 (1): 105–38.

———. 2002. *Bitter fruit: The politics of black-Korean conflict in New York City*. New Haven: Yale University Press.

———. 2004. Imagining race and nation in multiculturalist America. *Ethnic and Racial Studies* 27: 987–1005.

Kim, Claire Jean, and Taeku Lee. 2001. Interracial politics: Asian Americans and other communities of color. *PS* 34: 631–37.

Kingdon, John W. 1995. *Agendas, alternatives, and public policies*. New York: Harper Collins.

Knight, Heather. 2005a. Chinese Americans renew school placement push: Court-ordered desegregation system sends many students to campuses across town. *San Francisco Chronicle*, March 31.

———. 2005b. Ackerman says she plans to stay: Schools chief, new board president to talk. *San Francisco Chronicle*, 21 January.

Kreck, Carol. 2001. Parents demanding more school clout. *Denver Post*, 15 July 2001.

Lai, James S. 2005. The suburbanization of Asian American politics. In *National Asian Pacific American political almanac 2005–2006*, 7–10. Los Angeles: UCLA Asian American Studies Center.

Lamdin, Douglas J., and Michael Mintrom. 1997. School choice in theory and practice: Taking stock and looking ahead. *Education Economics* 5: 211–44.

Leal, David L., Valerie Martinez-Ebers, and Kenneth J. Meier. 2004. The politics of Latino education: The biases of at-large elections. *Journal of Politics* 66: 1224–44.

LEARN. *The learning curve*. Vol. 1, Issue 2.

LEARN Collection. Series 2: Implementation. Collection No. CSLA-14. Loyola Marymount University: Center for the Study of Los Angeles.

Lewis Mumford Center for Comparative and Urban Regional Research. Metropolitan racial and ethnic change-Census 2000. http://mumford.albany.edu/census/WholePop/ WPsegdata.htm.

Li, Wei. 1998. Anatomy of a new ethnic settlement: the Chinese ethnoburb in Los Angeles. *Urban Studies* 75: 479–501.

Lieberman, Robert C., Anne L. Schneider, and Helen Ingram. 1995. Social construction (continued). *American Political Science Review* 89: 437–46.

Lien, Pei-te. 2001. *The making of Asian America through political participation*. Philadelphia: Temple University Press.

Lien, Pei-te, M. Margaret Conway, Taeku Lee, and Janelle Wong. 2001. The mosaic of Asian American politics: Preliminary results from the five-city post-election survey. Paper presented at the Midwest Political Science Association, Chicago, IL.

Lien, Pei-te, M. Margaret Conway, and Janelle Wong. 2003. The contours and sources of ethnic identity choices among Asian Americans. *Social Science Quarterly* 84: 461–81.

———. 2004. *The politics of Asian Americans*. New York: Routledge.

Logan, John R. 2001. *From many shores: Asians in Census 2000*. University at Albany: Lewis Mumford Center for Comparative Urban and Regional Research.

———. 2002. *Hispanic populations and their residential patterns in the metropolis*. University at Albany: Lewis Mumford Center for Comparative Urban and Regional Research.

Lowi, Theodore J. 1979. *The end of liberalism*. 2nd ed. New York: Norton.

Malen, B., R. T. Ogawa, and J. Kranz. 1990. What do we know about school-based management? A case study of the literature—a case for research. In *Choice and control in American education, vol. 2, The practice of choice, decentralization and school restructuring*, ed. W. H. Clune and J. F. Witte, 289–342. London: Falmer Press.

Marquez, Benjamin. 1993. *LULAC: The evolution of a Mexican American political organization*. Austin, TX: University of Texas Press.

Marschall, Melissa J. 2001. Does the shoe fit? Testing models of participation for African-American and Latino involvement in local politics. *Urban Affairs Review* 37: 227–48.

Massey, Douglas S., and Nancy A. Denton. 1993. *American apartheid: Segregation and the making of the underclass*. Cambridge, MA: Harvard University Press.

Maynard-Moody, Stephen. 1989. Beyond implementation: Developing an institutional theory of administrative policy-making. *Public Administration Review* 49 (March/April): 137–42.

McCabe, Barbara Coyle, and Janet Coble Vinzant. 1999. Governance lessons: The case of charter schools. *Administration and Society* 31: 361–77.

McClain, Paula D. 1993. The changing dynamics of urban politics: Black and Hispanic municipal employment—is there competition? *Journal of Politics* 55 (2): 399–414.

McClain, Paula D., and Albert K. Karnig. 1990. Black and hispanic socioeconomic and political competition. *American Political Science Review* 84 (2): 535–45.

McClain, Paula D., and Joseph Stewart Jr. 1998. *Can we all get along?: Racial and ethnic minorities in American politics*. Boulder, CO: Westview Press.

McClain, Paula D., and Josepth Stewart Jr. 2002. 3rd ed. *Can we all get along?: Racial and ethnic minorities in American politics*. Boulder: Westview Press.

McDermott, Kathryn A. 2000. Barriers to large-scale success models for urban education reform. *Educational Evaluation and Policy Analysis* 22 (1): 83–89.

Medler, Alex. 2004. The charter school movement: Complementing or competing with public education? In *The emancipatory promise of charter schools: Towards a progressive politics of school choice*, eds. Eric Rofes and Lisa M. Stulberg, editors. 189–217. New York: SUNY Press.

Meier, Kenneth, Eric Gonzalez Juenke, Robert D. Wrinkle, and J. L. Polinard. 2005. Structural choices and representational biases: The post-election color of representation. *American Journal of Political Science* 49 (4): 758.

Meier, Kenneth, and Joseph Stewart Jr. 1991. *The politics of Hispanic education*. Albany, NY: State University of New York Press.

Meier, Kenneth, Joseph Stewart Jr., and Robert E. England. 1989. *Race, class, and education: The politics of second generation discrimination*. Madison, WI: University of Wisconsin Press.

Meyer, John W., and Brian Rowan. 1977. Institutional organization: Formal structure as myth and ceremony. *American Journal of Sociology* 83: 340–63.

Meyer, John W., W. Richard Scott, and Terrence E. Deal. 1981. Institutional and technical sources of organizational structure: Explaining the structure of educational organizations. In *Organization and the human services: Cross-disciplinary reflections*, ed. Herman Stein, 151–79. Philadelphia: Temple University Press.

Mintrom, Michael. 2000. *Policy entrepreneurs and school choice*. Washington, DC: Georgetown University Press.

Mintrom, Michael, and Sandra Vergari. 1998. Policy networks and innovation diffusion: The case of state education reforms. *Journal of Politics* 60 (1): 116–26.

———. 1997. Political factors shaping charter school laws. Paper presented at the annual meeting of the American Educational Research Association, Chicago, IL.

Moe, Terry M. 1987. Interests, institutions, and positive theory: The politics of the NLRB. *Studies in American Political Development* 2: 236–99.

———. 1994. The "reinventing government" exercise: Misinterpreting the problem, misjudging the consequences. *Public Administration Review* 54: 111–22.

———. 2001. *Schools, vouchers, and the American public*. Washington, DC: Brookings Institution Press.

Moore, Joan, and Harry Pachon. 1985. *Hispanics in the United States*. Englewood Cliffs, NJ: Prentice Hall.

Morin, Richard. 1998. The three R's still stand. *The Washington Post National Weekly Edition*, August 10: 33.

Myrdal, Gunnar. 1944. *An American dilemma: The negro problem and modern democracy*. New York: Harper and Brothers.

Naimark, Susan. 2004. Unfinished business on school assignments. *Boston Globe*, 28 November.

Nathan, Joe. 1996. *Charter schools: Creating hope and opportunity for American education*. San Francisco, CA: Jossey-Bass.

National Center for Education Statistics. *Digest of education statistics*. Washington, DC: U.S. Dept. of Education. http://nces.ed.gov/programs/digest/ (multiple years available).

National Commission for Excellence in Education. 2002. *A nation at risk*.

National Conference of State Legislatures. *State tax and expenditure limits—2005*. http://www.ncsl.org/programs/fiscal/tels2005.htm.

National Council of La Raza (NCLR), National Council of La Raza's Charter School Development Initiative.

Nelson, Adam R. 2005. *The elusive ideal: Equal educational opportunity and the federal role in Boston's public schools, 1950–1985*. Chicago: University of Chicago Press.

Nelson Jr., William E. 1999. *Black Atlantic politics: Dilemmas of political empowerment in Boston and Liverpool*. Albany, NY: State University of New York Press.

Obmascik, Mark. 1998. Choice revolution hits DPS. *Denver Post*, 25 January.

Orfield, Gary, chair. 1992. Desegregation and Educational Change in San Francisco: Findings and Recommendations on Consent Decree Implementation. Expert's report, submitted to the court.

Orfield, Gary, and Chungmei Lee. January 2005. *Why segregation matters: Poverty and educational inequality*. Cambridge, MA: The Harvard Civil Rights Project.

Orfield, Gary, and Susan E. Eaton. 1996. *Dismantling desegregation: The quiet reversal of Brown v. Board of Education*. New York: The New York Press.

Orr, Marion. 1992. Urban regimes and human capital policies: A study of Baltimore. *Journal of Urban Affairs* 14 (2): 173–87.

Orren, Karen, and Stephen Skowronek. 1989. *Studies in American political development*. New Haven, CT: Yale University Press.

Paris, David C. 1995. *Ideology and educational reform*. Boulder, CO: Westview Press.

Pedescleaux, Desiree, Jorge Ruiz-de-Velasco, Lana Stein, and Clarence Stone. 1994. Urban education as an area of reform. Paper presented at the annual meeting of the American Political Science Association.

Peterson, Paul E. 1981. *City limits*. Chicago: University of Chicago Press.

———. 1985. *The politics of school reform, 1870–1940*. University of Chicago Press.

Pew Hispanic Center/Kaiser Family Foundation. 2004a. *National survey of Latinos: Education*. http://pewhispanic.org/reports.

———. 2004b. *National survey of Latinos: Politics and civic participation*. http://pewhispanic.org/reports.

Pierson, Paul. 1994. *Dismantling the welfare state? Reagan, Thatcher, and the politics of retrenchment*. New York: Cambridge University Press.

Pinderhughes, Dianne. 1987. *Race and ethnicity in Chicago politics: A re-examination of pluralist theory*. Urbana, IL: University of Illinois Press.

Piper, Bill. 2001. A brief analysis of voter behavior regarding tax initiatives, from 1978 to March 2000. Initiative and referendum institute working paper. Initiative and Referendum Institute, Washington, DC: Citizen Lawmaker Press. http://www.cato.org/ pubs/pas/pa-213.html.

Piton Foundation. 2000. *Improving public education in Denver*. Denver: Piton Foundation.

———. 2002. Improving public education in Denver. *The term paper*, vol. 1. Denver: Piton Foundation.

Poppen, Julie. 2005a. Study claims unfair discipline at DPS: Padres Unidos findings say minorities targeted more often than Anglos. *Denver Post*, 24 March.

———. 2005b. It's time for Hispanic to lead DPS, some community leaders say. *Denver Post*, 23 March.

Portz, John. 1994. *The politics of education reform in Boston*. A paper presented at the Annual Meeting of the Urban Affairs Association, New Orleans, March 4–5.

———. 1996. Problem definitions and policy agendas: Shaping the educational agenda in Boston. *Policy Journal Studies* 24: 371–86.

Portz, John, Lana Stein, and Robin R. Jones. 1999. *City schools and city politics: Institutions and leadership in Pittsburgh, Boston and St. Louis*. Lawrence, KS: University Press of Kansas.

Powell, Walter W., ed. 1987. *The nonprofit sector: A research handbook*. New Haven, CT: Yale University Press.

Powell, Walter W., and Paul J. DiMaggio, eds. 1991. *The new institutionalism in organizational analysis*. Chicago: The University of Chicago Press.

Public Agenda. 1999. On thin ice: How advocates and opponents could misread the public's view on vouchers and charter schools. http://www.publicagenda.org.

———. Race: Bills and proposals. http://www.publicagenda.org.

———. 2004. Race: People's chief concerns. http://www.publicagenda.org/issues/ pcc_detail.cfm ?issue_type=race&list=1

Public Policy Institute of California (PPIC). 2002. *Who's your neighbor? Residential segregation and diversity in California*. San Francisco: PPIC.

Purdam, Todd S. 2000. Moving heaven and earth for the City of Angels. *New York Times*, 12 August.

Putnam, Robert D. 1993. *Making democracy work: Civic traditions in modern Italy*. Princeton, NJ: Princeton University Press.

Putnam, Robert D. 2000. *Bowling alone: The collapse and revival of American community*. New York: Simon and Schuster.

Quality counts 1998. *Education Week*. 8 January.

Rabrenovic, Gordana. 1995. Education reform and charter schools: The case of charter schools in Massachusetts. In *Innovations in Urban Education: The impact of research on practice in schools 2*, Center for Innovation in Urban Education, Northeastern University.

Ramakrishnan, S. Karthick. 2005. *Democracy in immigrant America: Changing demographics and political participation*. Stanford, CA: Stanford University Press.

Reed, Adolph. 1995. Demobilization in the new black political regime: Ideological capitulation and radical failure in the postsegregation era. In *The bubbling cauldron: Race, ethnicity, and the urban crisis*, ed. Michael Peter Smith and Joe R. Feagin, 182–208. Minneapolis, MN: University of Minnesota Press.

Regalado, James. 1988. Latino representation in Los Angeles. In *Latino empowerment: Progress, problems, and prospects*, ed. Roberto Villareal, Norma Hernandez, and Howard Neighbor, 91–104. New York: Greenwood Press.

Reich, Robert. 1991. *The work of nations*. New York: Knopf.

Reilly, Adam. 2004. Late assignment: Boston's efforts to balance school choice with a neighborhood system are behind schedule and politically explosive. *The Boston Phoenix*, 16–22 July 2004.

Rich, Wilbur. 1996. *Black mayors and school politics*. New York: Garland.

Rochefort, David A., and Roger W. Cobb. 1994. Problem definition: An emerging perspective. In *The politics of problem definition*, ed. David A. Rochefort and Roger W. Cobb, 1–31. Lawrence, KS: University Press of Kansas.

Rofes, Eric. 1998. *How are school districts responding to charter schools? A study of eight states and the District of Columbia*. Berkeley: Policy Analysis for California Education.

Romer, Paul M. 1994. The origins of endogenous growth. *The Journal of Economic Perspectives* 8: 3–22.

Salamon, Lester M. 1981. Rethinking public management: Third-party government and the changing forms of government action. *Public Policy* 29: 255–75.

Salamon, Lester M., and Helmut K. Anheier. 1994. *The emerging sector: The nonprofit sector in comparative perspective—an overview*. Baltimore: Johns Hopkins University Institute for Policy.

San Miguel, Guadalupe. 1987. *Let them take heed: Mexican Americans and the campaign for educational equality in Texas, 1910–1981*. Austin, TX: University of Texas Press.

Schattschneider, E. E. 1960. *The semi-sovereign people*. Hinsdale, IL: Dryden Press.

Schmidt, Ronald Sr. 2000. *Language policy and identity politics in the United States*. Philadelphia: Temple University Press.

Schneider, Anne, and Helen Ingram. 1997. *Policy design for democracy*. Lawrence, KS: University Press of Kansas.

———. Social construction of target populations: Implications for politics and policy. *American Political Science Review* 87 (2): 334–47.

Schwab, Jeremy. 2005. Task force unveils new measures of school quality. *The Boston-Bay State Banner Online*, 10 February 2005.

Schwartz, Stephen. 1997. Anti-desegregation bid rejected: Judge refuses to end race-based school admissions. *San Francisco Chronicle*, 7 May.

Sege, Irene. 1991. Census tells tale of two Bostons. *Boston Globe*, 1 May.

Shanker, Albert. 1998. Address at the national press club. 31 March.

———. 1988. Where we stand. *New York Times*, 10 July.

Shepsle, Kenneth A. 1986. Institutional equilibrium and equilibrium institutions. In *Political science: The science of politics*, ed. Herbert Weisberg, 51–81. New York: Agathon Press.

Sherry, Allison. 2004. CSAPs show "miniscule improvements." *Denver Post*, 3 August.

Shklar, Judith N. 1998. *American citizenship: The quest for inclusion*. Cambridge, MA: Harvard University Press.

Sidney, Mara S. 2002. The role of ideas in education politics: Using discourse analysis to understand barriers to reform in multi-ethnic cities. *Urban Affairs Review* 38: 253–79.

Sidney, Mara S. 2003. *Unfair housing: How national policy shapes community action*. Lawrence, KS: University Press of Kansas.

Singer, Audrey. 2004. The rise of the new immigrant gateways. *Living cities census series*. Washington, DC: Brookings Institution.

Skocpol, Theda. 2004. *Diminished democracy: From membership to management in American civic life*. Norman OK: University of Oklahoma Press.

Smith, Michael P. and Joe R. Feagin, eds. 1995. *The bubbling cauldron: Race, ethnicity and the urban crisis*. Minneapolis, MN: University of Minnesota Press.

Smith, Rogers M. 1993. Beyond Tocqueville, Myrdal and Hartz: The multiple traditions in America. *American Political Science Review* 87 (3): 549–66.

Smith, Steven R. 1994. Social capital, community coalitions and the role of institutions. Presented at the annual meeting of the American Political Science Association, New York, NY.

Smith, Steven Rathgeb, and Michael Lipsky. 1993. *Nonprofits for hire: The welfare state in the age of contracting*. Cambridge, MA: Harvard University Press.

Sonenshein, Raphael. 1993. *Politics in black and white*. Princeton, NJ: Princeton University Press.

———. 1997. Post incorporation politics in Los Angeles. In *Racial politics in American cities*, 2nd ed., eds. Rufus Browning, Dale Rogers Marshall, and David Tabb, 41–64. New York: Longman Press.

Stanfield, Rochelle L. 1993. Reform by the book. *National Journal* 25 (4 December): 2885–87.

States' Impact on Federal Education Policy Project. 2006. *Federal education policy and the states, 1945-2004*. New York State Archives.

Steinmo, Sven, Kathleen Thelen, Frank Longstreth and Peter Lange, eds. 1992. *Structuring politics: Historical institutionalism in comparative analysis*. Cambridge: Cambridge University Press

Stevens, M. 1994. Signs of black students' progress scarce, council reports to DPS. *Denver Post*, 4 November.

Stoker, Gerry. 1995. Regime theory and urban politics. In *Theories of urban politics*, ed. David Judge, Gerry Stoker, and Harold Wolman, 54–71. London: Sage Publications.

Stone, Clarence N. 1986. Race, power and political change. In *The egalitarian city*, ed. Janet K. Boles, 200–23. New York: Praeger.

———. 1989. *Regime politics: Governing Atlanta, 1946–1988*. Lawrence, KS: University Press of Kansas.

———. 1998. Civic capacity and urban school reform. In *Changing urban education*, ed. Clarence Stone, 250–73. Lawrence, KS: University Press of Kansas.

Stone, Clarence N., Jeffrey Henig, Bryan Jones, and Carol Pierannunzi. 2001. *Building civic capacity: The politics of reforming urban schools*. Lawrence, KS: University Press of Kansas.

Stone, Clarence N., Robert K. Whelan, and William J. Murin. 1986. *Urban policy in a bureaucratic age*. 2nd ed. Englewood Cliffs, NJ: Prentice-Hall.

Stone, D. 1989. Causal stories and the formation of policy agendas. *Political Science Quarterly* 104: 281–300.

Suro, Roberto. 2002. *Latino growth in metropolitan America: Changing patterns, new locations*. Washington, DC: The Brookings Institution, Center on Urban and Metropolitan Policy and the Pew Hispanic Center.

Taebel, Delbert. 1978. Minority representation on city councils. *Social Science Quarterly* 59: 142–152.

Tench, Megan. 2003. Parents slam policy on school assignment. *Boston Globe*, 14 May.

———. 2004. Busing proposals draw fire on 2 sides. *Boston Globe*, 20 September.

Teske, Paul. 2005. *Stepping up or bottoming out? Funding Colorado's schools*. Denver: Donnell-Kay Foundation. http://www.dkfoundation.org.

Thelen, Kathleen, and Sven Steinmo. 1992. Historical institutionalism in comparative politics. In *Structuring politics: Historical institutionalism in comparative analysis*, eds. S. Steinmo, K. Thelen, and F. Longstreth, 1–32. Cambridge: Cambridge University Press.

Timberlake, Jeffrey M. 2002. Separate, but how unequal? Ethnic residential stratification, 1980 to 1990. *City and Community* 1: 251–66.

Tocqueville, Alexis de. 1958. *Democracy in America*. New York: New American Library.

Tyack, David, and Larry Cuban. 1995. *Tinkering toward utopia: A century of public school reform*. Cambridge, MA: Harvard University Press.

Ucelli, Marla. 2001. From school improvement to systemic reform. Paper presented at the Symposium on Leveraging Change: An emerging framework for education equity, sponsored by the Rockefeller Foundation and the Comer School Development Program, Washington, DC.

UCLA Asian American Studies Center. 2005. *National Asian Pacific American political almanac 2005–2006*. Los Angeles: UCLA Asian American Studies Center.

Uriarte, Miren, and Lisa Chavez. 2000. *Latino students and the Massachusetts public schools*. Mauricio Gaston Institute for Latino Community Development and Public Policy, University of Massachusetts at Boston.

Usansky, Margaret R. 1994. Segregated schools are once again the norm. *USA Today*, 12 May.

U.S. Department of Commerce, Bureau of the Census. 1998. *The Asian and Pacific Islander population in the United States*. http://www.census.gov/population/www/socdemo/race/api98.html.

———. 1993. *We, the American Asians*. Washington, DC.

———. 1993. *We, the American Hispanics*. Washington, DC.

———. 1994. *Statistical brief: Blacks in America—1992*. Washington, DC.

———. 1995. *Statistical brief: The nation's Hispanic population—1994*. Washington, DC.

———. 1995. *Statistical brief: Housing in metropolitan areas—Asian or Pacific households*. Washington, DC.

U.S. Department of Education. 1998, 1999, 2000, 2001. *National study of charter schools*. Washington, DC.

———. 2001. *Challenge and opportunity: Impact of charter schools on school districts*. Washington, DC.

Vaishnav, Anand, and Sasha Talcott. 2003. Boston talks about ending school busing. *Boston Globe*, 9 October.

Virgil, Maurilio. 1987. *Hispanics in American politics: The search for political power*. Lanham, MD: University Press of America.

Vouchers Revisited: DPS vs. private schools: Where's the best education? 1997. *Denver Post*, 13 July.

Waldinger, Roger, and Mehdi Bozorgmehr. 1997. *Ethnic Los Angeles*. New York: Russell Sage Foundation.

Warren, Christopher L. 1997. Hispanic incorporation and structural reform in Miami. In *Racial politics in American cities*, 2nd ed., eds. Rufus P. Browning, Dale Rogers Marshall, and David H. Tabb, 223–58. New York: Longman.

Weiss, Janet A. 1989. The powers of problem definition: The case of government paperwork. *Policy Sciences* 22: 97–121.

Welch, Finis, and Audrey Light. June 1987. *New evidence of school desegregation*. Washington, DC: U.S. Commission on Civil Rights, Clearinghouse Publication 92.

Wells, Amy Stuart, and Janelle Scott. 1999. Charter schools as postmodern paradox: Rethinking social stratification in an age of deregulated school choice. *Harvard Education Review* 69: 172–204.

Wessman v. Gittens. 160 F. 3 d. 790, 130 Ed. Law Rep. 1009 (1st Circuit, 1999).

Whitmire, Richard. 1997. Troubled schools "reconstituted." *Denver Post*, 30 November.

Williams v. State of California. 2004. Settlement Implementation Agreement. Case No. 312236, Superior Court, San Francisco, State of California, August 12.

Wilson, William Julius. 1996. *When work disappears*. New York: Vintage.

Winant, Howard. 1995. Dictatorship, democracy, and difference: The historical construction of racial identity. In *The bubbling cauldron: Race, ethnicity and the urban crisis*, ed. J. R. Feagin and M. P. Smith, 31–49. Minneapolis, MN: University of Minnesota Press.

Wirt, Frederick M. 1974. *Power in the city: Decision making in San Francisco*. Berkeley, CA: University of California Press.

Wirt, Frederick M., and Michael W. Kirst. 2001. *The political dynamics of American education, second edition*. Berkeley, CA: McCuthan Publishing Corporation.

Witcher, T. R. 1997. Forward to the past: What will happen when Denver's model of integration, Manual High, returns to the old days of segregation? *Westword*, January 23.

Wolfinger, Raymond. 1974. *The politics of progress*. Englewood Cliffs, NJ: Prentice-Hall.

Wong, Janelle. 2000. The effects of age and political exposure on the development of party identification among Asian American and Latino immigrants in the United States. *Political Behavior* 22: 341–71.

Wood, Elaine. 1997. S.F. schools on a winning streak. *Los Angeles Times*, 26 August.

Yanow, Dvora. 1995. Editorial practices of policy interpretation. *Policy Sciences* 28: 111–26.

Yzaguirre, Raul. 2002. Educational status of Latino children. National Council of La Raza. http://www.nclr.org/content/viewpoints/detail/1310/.

Zax, Jeffrey S. 1990. Election methods and blacks and Hispanic city council membership. *Social Science Quarterly* 71 (2): 339–55.

NOTES

PREFACE

1. We thank an anonymous reviewer for this characterization.

2. Funding for the eleven-city Civic Capacity and Urban Education project (Clarence N. Stone, University of Maryland, Principal Investigator; Jeffrey Henig, Columbia University, Co-Principal Investigator; Bryan Jones, University of Washington, Co-Principal Investigator) was provided by the Education and Human Services Directorate, National Science Foundation (RED9350139). Project data are available through the Center for American Politics and Public Policy (CAPP), University of Washington, http://depts. washington.edu/ampol.

3. We recognize the impressive and burgeoning literature seeking to move beyond black/white paradigms (e.g., Ancheta 1998; Kim 1999, 2002; Schmidt 2000; Lien 2001; Lien et al. 2001, 2004); our aim is to contribute a theoretically grounded, empirical analysis of local multiethnic politics to this effort.

CHAPTER ONE

1. These stories are drawn from Judy and Ronnie Young and Sherrie and Kermit Queenan in "DPS vs. private schools: Where's the best education?" *Denver Post* July 13, 1997: 1E.

2. The Queenans are plaintiffs in the 1997 class action suit against DPS schools demanding vouchers for low income students in the face of poor training of basic skills to poor and minority students.

3. There are multiple terms in common use to distinguish different ethnic and racial groups. We primarily employ black and/or African American, Latino, and Anglo and/or white on an interchangeable basis to refer to different groups unless our data source or respondents specify a particular term.

4. We refer to "new school constituencies" to highlight the increasing Latino and Asian presence in urban public schools relative to black and white students. These broad categories obscure significant variation within each category, articulated in each of our cities by references to the number of languages spoken in each district. "New" refers to their emerging presence in urban public schools; it also reflects the presence of new immigrant student populations across racial and ethnic categories.

5. We appreciate this felicitous phrasing suggested by an anonymous reviewer.

6. While not among top ten metropolitan areas with the largest immigrant populations (as reported in Camorata 2002), the Denver MSA's foreign-born population nearly doubled during the 1990s (Singer 2004). See Bluestone and Stevenson (2000) for a discussion of globalization impacts on Boston; Waldinger and Bozorgmehr (1997) and Bobo et al. (2000) on Los Angeles; Clark (2003, 1998) on Los Angeles and San Francisco; and Hero and Clarke (2002) on Denver.

7. Among our cases, Los Angeles was an exception to this pattern in the 1990s with Hispanics as a plurality; the 2000 Census reveals Hispanics as a majority, with white students significantly underrepresented in the school population.

8. In a 2004 Pew Center national survey, few respondents were aware of the No Child Left Behind (NCLB) program but Latinos (67 percent), African Americans (69 percent) and whites (73 percent) supported the general principles of the NCLB legislation, including reliance on state performance standards. Latino and African Americans did not, however, agree with NCLB provisions encouraging parents with children in failing schools to move them to other schools. In contrast to whites (35 percent), Latino (62 percent) and African American (53 percent) respondents emphasize improvement of the existing schools and the continued attendance of students.

9. Given the collaborative nature of this project, this book is coauthored. The analysis draws on research by each city "team" but we each authored individual chapters, as follows: One (Clarke), Two (Hero and Sidney), Three (Clarke), Four (Hero), Five (Sidney), Six (Fraga and Erlichson), Seven (Hero and Fraga).

CHAPTER TWO

1. Changes in the Census categories for race and multiple racial identities complicate comparisons of Asian conditions over time. The 1990 Census was the last one to consider Asian Pacific Islanders as a single race and also to not ask respondents if they consider themselves to be characterized as more than one race or ethnicity (UCLA 2005, 39). The current use of the term Asian Pacific American or Asian American is defined as anyone of part-Asian or part–Native Hawaiians and other Pacific Islanders (NHPI) descent, which includes all mixed race ancestry (ibid.). See U.S. Census 2000 SF2 Table PCT1 for details.

2. These Democratic vote figures are higher than those reported by, for example, the National Election Pool; many analysts argue that multilingual exit polls, often conducted by Asians, provide more accurate data than mainstream voter surveys (UCLA 2005, 48; see also Lien 2001; Lien et al. 2004; http://www.aaldef.org).

3. As a result of the 1992 TABOR limits, per pupil funding for K–12 education in Colorado plummeted below the national average; by 2001 Colorado dropped to 50th in the nation in per-pupil funding as a percentage of state income (Great Education Colorado). Amendment 23 also established the State Education Fund, funded by 0.33 percent of Colorado's state income tax and not subject to TABOR limits, as the mechanism for meeting Amendment 23 obligations.

4. We appreciate Alex Medler's bringing this caveat to our attention in his careful reading of an earlier version.

5. We sketch the basic features of the desegregation context in each city here; Chapter 6 provides more detail, particularly on the institutional dynamics in each city.

6. Our account of Los Angeles draws on Fernando Guerra and Mara Cohen (1994).

7. Our account of Boston draws on Nelson 1999; Portz 1994; Portz 1996; Portz et al. 1999 and the generous comments on our manuscript by John Portz. We are responsible for any inaccuracies.

CHAPTER THREE

1. In 2001 the National Council of La Raza (NCLR), the largest national Hispanic advocacy organization, established a Charter School Development Initiative to assist Latino-serving community-based organizations to start new charters congruent with the educational needs of local Latino communities. Through planning, technical assistance, and implementation grants, NCLR hopes to support up to fifty new charter schools by 2005. In 2002, the Bill and Melinda Gates Foundation awarded NCLR $6.7 million for fifteen new charter schools to be established over a five-year period in California. Although NCLR is not a membership-based group, and not necessarily representative of Latino priorities, it is a long-standing and influential organization within the Latino community. School reform politics, like other political arenas, is increasingly dominated by what Theda Skocpol (2004) refers to as "wallet" as opposed to "membership" groups, that is, groups relying more on the dues than the active support of their members. Thanks to Alex Medler for his comments on the evolutionary aspects of policy support for school reforms.

2. Alex Medler brought this prospect to our attention in reading an earlier version of this chapter; we appreciate his observations. The Denver Public School system is currently converting a school labeled as "failing" by state standards into a charter school with specialized programs.

3. Shortly after CDMs were created, the state legislature passed a law in 1993 calling for statewide standards and testing; in the first round of the Colorado Student Assessment Program, administered in 1996, just a third of Colorado fourth-graders tested proficient in writing and 57 percent were proficient or advanced in reading (Bingham 1997). Scores for DPS were significantly lower, with students of color faring poorly. Thus DPS is held accountable for student performance by one legislative initiative while another devolves important responsibilities to school-based committees. After eleven years, DPS and the teachers union formed a commission to assess the future

of CDMs in the face of dwindling activity and confusion over the intended focus and purview of CDMs (Hubler 2002).

4. See U.S. District Court, 1992, 48–50.

5. These diverse roots were brought to our attention by Alex Medler (Johnson and Medler 2000).

6. By fall 2001, California had 358 charter schools (compared to Arizona's 419), Colorado had 88, and Massachusetts had 43 after lifting its original cap (Center for Education Reform 2001). With the explosive growth in charter schools, these states now account for a little more than 20 percent of the total number of charter schools nationally.

7. One study found that California charter schools enroll 53 percent minority students; similarly, another study found that 48 percent of Massachusetts charter school students are minorities, 39 percent qualify for the free lunch program, and 18 percent speak a language other than English as their primary language, all well above state averages for these categories (CER 1998a).

8. The National Council of La Raza organization now funds Latino groups for charter school startups.

9. Despite local resistance, state officials continue to press forward with Commonwealth Charter Schools. By 2004, fifteen Commonwealth Charter schools were operating in Boston. As feared, the per-pupil formula in which public funding follows the student cost the Boston public schools an estimated forty million dollars as of 2004.

10. The more visible local organizations work across districts throughout the state. The Public Education Coalition (PEC) is one of fifty-eight nonprofit education funds operating in twenty-six states; it has an annual budget of eight hundred thousand dollars contributed by a dozen foundations and more than two hundred businesses, corporations, and individuals in the Denver area. PEC emphasizes a School Renewal Project providing funds and technical assistance to eighteen schools attempting to rethink their structure and curriculum and a Literacy League using master teachers and "lab classrooms" to provide teacher training in reading and writing skills. The Colorado Alliance of Business began a School Restructuring Initiative in 1988 to help develop a model for restructuring processes and to build bridges between schools and the business community. It has a staff of eleven, an annual budget of over eight hundred thousand dollars, and over two hundred eighty members including foundations, bank, retail and wholesale firms, and service industries (ibid., 19).

11. Our discussion of Los Angeles draws on Fernando Guerra and Mara A. Cohen's case study for the Civic Capacity project *Educational Restructuring in Los Angeles* (1994).

12. Throughout, our discussion of San Francisco is drawn from Luis Fraga and Bari Erlichson's case study for the Civic Capacity project, *The Politics of Educational Reform in San Francisco* (1994); see also Fraga et al. 1998.

13. Many choice advocates, for example, Terry M. Moe, would argue that choice is the pathway to more equitable education outcomes.

14. In a bid to realign the rhetorical balance between reform and resources, Philadelphia Mayor Ed Rendell and city officials recently sued the state government, charging that state education aid formulas discriminate against minority students and violate federal civil rights laws (Dionne 1998a). Although state courts have ordered school finance reforms in California (1971) and Massachusetts (1993) and fourteen other states in the twenty-five years since the 1971 *Serrano v. Priest* decision (Colorado enacted legislative reform without court intervention in 1973) (Evans, Murray, and Schwab 1997), these fiscal disparities persist despite increased state shares of education costs.

15. Dan Lewis, Northwestern University, made this observation in commenting on our work at a panel of the Western Political Science Association Annual Meeting, San Francisco, March 1996.

CHAPTER FOUR

1. Miami, where the Latino population is predominantly Cuban, is a notable exception where Latinos are more politically influential than blacks (see Croucher 1997; Warren 1997).

2. From their websites, visual evidence suggests the following school board composition in 2005: In the SFUSD, three of seven Board of Education members are Asian, one Latino, three white. In the LAUSD, one of seven Board of Education members is African American, one Latino, five white. In the DPS district, two of seven Board members are Latino, one African American, four white (there are four seats up for reelection in Nov. 2005). In BPS, three of seven school committee members are African American, one Latino, three white. See also, UCLA *National Asian Pacific American Political Almanac 2005—2006*.

CHAPTER FIVE

1. See Methodological Appendix for the numbers of interviews per city, per respondent category, and by racial or ethnic group. The appendix also provides a copy of the interview protocol, and describes how respondents were chosen for this study.

2. Transcribed interviews constitute a rich data set but are challenging to analyze in their fullness. NUD•IST enables the analyst to reduce and aggregate data so patterns are evident, while maintaining access to individual voices and the nuances of meaning they express. The analyst uses the software by of coding portions of text, analyzing patterns of codes, and then swiftly collecting similarly coded text to read once again. This iterative process means that the analyst checks for the reliability of the codes and probes the data for further variations. Unlike survey data, coding categories are not imposed through a preset format of questions, but emerge from the respondents themselves. Unlike regression analysis or content analysis, data are not reduced to numbers, but consist simultaneously in numeric and textual forms. That is, one can not only count frequencies of codes but also read the text that codes represent.

CHAPTER SIX

1. Sociologists who study organizations and institutions have contributed a wealth of understanding of schools as institutions. See Meyer and Rowan (1977) and Meyer, Scott, and Deal (1983).

2. For a fuller discussion of the history of the *Brian Ho v.* SFUSD case see Fraga, Erlichson, and Lee (1998, 66–90).

3. Under the agreement, race and ethnicity cannot be used "except as related to the language needs of the student or otherwise to assure compliance with controlling federal or state law" (*Ho v.* SFUSD, 11).

CHAPTER SEVEN

1. This section draws on Cuban's work.

METHODS APPENDIX

1. Funding for this project was provided by the Education and Human Services Directorate, NSF (RED9350139).

INDEX

ABOUT THE AUTHORS

Susan E. Clarke is Professor of Political Science, University of Colorado at Boulder.

Rodney E. Hero is Packey J. Dee III Professor of American Democracy, Department of Political Science, University of Notre Dame.

Mara S. Sidney is Associate Professor of Political Science at Rutgers University-Newark.

Luis R. Fraga is Associate Professor, Department of Political Science, and by courtesy, School of Education, Stanford University.

Bari A. Erlichson is a classroom teacher in Plainfield NJ.